D1602545

Globalism
and Comparative
Public Administration

PUBLIC ADMINISTRATION AND PUBLIC POLICY
A Comprehensive Publication Program

EDITOR-IN-CHIEF
EVAN M. BERMAN
Distinguished University Professor
J. William Fulbright Distinguished Scholar
National Chengchi University
Taipei, Taiwan

Founding Editor
JACK RABIN

RECENTLY PUBLISHED BOOKS

Globalism and Comparative Public Administration, Jamil Jreisat

Government Budgeting and Financial Management in Practice: Logics to Make Sense of Ambiguity, Gerald J. Miller

Globalism and Comparative Public Administration, Jamil Jreisat

Energy Policy in the U.S.: Politics, Challenges, and Prospects for Change, Laurance R. Geri and David E. McNabb

Public Administration in Southeast Asia: Thailand, Philippines, Malaysia, Hong Kong and Macao, edited by Evan M. Berman

Governance Networks in Public Administration and Public Policy, Christopher Koliba, Jack W. Meek, and Asim Zia

Public Administration and Law: Third Edition, David H. Rosenbloom, Rosemary O'Leary, and Joshua Chanin

Public Administration in East Asia: Mainland China, Japan, South Korea, and Taiwan, edited by Evan M. Berman, M. Jae Moon, and Heungsuk Choi

Handbook of Public Information Systems, Third Edition, edited by Christopher M. Shea and G. David Garson

Science and Technology of Terrorism and Counterterrorism, Second Edition, edited by Tushar K. Ghosh, Mark A. Prelas, Dabir S. Viswanath, and Sudarshan K. Loyalka

Bureaucracy and Administration, edited by Ali Farazmand

Performance-Based Management Systems: Effective Implementation and Maintenance, Patria de Lancer Julnes

Handbook of Governmental Accounting, edited by Frederic B. Bogui

Labor Relations in the Public Sector, Fourth Edition, Richard Kearney

Understanding Research Methods: A Guide for the Public and Nonprofit Manager, Donijo Robbins

Contracting for Services in State and Local Government Agencies, William Sims Curry

State and Local Pension Fund Management, Jun Peng

Available Electronically
PublicADMINISTRATION*netBASE*

Globalism
and Comparative
Public Administration

Jamil Jreisat

CRC Press
Taylor & Francis Group
Boca Raton London New York

CRC Press is an imprint of the
Taylor & Francis Group, an **informa** business

CRC Press
Taylor & Francis Group
6000 Broken Sound Parkway NW, Suite 300
Boca Raton, FL 33487-2742

© 2012 by Taylor & Francis Group, LLC
CRC Press is an imprint of Taylor & Francis Group, an Informa business

---

Library of Congress Cataloging-in-Publication Data

Jreisat, Jamil E.
    Globalism and comparative public administration / Jamil Jreisat.
        p. cm. -- (Public administration and public policy ; 161)
    Rev. ed. of: Comparative public administration and policy. 2002.
    Includes bibliographical references and index.
    ISBN 978-1-4398-5458-7 (hardcover : alk. paper)
    1. Public administration. 2. Comparative government. 3. Public
administration--Cross-cultural studies. I. Jreisat, Jamil E. Comparative public
administration and policy. II. Title. III. Series.

JF1351.J73 2012
351--dc23
                                               2011027774

Visit the Taylor & Francis Web site at
http://www.taylorandfrancis.com

and the CRC Press Web site at
http://www.crcpress.com

Contents

Foreword

Public administration has become an increasingly international and comparative field of study and practice. First, these twin perspectives have done much to enrich public administration theory in the past generation. The number of refereed journal articles, the range of scholarly journals, and the breadth of their subject matter have increased remarkably since Huddleston's (1984) and Cayer and Van Wart's (1990) summaries and analysis of extant literature to what is available to contemporary scholars (Fitzpatrick et al., 2010). Second, the inclusion of international and comparative perspectives have been of inestimable value in the development of public administration theory, particularly the development and testing of hypotheses reflecting the importance of cross-national characteristics as independent or intervening variables. Third, and despite the preponderance of refereed journals published in the United States and Europe, these increases in the amount of international and comparative research have fostered fundamental changes in how we teach public administration. Although the newly updated National Association of Schools of Public Affairs and Administration (NASPAA) standards do not require a focus on the international, they do emphasize the importance of teaching public administration and affairs from a comparative perspective, as defined by the mission and objectives of a particular graduate degree program (NASPAA, 2009). Fourth, they have fundamentally altered the practice of public administration in its varied aspects—policy development, program implementation, and political leadership. We are arguably the first generation in world history with the ability to use information and communications technologies to share information, resolve conflicts, and make decisions at a global level. It is clearly the responsibility of intellectual and political elites to use this capability toward political, social, economic, and environmental sustainability (Argyriades and Pichardo Pagaza, 2009).

Several years ago, President Obama raised expectations that the United States might begin to rebuild its reputation as a member of the world community. Outside events beyond our control may prevent us from taking advantage of this opportunity. At a minimum, these include the faltering global economy, the emergence of China as our global competitor, and similar advances in India, Brazil, and Russia. But if U.S. public administrators are to respond effectively when elected and appointed officials do ask their help with policies and programs, we need to anticipate the internal challenges this entails. Today, U.S. international public administration is beset by diverse approaches, ambitious goals, and operational complexities. Despite these challenges, when elected and appointed officials do ask for help, U.S. public administrators can respond by defining U.S. public administration as purposive, data-driven, performance-oriented, and sustainable smart practices. This means reconnecting the approaches, seeking pragmatic not dogmatic solutions, conducting action research based on quantitative and qualitative data, connecting research results with policy outcomes and policy influences, and preparing globally competent administrators and organizations (Klingner, 2009).

This book is a unique contribution, not only for its focus on an important topic but also because it provides students and scholars with a comprehensive and conceptually focused view of the field. It is an analytical, evaluative, exhaustive, and balanced approach to critical dimensions of modern governance. In this magnificent book, Dr. Jamil Jreisat demonstrates that he has the heart and the head required to show how our newly won international and comparative perspectives on public administration require better leadership, policy making, and program implementation and shows how these can be achieved in the real world.

Donald Klingner
Distinguished University Professor
School of Public Affairs, University of Colorado
Former President, American Society for Public Administration

References

Argyriades, D., and I. Pichardo Pagaza, eds. 2009. *Winning the Needed Change: Saving Our Planet Earth—A Global Public Service.* New York: IOS Press, International Institute of Administrative Sciences Monographs, Volume 30.

Fitzpatrick, J., M. Goggin, T. Heikkila, D. Klingner, J. Machado, and C. Martell. 2010. Comparative public administration: Review of the literature and agenda for future research. Paper presented at the Annual Meeting of the American Political Science Association, September 2–5.

Huddleston, M. 1984. *Comparative Public Administration: An Annotated Bibliography.* New York: Garland Publishing, Inc.

Klingner, D. 2009. Using US public administration to support global development. *Journal of Regional Studies and Development, 18* (2): 1–30.

NASPAA (2009). *NASPAA Standards 2009: Defining Quality in Public Affairs Education.* Washington, DC: National Association of Schools of Public Affairs and Administration. Available at http://www.naspaa.org/accreditation/standard2009/main.asp. Accessed May 1, 2009.

Van Wart, M., and N. J. Cayer. 1990. Comparative public administration: Defunct, dispersed, or redefined? *Public Administration Review, 50* (2): 238–248.

Preface

I have many reasons for writing this book. Public administration is one of the most exciting and dynamic fields of knowledge in the social sciences. The comparative approach provides depth and breadth essential for transforming public administration to a field of universal learning and practice. Yet, today's graduate students, and many public administration academicians, have limited opportunities to develop real understanding of the conceptual evolution and the changing contextual relationships of their field. The education establishments offer little exposure to the full spectrum of public administration theory and practice and the influences that shaped them. Current curricula rarely account for the contributions of comparative and development public administration that opened up the field of public administration to the total human experience worldwide.

This book is a major revision and extension of my earlier work *Comparative Public Administration and Policy* (Westview, 2002). This edition includes new chapters that focus on trends and developments not covered in the earlier work. Globalism, governance, and global ethics are among the topics that receive added attention. Within the emerging global patterns of decision making, better understanding of earlier contributions to comparative public administration is vital for explaining the current and for refining future research. Existing and evolving human insights, concepts, and experiences are crucial inputs into the imperatives of administrative theory and practice.

The examination and analysis of comparative public administration from the classic period of the 1960s to the present are an attempt to synthesize and to link the literature with current critical developments. This work is neither an edited handbook on selected individual countries nor a collection of articles by different authors looking at different aspects of the subject. It is not a campaign for a particular framework to the exclusion of others either. Rather the book aims to provide an integrated, historical, analytical, and realistic view of the comparative public administration perspective and its rationale. The overwhelming influence of globalism and the growing interdependence among countries, facilitated by revolutionary technological changes such as the Internet, are transforming modern living and challenging social sciences in general. Yet, institutions and systems of governance, particularly public administration, have not demonstrated sufficient capacity to solve complex national and global problems and challenges in areas such as finance, trade, security, human rights, and the environment.

Finally, I have personal reasons for writing this book. I have devoted a major part of my time and energies studying, researching, and teaching comparative public administration. Teaching graduate students and training public managers from many countries and cultures convinced me that applying the comparative method in presenting, explaining, and analyzing public management is an effective method for stimulating interest and creative management thinking. Also, I have known and interacted personally with several scholars regarded as pioneers of the field (many of whom became personal friends). As a doctoral student and as a faculty member at the University of Pittsburgh, I participated in the creation and the subsequent conferences of the Comparative Administration Group (CAG) and experienced the early debates and discussions that articulated mission, motivation, and parameters of the comparative studies. The questions of relevance and synthesis that I raised in my article in the *Public Administration Review* (1975) are still valid. At the present, I believe that an evolved and adapted comparative administration is the venue for leading public administration heritage through an inevitable phase of internationalization. Public administration has to reexamine its imperatives. Concepts and practices of leadership, ethics, accountability, and performance management are not American or European administration anymore. They are objectives and values of professional administrative practices everywhere. Despite the denials, the comparative perspective has been transforming public administration to a field of inquiry beyond provincial and ethnocentric tendencies to a universal subject of research, teaching, and practice. The global context, the information revolution, and democratization trends in various parts of the world are reshaping public organizations and changing governance.

Acknowledgments

I would like to thank the Westview Press of the Perseus Books Group for reverting to me all rights to my book *Comparative Public Administration and Policy*, which allowed me to incorporate my previous work in this volume.

Over the years, my students were always an inspiration and often a challenge. I am grateful to my graduate students in the Public Administration Program at the University of South Florida and in many other places where I taught and trained in public administration. Their curiosity, questions, and research projects have always been intellectually stimulating.

The unknown soldiers in publishing a book like this may not be known to the readers, but, in this case, I feel particularly fortunate to have Lara Zoble (CRC Press, New York) as my editor. Her expertise, professionalism, and consideration are exemplary. She knows what matters in the business of publishing and I am grateful for her help throughout. I am also thankful to others at CRC Press who have been most helpful, particularly Joselyn Banks-Kyle, project coordinator, and Frances Weeks, project editor.

Author

Jamil Jreisat is a professor of public administration and political science in the Department of Government and International Affairs at the University of South Florida. He is the author of over 100 books, chapters, and articles in public administration theory and process, comparative public administration, and development administration with focus on the Arab states. Professor Jreisat is an internationally recognized expert who consulted to the World Bank, UNDP, German Technical Assistance (GTZ), and the Institute of Development Administration of the League of Arab States. He serves on the editorial boards of several professional publications, and is the associate editor of the *Journal of Asian and African Studies.* Professor Jreisat is the recipient of many awards including the USF Award for Professional Excellence.

Chapter 1

Governance and Globalism

I want to rebuild this government. Rebuild it by bringing back competence; rebuild it by bringing back integrity; rebuild it by bringing back performance; by bringing back people of talent; by bringing back people of goodwill; rebuild it by bringing back professionalism and respect.

**New York Governor Andrew Cuomo,
Inaugural Address, 2010**[1]

Introduction

To fulfill its professional responsibilities and to serve its authoritative obligations, public administration as a profession continues to evolve and to search for the most appropriate knowledge and competence. Early in the previous century, development of the administrative state within the industrial nations was a major adjustment that changed the structure and the functioning of contemporary governance. As Kettl and Fesler (1991) note, increasing citizens' demands of government for delivery of public services as well as for securing and protecting the general welfare have led to a multiplicity of administrative agencies, a large number of civil servants, and swelling government budgets to pay for what citizens want, and for developing the administrative capacity to meet such expectations. This brought us into a new phase of governance, characterized as "the administrative state." Dwight Waldo was one of the earliest to use the term in the title of his seminal work *The Administrative State* (1948). Since then, extensive literature focused on the administrative state and its profound effect on society, such as Emmette Redford's *Democracy and the Administrative State* (1969), Fritz Morstein Marx's *The Administrative State* (1957), John Rohr's *To Run a Constitution: The Legitimacy of the Administrative State* (1986), and others.

The Industrial Revolution and subsequent technological advancements revolutionized production with greater use of machines. This created new needs for rationalized organizational management, public or private, through design, planning, measurement, and regularity in production. Two profound changes in the business sector transformed corporate governance, permanently:

1. Professionalizing corporate management, mainly by separating ownership and management. The landmark study by A. Berle and G. Means, *The Modern Corporation and Private Property* (1932, revised 1968), has been credited with causing significant developments in legal and economic theory. The study is also credited with changing the U.S. public policy and helping ratification of the law that created the Securities and Exchange Commission.
2. The development of organization and management concepts and frameworks, such as the *Scientific Management* movement (Taylorism) in the first decade of the last century, was specifically aimed to improve organizational capacities for production and performance in the manufacturing firms.

As critical systems of production and service, organizations inspired many theories and practices seeking to achieve valid and universal approaches to managing complex organizations. In this genre are the theories of *Scientific Management*, *Administrative Management*, and the *Bureaucratic Model* that have been referred to as traditional, classic, rational, or machine models (Jreisat 1997). Afterward, an assortment of concepts grounded in the *Human Relations* perspective directed research on organization theory and process into areas of human behavior that were not familiar in earlier literature. The end result, organization theory and practice, gained importance in teaching and research, particularly for the growing number of large organizations in society performing key roles and objectives. The wide acknowledgment of the impact of organizations on modern society led to the characterization of "the organization society" (Presthus 1978).

By the end of World War II, the authority of the state had expanded and its legal and administrative powers had increased. This was facilitated by growing resources (financial and human), war, the welfare system, and the need to regulate the market and the production systems to safeguard the common interest. In the United States, the "New Deal" policies and programs of the 1930s exemplify the conceptual and practical shift in governance. The change necessitated adapting and improving public administration capacity, affirming what Woodrow Wilson recognized in the 1880s—that public administration is "the cutting edge of government" and is "government in action."

Governance

Definition Issue

The considerable effects of governance on society have attracted wide interest in the literature, conveying diverse conceptualizations and definitions (Ahern 2002; Jain 2002; Hyden 2002; Jreisat 2001a; Pierre 2000; Nye and Donahue 2000). Regardless of how governance is perceived, public administration is a component of significance, though with variable levels of capacity and professionalism. The association of politics and administration within governance is intrinsic; each profoundly reflects the image and values of the other. This connection is more real today because conventional jurisdictional boundaries of administration no longer have the same relevance as in the past in explaining what happens with formulation and implementation of policy (Hyden 2002: 14). Public administration is the operational dimension of governance, providing the tools for efficient and effective implementation of policies and decisions. Governance can be powerless without the instruments to carry out its policies. "A strategy paper without a road map is a paper, not a strategy; a decision without implementation is a wish not a decision" (Schiavo-Campo and McFerson 2008: 3).

While one conception of governance refers to empirical manifestation of state adaptation to its external environment, another denotes representation of coordinated social systems and the role of the state in the pursuit of collective interests through traditional, institutional channels (Pierre 2000: 3). Yet another conception focuses on "the extent and form of [governance] intervention and the use of markets and quasi-markets to deliver 'public' service" (Rhodes 2000: 55). A distinction is also made between "old governance," focusing on how and what outcomes are conceivable, and recent or new governance, conceived in terms of comparative politics and whether concepts "can 'travel' across a range of political systems and still have substantial meaning and validity" (Peters 2000: 50). "In much of the public and political debate, governance refers to sustaining co-ordination and coherence among a wide variety of actors with different purposes and objectives such as political actors and institutions, corporate interests, civil society, and transnational organizations" (Pierre 2000: 3–4).

Governance is an organizing inclusive function that encompasses, in addition to central government, other players who share the responsibilities such as local authorities, business, interest groups, voluntary organizations, and a variety of civic associations (Klingner 2006). Thus, governance is a system of many dimensions, continually evolving and adapting its complex web of structures, processes, policies, behaviors, traditions, visions, and outcomes. The United Nations Development Program defines governance "as the exercise of economic, political, and administrative authority to manage a country's affairs at all levels, comprising the mechanisms, processes, and institutions through which that authority is directed" (UNDP 2007: 1).

The term *governance* is derived from the Greek *to steer*, the process by which a society or an organization steers itself (Rosell 1999: 1). Despite the apparent conceptual amorphousness, it is possible to analyze governance through its constant rudiments of structure, process, and outcome:

- *Structure* is the standard features and forms of the authority system in practice. Usually, structures reveal specific attributes of the system such as centralized or decentralized authority, type of organizational and institutional setting, specificity of functions performed, and the overall authority pattern that connects all such structural essentials for performance. The capacity of institutional structures to perform the diverse functions of governance is a crucial measure of effectiveness. Also, the structure signifies the extent of representation of the people and the legitimacy of the authority system itself.

- *Process* defines the rules and operational methods of decision making. In theory, the process promotes fairness and legitimacy of outcomes of public policy and advances the common interests. In reality, however, outcomes of the process often vary from expectations, specially when the process becomes captured by powerful special interests, and serves mainly to accommodate the objectives of organized interest groups. Although basic processes of governance are designated by law or constitution, other factors may have important modifying effects such as tradition and precedent. Still, an open and transparent process indicates real responsiveness to citizens' preferences and attempt at sound reasoning in decision making. An impartial process raises confidence in the integrity of governance.

- *Outcome* is the measured quality and quantity of the overall results of governance performance, particularly in serving the collective interest, delivery of public services, managing sustainable development, and improving the effectiveness of a civil society. Outcomes exemplify accountability of public decision making and illustrate the level of commitment to equity in the distribution of benefits and delivery of public services as well as the uniformity in the application of law and justice in the society.

Shifting Role of Governance

Governance has wide-ranging effects on its people; it has major responsibilities of coping with external challenges as well as making decisions that affect the welfare and security of the society. Focus on governance encourages people to think beyond the daily routine or the need for only incremental steps that do not call for change in existing rules. Like strategic management, Hyden (2002: 18) points out, governance becomes a way of looking at a problem in the context of the "big picture" of adapting systems of rules to changes in the environment. Effective leaders, therefore, continually search to find consensual and creative solutions to problems encountered by their constituents.

A system of governance is neither a static nor a preset condition. Invariably, the system, the process, and the outcome of governance change, distinctly rather than uniformly. After examination of administrative reform in fourteen countries, Manning and Parison conclude: "Circumstances dictated action, but leverage available to reformers—the points of entry to comprehensive reform programs—and the malleability of basic public sector institutions varied considerably among countries" (2004: xv). Refinements and realignments of governance structures and functions take place with change of internal conditions such as change of leadership or in response to citizens' demands. While external pressures and global challenges have also been a source of systemic change in governance, such outside pressures tend to promote value-laden propositions that reflect external values, as those of donor countries, thus generate domestic resistance and contentions.

Mediating issues of change is a prime test and a reliable indicator of the effectiveness and competence of leadership. Leadership, attitudes, values, tradition, and overall political culture influence what and how change in governance is attained. Leadership and political culture are mainly emphasized because of the realization that societies change far more meaningfully through negotiation, reconciliation, and consensus building than through upheaval or external pressures. "A growing body of work suggests that important changes often take place incrementally and through seemingly small adjustments that can, however, cumulate into significant institutional transformation" (Mahoney and Thelen 2010: xi).

Accumulation of incremental adjustments that result in gradual institutional transformation assumes an open and representative system of government with legitimate leadership that enjoys public trust and confidence in its competence and integrity. During the early days of 2011, the world witnessed in the Arab world a forceful public demand for reform. The popular uprisings were against autocratic leaders, rampant corruption, incompetent institutions, and inept public leaders and managers who have mainly been employed and appointed through nepotism and favoritism. Moreover, lack of freedom and economic opportunity pushed previously silent and frustrated young people to press forward for radical change of regime. From Tunisia and Egypt to Libya, Yemen, Bahrain and the rest of the Arab world, voices of massive public protests and acts of discontent forced political leaders out of office in some countries, and threatened others with similar destiny unless the system of governance is fundamentally reformed. Regardless of the wishes of the outside world, the Arab people from the inside of their countries provided the determination to change history.

The past few decades have been demanding for governance everywhere. Vigorous debates, assessments, and evaluations of the domestic and the international roles of governance were encouraged. During the 1980s and shortly after, the power of the state in the industrialized countries and its ability to address societal issues was challenged from within. The rapid ascendance of neoliberal regimes in several advanced democracies, regarded the state not as a source of collective action, or a base for solutions, but rather as a main source of many societal problems (Pierre 2000: 3). The thrust of this political thinking, and the ideological following it generated in various countries, was manifested in determined confidence in a monetarist economic policy supported by deregulation, privatization, drastic reductions of civil service, and the push to "reinvent government" and to manage it "businesslike." In the United States, an assertive neoconservative extremist group, with their own particular agenda, emerged within this camp pressing with a missionary zeal for minimum state intervention domestically, and a maximum intervention externally (Margolick 2010).

Thus, the private sector, spearheaded by multinational corporations, seemed to have won back at the global level the degree of freedom they had lost at the national level with the advent of the welfare state. At the global level, they did not encounter the equivalent of the state, an entity that can tax them, regulate them, and manage a redistributive process. This resulted in what Richard Falk (1999) refers to as "predatory globalization." These pressures encouraged the United States to walk away from international agreements at the turn of this century, undermining the concept and the practice of multilateralism, that has been "an underpinning of the global system since the end of World War II" (Prestowitz 2003: 22). In September 2002, the U.S. administration published the *National Security of the United States of America*, a report described as enshrining the doctrines of preventive war and overwhelming U.S. military superiority (Prestowitz 2003: 22). Even free trade among countries was often used to reward those who yield to certain hegemonic policies and to punish those who do not.

Forces of globalizing capital mounted pressures worldwide for sweeping privatization and contracting out public functions to business enterprises. During this period, the New Public Management (NPM) emerged to offer a new paradigm of entrepreneurial system of governance and administration based on the market criteria of efficiency and flexibility (Farazmand 2002: 132). The NPM was not an unqualified success story. The competitiveness envisioned to result from privatization and to increase efficiency rarely materialized. Instead, minimizing the role of the state and shrinking public service added greater complexity in the delivery process and made coordination even more difficult. The critics point out that globalizing capital promoted corruption, reduced accountability, violated territorial sovereignty, and left no room for any choice for people or nations but to succumb to the dictates of the globalizing corporate power structure (Farazmand 2002: 128–129; Gawthrop 1998; Korten 1995). Globalism changed the nature of the administrative state worldwide (Farazmand 1999: 510).

Eventually, diluting the power of the state undermined professional public management by reducing its regulatory oversight, pressing on it a "businesslike" and "bottom line" culture, and weakening its traditional values of representing and serving the collective interest. By 2008, the industrial countries and the rest of the world found themselves in the midst of one of the worst economic disasters in modern history. The neoliberal recipes not only proved to be vain but also brought many countries to the edge of financial ruin. In foreign affairs, the consequences were no less tragic: alienation of allies, undermining of international diplomacy, and costly military adventures as the invasion of Iraq in 2003 on false pretexts. Political leaders and their associates of ideologically inclined pressure groups, captivated by the "magic of the market," sought, with some success, to restrict the role of governance. The recipe of such perspective was a profound institutional restructuring to facilitate implementation of the measures of deregulation, privatization, reduction of civil service, and introduction of business managerial practices in government (Falk 1999; Pierre 2000: 2; Jreisat 2006). But, the huge size of business corporations compromised healthy competition, became impediments to innovation, and exerted corrupting influence in politics (Greider 2009: 11–12). Weakening anti-trust laws allowed concentration of economic power within a few corporate entities, which were deemed "too big to fail" and thus had to be bailed out by taxpayers' money.

Against a worsening economic crisis in 2008–9, reorientation of public policy toward broader collective interests restored some of the power of public authority. The internal economic disorder and global pressures required clarifying and redefining public policy objectives, analyzing and evaluating possible solutions, and authorizing new public policies. Among the most effective instruments of the newly promised state activism is fiscal policy that is directed to stimulate employment and achieve economic growth and stability. The state relies on the budget process (taxes and expenditures) and the regulatory framework to execute its major policies on the economy. The result of the economic crisis of 2008 was a plea to governments to assume greater responsibilities in ensuring orderly economic activities.

Activated governance requires effective managerial capacity to devise and implement solutions. But the tilted perception of the role of the state and its policies over the years created knowledge gaps and neglect. The new demands for pertinent knowledge and renewed administrative competence are not attainable through the traditional training and education. Broader views by managers and the ability to incorporate and integrate knowledge in their decisions have become imperatives in a fast-changing global context. As policy issues in areas such as health care, finance, labor migration, environment protection, and international agreements acquired higher importance, so did new administrative knowledge and skills.

An illustrative example of recent change of perspective on governance in the United States is reliance on contracting out that has been a pillar of neoliberal pro-business policies since the 1980s. Budget cuts announced by Secretary of Defense Robert Gates (May 2010) recognized that defense contractors are a "significant budgetary bloat." As reported, Gates also said, "We ended up with contractors supervising other contractors—with predictable results" (Jaffe 2010: A03).

> Among Gates' apparent targets for major cuts are the private contractors the Pentagon has hired in large numbers over the past decade to take on administrative tasks that the military used to handle. The defense secretary estimated that this portion of the Pentagon budget has grown by as much as $23 billion, a figure that does not include the tens of billions of dollars spent on private firms supporting U.S. troops in Afghanistan and Iraq. (Jaffe 2010: A03)

The shifting role of governance has instigated some of the most passionate political and economic debates in recent history. The economic crisis of 2008–9 caused the emergence of extreme positions on both sides of the political spectrum. On the left, serious doubts are expressed about the functionality of capitalism and the free market as viable systems. On the right, ominous warnings have been delivered about state activism, charging that it creates destructive huge public debts and invites socialism and communism. The politics of the middle has been struggling to govern throughout the democratic systems with no support from either political extreme. The dilemma is that a governing strategy with commitment to economic growth and job creation cannot succeed without public spending that adds to already huge public debts in many countries as it portends a tax increase in the future. The opposite strategy of deep cuts in public spending to reduce the size of government and public debt could cause deep recessions and impede economic growth.

An effective strategy of governing under conditions of economic stress requires pragmatism and reliance on empirical evidence far more than ideology or rigid dogma. Rational public policy formulation has to utilize all reasonable policy tools available such as spending cuts, tax increase, fiscal austerity, and stimulus spending, or the opposite of each, as the situation requires. Successful execution of any strategy of governance, however, has to be mindful of basic prerequisites: (1) maintenance of discipline, accountability, and transparency; (2) clear definition of the strategy, ensuring broad support and wide communication of the strategic vision; and (3) employment of an inclusionary approach, partnering with local governments, the private sector, and community organizations. Certainly, governance has an important role in building and developing the society; it is the size of resources used and the style of authority applied that, generally, raise questions and cause concerns.

What Is Good Governance?

How does one define, recognize, evaluate, or measure good governance? These are basic questions, continually asked by students, scholars, and practitioners alike. Predictably, many positive attributes of good governance can be identified. Good governance demonstrates capacity to aggregate and coordinate various interests to bring about agreements on policy action while managing political and administrative institutions with accountability and transparency. An operational and supportable vision of good governance is necessary for a consensus to emerge and for a system of measurement and evaluation of performance to be effective. Another compelling reason to search for a true understanding of transcendent qualities of good governance is to be able to articulate, design, and execute relevant reform strategies.

According to J. Ahrens, an explanation of good governance essentially refers to two of the most basic questions posed by political scientists since the foundation of their discipline: "Who governs?" and "How well?" (2002: 119). The first part of the question focuses on the issues of power and the distribution of power and resources in the society. The second part is primarily concerned with "good government," such as effective institutions, efficient methods of operation, and equitable policy outcomes (Ahrens 2002: 119). As a system, governance is continually changing, reflecting historical, political, cultural, educational, and economic circumstances. Appraisal of such a system has to consider many factors, particularly those that influence performance. Evaluation indicators have also to convey a high priority among these indicators to citizens' satisfaction and participation in decisions affecting them.

Measuring results requires relevant criteria that incorporate compatible principles and objectives with societal values and interests. Valid measurement has to determine degree of fidelity to these values in principle and in practice. Some widely conveyed core values of good governance are mutually reinforcing—that is, the flaw of one causes difficulties in another. The following are some examples:

- *Ethics and accountability* infuse all aspects of governance. The "connection between ethics and governance is immediate," Rohr (2000: 203) concludes. A report titled "Trust in Government" for the twenty-nine OECD countries provides a comprehensive overview of ethics measures, trends, promising practices, and innovative solutions taken by member countries. The report clearly affirms that public ethics are a prerequisite to and underpin public trust; they are a "keystone of good governance" (OECD 2000: 9). Whereas integrity and capacity have become a condition for good governance, checks and balance in the authority structure affirm accountability.
- *Creation of trust and promotion of shared values* such as sustained openness, transparency, and equal justice under the law. This means the following: (1) Relevant information is openly discussed, mass media are free to report, and professional exploration and learning processes are unbound in conducting their functions. (2) A study by the OECD concludes that measures of good government include the following: public servants' behavior is in line with the public purposes; citizens receive impartial treatment on the basis of legality and justice; public resources are effectively and properly used; decision-making procedures are transparent to the public; and procedures are in place to permit public scrutiny and redress (2000: 11). In brief, rules and legal standards for orderly conduct and progressive social transformation are constructed and impartially applied.
- *Competent and ethical leadership* is indispensable for establishing an overall framework of collective and strategic goals as well as reflecting shared values—both within government and across society. It is often said that "leadership defies simple formulations and easy solutions" (Beinecke 2009: 1). But, Donna Shalala offers a perspective that sums up the main functions of professional organizational leaders and managers as to "set standards, communicate a vision, choose staff based on competence and character, encourage team work, cultivate transparency, care about employees, and respond constructively to feedback" (2004: 349).

◾ *Decentralization.* Sharing authority and responsibility with local governments/authorities to improve access to public services, increase public participation, and enhance government responsiveness. "The present interest in decentralization is pervasive in that out of 75 developing and transitional countries with populations greater than 5 million, all but 12 claim to have embarked on some form of transfer of political power to local units of government" (UNDP 1997: 1). Furthermore, decentralization stimulates meaningful shifts in authority relationships to prevent its concentration at the top. Indirectly, decentralization weakens authoritarianism and supports forces of democratic values, economic competition, and global means of education and communication. Centralized systems of governance, perpetuated by tradition, culture, and other exceptional measures are often hesitant or slow buying into the decentralization reform.

Public administration faces its own challenges in coping with decentralization trends. The early legacy relied on models of organization and management that are hierarchical, applying command and control paradigms. Attempts to "reinvent" government and to emphasize total quality management, team building, performance measurement, and empowerment of employees have contributed significantly to a meaningful transformation of contemporary governance, even if application of these new organizational and managerial changes has hardly been uniform. The diffusion of techniques of organizational learning played an important role in ushering in a culture of governance that fosters delegation, representation, transparency, and accountability. This trend, however, has not been linear or painless. Although decentralization and delegation of authority improve efficiency, delegation may create problems of accountability and control when those receiving the greater authority are not appropriately prepared. Still, recent history shows that the power to govern has diffused away from the centralized autocratic rule to a broader base of elected representatives, professional public management, and active involvement of the governed (Michalski, Miller, and Stevens 2001: 7).

Ultimately, all factors presented so far in assessing good governance are as much valuable as they yield good results—namely, provide effective delivery of public services and enhance citizens' trust and satisfaction. The list of failures and deficiencies of governance in many parts of the world that did not adhere to core values can be quite lengthy. Too many political leaders fail to advance sustainable and equitable political and economic policies that are institutionally rather than personally based. Worldwide similarities of governance failures to respond effectively to the growing demands for integrity, protection of citizens' rights and liberties, and improving standards of living are remarkable.

Governance has been judged by the level of achievement of democratic ideals and a self-sustained economic growth by stimulating the private sector. Reliance on the private sector for steering socioeconomic development, however, assumes the presence of a lean state, thriving private sector in a civil society, and a non-monopolistic free domestic and world markets. Achieving this synergy requires other preconditions, particularly checks and balances in the market and a representative government. Actual experiences in many countries indicate absence of many of the key instruments of effective governance: lack of market competition and weak adherence to cherished societal values of liberty and the rule of law. Various studies and political declarations on governance and reform have not produced a universally accepted analytical framework or model. With a more precise meaning of governance, Hyden (2002: 17) argues, it is possible to distinguish between the distributive side of politics (how public resources are allocated), addressing the perennial question of "who gets what, when, and how," and the constitutive side that deals with the question of "who sets what rules, when, and how?" This distinction is particularly important to countries emphasizing policies for sustainable development. The conventional needs approach that has dominated international development assistance, for example, relies more on the distributive side, and does not ask for changes in the rules of the game to achieve its objectives (Hyden 2002: 17). Yet, sustainable development that focuses on empowerment and enhanced access to resources also requires a change in the rules, and, by implication, a shift in power relations.

In sum, governance has identifiable qualities with multiple dimensions. Analysis and measurement techniques in the past decades made it possible to delineate some of the crucial qualities and attributes of good government that have received wide recognition and acceptance. The following UNDP (1997: 4) list is inclusive and representative of the literature:

UNDP List of *Core Characteristics* of Good Governance

Participation: All men and women have a voice in decision making.

Rule of Law: Legal frameworks are fair and enforced impartially.

Transparency: Free flow of information and enough information provided.

Responsiveness: Institutions and processes serve all stakeholders.

Consensus Orientation: Differing interests are mediated to reach broad consensus on what is the common good.

Equity· All men and women have opportunities to improve or maintain their well-being.

Effectiveness and Efficiency: Processes and institutions produce results that meet needs.

Accountability: Public decision makers, private sector, and civic society organizations are accountable to constituents.

Strategic Vision: Leaders and the public share a long-range perspective on the good society.

Legitimacy: Authority is consistent with established legal and institutional frameworks.

Resource Prudence: Resources are managed and used to optimize the well-being of people.

Ecological Soundness: The environment is protected and regenerated for sustainability.

Empowering and Enabling: All in society are empowered to pursue legitimate goals.

Partnership: Governance is a whole-system responsibility that involves institutionalized mechanisms and processes for working in partnerships with non-governmental parties.

Spatially Grounded in Communities: Multi-level systems of people are empowered to be self-reliant, self-organizing, and self-managing within the autonomy of local communities.

Measuring Governance

This is a difficult question for many reasons. Practices of governance continually change, sometime precipitously, invalidating the result of measurement by the time it was completed. Other aspects of governance generate particular dilemmas, defying measurement efforts. Over conformance and excessive compliance with rules and procedures, for example, create rigidities, undermine creativity, and weaken overall performance of basic duties. Procedural accountability cannot substitute for performance accountability. Many efforts to measure good governance and determine its qualities—such as effectiveness, efficiency, accountability, and ethics—are approximations or judgments that may have been subjected to particular predispositions. Measurement, however, is helpful in raising awareness, informing decisions, pointing out trends, and underscoring strategies for improvement. The following are some examples of notable measurement projects:

- *Worldwide Governance Indicators* have been developed by the World Bank, *as an attempt to build regular governance indicators that can be a crucial tool for policy analysts and decision makers. The indicators seek to facilitate benchmarking and measurement of performance.* The World Bank Institute relies on a set of standards for effective governance that consist of six measures: (1) Voice and Accountability, (2) Political Stability and Absence of Violence, (3) Government Effectiveness, (4) Regulatory Quality, (5) Rule of Law, and (6) Control of Corruption.[2]
- *The UNDP* (January 1997) published a policy document titled *Governance for Sustainable Human Development*, articulating commitment to supporting national efforts for good governance for sustainable human development. The policy document followed UNDP's first attempt to define the parameters of good governance in a 1994 in Initiatives for Change, which stated that "the goal of governance initiatives should be to develop capacities that are needed to realize development that gives priority to the poor, advances women, sustains the environment and creates needed opportunities for employment."[3] The UNDP also launched other initiatives to develop governance indicators that provide guidance and technical assistance in governance. Two particular programs have been the focus of field research and have significant practical thrusts: (1) The UNDP Governance Indicators Program (2007) is jointly

produced with the Oslo Governance Center to provide a "User's Guide" that measures the performance of governments, the quality of public institutions, and people's perceptions of various aspects of governance. This report points out that "an indicator does not have to come in numeric form" such as classification of countries as free or not free. (2) Program on Governance in the Arab Region (POGAR), initiated in early 2000, to promote capacity building of governance institutions including legislatures, judiciaries, and civil society organizations. Advice and assistance have primarily focused on three main aspects of governance: participation, rule of law, and transparency and accountability.[4]

▪ A report by Lonti and Woods (2008) for the OECD countries sets some specific ideas on measuring governance. The project emphasizes collecting "core data that should enable comparative institutional arrangements and performance" and shed some light on difference in institutional performance. Comparative data, it is claimed, "enable countries to better understand their own practices, to benchmark their achievements through international comparisons and to learn from experiences of other countries facing similar challenges" (Lonti and Woods, 2008: 7). The study underscores the importance that core data be as stable as possible to detect trends. Core data suggested includes indicators on government revenue and expenditure structures, employment and compensation, executive government outcomes, and budget procedures.

Other measurement attempts include those by the following:

▪ *Transparency International* has developed various indexes on ethical, transparent, and accountable systems of governance. Progress in fighting corruption at the international level considerably relies on such measurement and benchmarking. The most widely recognized in this regard is the Corruption Perception Index that covered 180 countries in 2010. Primarily, Transparency International "seeks to provide reliable quantitative diagnostic tools regarding levels of transparency and corruption at the global and local levels."[5]

▪ *Freedom House Survey* measures progress in developing political freedoms. The index is widely used by news agencies and researchers and has exclusively reported expert opinions on 192 countries since 1955. Experts, generally not based in the country, allocate a country rating based on responses to a series of questions. The scores for political rights, civil liberties, and combined freedom index run from 1 to 7, with 1 being most free and 7 being least free.

▪ *Newsweek's rankings* of "The Best Countries in the World" is worthy of note as a measurement initiative that claims to achieve more than measuring various aspects of countries by putting these aspects together (*Newsweek* 2010,

August 23 & 30: 31–42). The *Newsweek* survey, utilizing a team of experts, selected "five categories of national wellbeing—education, health, quality of life, economic competitiveness, and political environment—and compiled metrics within these categories across 100 nations" (2010: 31). Despite the difficulty of gathering comparative data, the magazine acknowledges that the outcome was a "snapshot" of how countries looked in 2008 and 2009. The top four countries in this ranking are Finland, Switzerland, Sweden, and Australia. The bottom four were Zambia, Cameron, Nigeria, and Burkina Faso. The United States was ranked number 11 (*Newsweek* 2010, August 23 & 30: 32–33).

Question of Democratic Governance

The classification of countries as democratic and nondemocratic governance in the literature and by mass media tends to group together under one descriptive term significantly different systems with diverse forms and practices. Democratic constitutional monarchies of Spain, UK, and the Netherlands, for example, are not the same as the democratic presidential systems of the United States or France. The variation is far greater among non-Western, large systems such as Japan, China, Brazil, Mexico, Egypt, India, South Africa, and Indonesia. Over the years, *democracy* has been loaded with meanings and conceptions, even myths and ideologies that obscure its real values and attributes. The term *democracy* is one of the most widely used and abused characterizations of governance. "The smug assertion that liberal democratic regimes alone are morally acceptable cannot be sustained," as Rohr (2000: 215) points out. Not only would this be unrealistic, Rohr argues, "but, more importantly, it would be a form of historical imperialism that stands aloof in self-righteous judgment on how the vast majority of human beings have organized their civic lives over the centuries." This does not mean one may not favor a liberal democracy over authoritarian rule. It means, however, that the moral excellence of a liberal democracy cannot deprive a centralized or authoritarian system of moral legitimacy (Rohr 2000: 215).

The attempt to define operationally what a democratic government looks like runs into many obstacles and easily gets shrouded with ethnic and cultural biases. A common description of democratic governance is as follows: "In the modern world there are no democracies without constitutions" (Chapman 2000: 221). This includes written and unwritten constitutions that encompass customs and conventions. But, while Chapman recognizes constitutions and elections as determinants of the legitimacy of governance, many examples exist of systems of governance that conduct regular elections and have constitutions but lack fidelity to democratic values. Conducting a national election and having a constitution is not a sufficient indicator or does not constitute qualification for classifying a state as democratic. Does governance remain democratic when it fails to recognize the particularities of its minorities, oppresses them, practices open racism, or habitually disregards international laws and conventions? Would a system of governance remain democratic when declaring itself as a Muslim, Jewish, or Christian state, providing policy preferences to those who are members of the faith and, by such actions, placing in disadvantage citizens who are not of the same faith or actively discriminating against them?

These and similar questions should modify or qualify an absolutist perspective of democracy. To be sure, a constitution is a basic document that specifies the main structures and functions of a governance system, but history is replete with examples of totalitarian systems that have constitutions and conduct election. Many examples indicate that governance systems that seek to melt away or exclude certain citizens on the basis of gender, religion, ethnicity, culture, or race, if not reformed, tend to drift to greater chauvinistic, nationalistic, and extremist practices. Regardless, a constitution does enhance the democratic characteristics of a governance system when such a constitution, explicitly, affirms unfettered equality under the law of all citizens. While a constitution safeguards the principle of equality in word and indeed it should, also, ensure genuine representation of citizens through free and fair election (Jreisat, 2004).

Concluding that "more countries than ever before are working to build democratic governance," the UNDP has been promoting democracy through reform and development of institutions and processes that are more responsive to the needs of ordinary citizens. This approach also seeks to build partnerships and to share ways to promote participation, accountability, and effectiveness at all levels. "We help countries strengthen their electoral and legislative systems, improve access to justice and public administration, and develop a greater capacity to deliver basic services to those most in need."[6] Actually, it is ineffective and corrupt governance, particularly in developing societies, that has been blamed for conditions of poverty, economic stagnation, lack of political stability, confused priorities, and being an obstacle to sustainable development (Jreisat 2004; Donahue and Nye 2003; Werlin 2003: 332). In contrast, as Rosell (1999: ix) explains, the ability of a society to prosper in a world of rapid change will largely depend on its ability to develop a more participatory and a more effective governance system.

Globalization

Globalization has mainly been defined in terms of linkages, integration, interdependence, and connectedness among economies, peoples, cultures, and countries. Certainly, goods and services produced in one country are increasingly obtainable anywhere in the world. International travel, finance, communication, and a variety of exchanges are made simple and fast. Nevertheless, the consequences of globalization have been grounds for high praise as well as criticism and resentment. The subject is particularly complicated because it has many aspects and dimensions and its effects are felt worldwide. These are different perspective on globalization:

Economic-Based Globalization

The major premise of this perspective on globalization is based on economic factors such as free trade, banking, investment, labor, and transfer of capital. The reference is specifically to global capitalism that furthers the integration of national economies into the international economy. Economic globalization gained particular notoriety or influence since the 1980s, with the ascendancy of the prescriptions promoted by what is known as "neoliberalism," or the "Washington consensus," affirmed and enhanced by policies of the International Monetary Fund and the World Bank. Globalization is regarded as a continuing process of capital accumulation that has been going on for a long time and only recently intensified as a result of technology (Farazmand, 1999: 512).

As pointed out above, the neoliberal economic perspective promoted public policies of "privatization, minimizing economic regulations, rolling back welfare, reducing expenditures on public goods, tightening fiscal discipline, favoring free flow of capital, strict control on organized labor, tax reductions, and unrestricted currency repatriation" (Falk 1999: 1–2). Actually, in recent years, these prescriptions have given globalization some of its most publicly known characteristics. Adherence to this neoliberal school inevitably results in global competitiveness for advantages in trade, investment, and free flow of capital across borders. In the end, there are winners and losers within such a competitive environment. In the past, multinational corporations and economies of industrial countries have been the main beneficiaries.

The economic thrust, fueled by overcoming trade and investment barriers, also displayed enormous flexibility and adaptation. Many more U.S. companies have offices and factories around the world. *Outsourcing* means that companies are going outside their organizational or national boundaries for products and services that once were produced by the company's employees. "Companies can outsource technology services, customer service, tax services, legal services, accounting services, benefit communications, manufacturing, and marketing" (Locker and Kienzler 2008: 20). American companies have been doing business abroad for a long time, but never before has it been so important that many large companies generate more than half of their sales in foreign countries.

Moreover, labor unions, parochial and protectionists in the past, have now become significant forces for globalization. An announcement in Ottawa, Canada (mid-April 2007) "signaled a radical new direction for the global economy. The United Steelworkers … entered into merger negotiations with two of Britain's largest unions … to create not only the first trans-Atlantic but the first genuinely multinational trade union" (Myerson 2007: 16A). This Ottawa declaration broke new ground in labor adaptation to the globalization of capital, a transition that began in the 1990s. Other unions such as the Communications Workers of America have been negotiating with similar unions in Europe and elsewhere. As steel production has become a global enterprise, the union formed alliances with mining and manu-facturing unions in Brazil, South Africa, Australia, Mexico, Germany, and Britain (Myerson 2007). In part, such alliances among unions have been prompted by the fact that their employers are global or multinational companies.

The impact of globalization is not unidirectional. Currently, labor laws and labor migration are hot issues in the West, actually contradicting commitments of some countries to globalization. This irony was illustrated in a headline about labor migration in *Business Week* (June 4, 2007: 40): "Globalization vs. Migration Reform: Can we have free flow of goods and capital without free flow of labor?" asked the business journal. Today, many countries in Europe, the United States, and the Arab world are wrestling with this problem. "One view of the world seems to be tearing down walls that separate countries; other view builds them up" (*Business Week*, June 4, 2007: 40). It is true that the United States and the Europeans are losing jobs, and that is posing a problem, since the companies are outsourcing work to the Asian countries because the cost of labor is low and this increases profits to corporations, considerably. There is immense pressure on the employed workers in the West who are always under the threat of the business being outsourced. Corporations are building up units in other countries equally well equipped as they have done in their own country, thus transferring the technology, the quality of the product, and the type of management to other countries. Other consequences that have been echoed in mass media in the past few years include the notion that globalization is leading to the invasion of communicable diseases, social degenera-tion, excessive corporate power, and, for nations at the receiving end, giving up the reins to a foreign company that might lead, again, to a subtle, sophisticated form of colonization.

Information Technology–Based Globalization

The appeal of technological innovation, and the recent worldwide popularization of electronic tools and products, underlines the depiction of globalization as driven by recent achievements in information and communication technologies (ICT). These advancements have precipitated an "information revolution," changing relation-ships, and improving global interconnections. The utility and the cumulative effect of ICT are tangible as they are universal. Actually, many changes in marketing, finance, dissemination of information, and methods of public and private manage-ment have been credited to ICT.

Applications of information technology (IT) in governments, particularly in managing public organizations, have resulted in shortened distances, saved time, expanded outputs, and increased freedom in crossing boundaries, and have over-come cultural, political, and institutional barriers. "Information technology is changing *everything* about the world in which we live with impacts that are both deep and diverse" (Rahm 1999: 75). The Internet, e-mail, Web pages, fax machines, printers, videoconferencing, and numerous other tools profoundly changed information flow and dissemination and markedly enhanced global communication. A particularly noteworthy effect of modern technology is "the shift to a knowledge economy, much deeper global integration, and a transformation in humanity's relationship to the environment" (Michalski, Miller, and Stevens 2001: 7). In brief, the ease of information communication stimulated the emergence of the knowledge society and a fundamental reshaping of the global interaction.

Whereas public administration has been emphasizing performance, benchmarking, and measurement of results, there is increasing reliance on information sources and on IT as elements of discovery and realization of the organization's strategic goals (Klingner 2009). Coordination and institutionalizing information systems, however, compel organizations to also confront specific challenges: (1) the choice of technology that is most relevant and economical to the organization; (2) the quality and relevance of data gathered and transmitted by technology; (3) the interconnectivity, across organizations and across cultures, that expands the horizons of management beyond the traditional boundaries.

Broad View of Globalization

Globalization is also viewed through wide-angle lenses that reflect a panoramic picture of its processes, continually stimulating "the thickening of interdependence" (Keohane and Nye 2000: 21). Although the growing interdependence is enhanced by electronic innovation, certainly it is not invented or created by these processes. In this analysis, globalization is more than economics or technology. Issues of environment, human rights, education, security, and ethics, to mention only a few policies, seem to transcend distances, cultures, and borders as well. Also, globalization has very ancient roots (Farazmand 1999). The British empire, for example, on which "the sun never set" by domination of others, crumbled amid the devastation of World War II, and the struggle for independence by the colonies.

Today, effective globalization can be realized through international cooperation rather than unilateral coercive or imperial powers. A serious challenge to nation-states, in the sphere of economics and beyond, is the increasing influence of transnational organizations such as the United Nations, the World Trade Organization (WTO), the North American Free Trade Agreement (NAFTA), and the World Bank. Similarly, actions by regional associations such as the European Union, the Organization of American States (OAS), the League of Arab States, the Union of African States, and others, all require profound adjustments in the traditional role of governance (Pierre 2000: 5). Technological innovations have blurred organizational and state boundaries inducing a continual search for new and more realistic forms of governance to suit the global age. Even if the central government in any society remains holding the greater powers and responsibilities, facilitated by civil and military services, globalization of capital has undermined territorial sovereignty and central control. To succeed in an interconnected and rapidly changing world, societies need "to develop learning-based governance and decision making systems" (Rosell 1999: ix) where more people can participate in systems capable of operating effectively across shifting boundaries.

As in any social system, the most reliable source of change is knowledge and education. Not only because "knowledge is power," but also the production and application of social and scientific knowledge harnesses social organization to economic growth as it assists policy-makers and managers in their managerial activities (Mahon and McBride 2009: 83). An organization that can create, synthesize, legitimate, and disseminate useful knowledge can play a significant role in state and global governance. The image of an information society, however, is far more involved than processing information; it is also the end result of the interplay and the dynamics of many qualitative and quantitative factors that converge to produce a changed society.

Information and knowledge are also essential for enhanced efficiency and effectiveness of both public and private organizations. But the negative side effects of the use of information technology have to be restrained as well from violations of citizens' privacy. The public outcry in the United States, for example, pressured lawmakers "to protect consumers from shady operators and commercialization run amok" (Dunham 2003: 40). Consumers are demanding that legislators rein in spammers jamming e-mail systems, telemarketers interrupting family time, and credit companies trading in consumer financial data and routinely intruding in the privacy of people (Dunham 2003: 40). New technology saves time, but information overload has become a problem. Employees are becoming overwhelmed with all the information available, particularly with the amount of e-mail and marketing messages and the threats to security and privacy (Locker and Kienzler 2008: 15–16).

Still, the deepening global interdependence reinforced mutual relationships among countries to unprecedented levels of "worldwide interconnectedness in all aspects of contemporary social life, from the cultural to the criminal, the financial to the spiritual" (Crocker 2002: 15). In their futuristic study for OECD countries on *Governance in the 21st Century*, Michalski, Miller, and Steven (2001: 8) claimed that technological breakthroughs and market-driven economic transformation have been potent forces in extending and deepening relationships of market forces. They regard the global economy as influenced by three sets of powerful changes that will sustain growth and wealth creation in the future: "the shift to a knowledge economy, much deeper global integration, and a transformation in humanity's relationship to the environment." From this perspective, the rules and behaviors that shape the making and implementation of public decisions are also expected to change.

It is important to point out that globalization trends do not move in a linear path, continually intensifying and speeding up. The position of globalization enthusiasts or "hyperglobalists," as David Crocker refers to them, is that the phenomenon of globalization is an historically unprecedented and powerful set of processes that certainly result in a more interconnected and organizationally multifaceted world (Crocker 2002: 16). Skeptics, on the other side, argue that regional trading blocs may become alternatives to globalization. The global economic and financial crisis of 2009 is described as "the worst global economic downturn of the post–World War II era; it is the first serious global downturn of the modern era of globalization" (Stiglitz 2009: 11). The crisis has become a real challenge to global economic integration, cross-boundary financial investment, and multinational corporate power. Also, the economic crisis underlined the fact that with "globalization not only do good things travel more easily across borders; bad things do too" (Stiglitz 2009: 11). One of those negative consequences is that prosperity has not been shared and the gap in wealth and economic growth between developed and developing countries has not been reduced; in many cases it has increased.

In brief, globalization is an indisputable reality. Perfectly equitable globalization, however, remains an illusion. Some important beginnings have been made by institutions such as the World Trade Organization to head off trade wars; UN agencies and international offices also set up frameworks to protect against abuse and to legitimate lawful economic, political, and social interactions within established methods (Rosell 1999: 21, 22). Nevertheless, the world was not spared the outcomes of the financial disaster of 2008–9. Now, we see reaffirmation of the role of governance for repairing the damage, protecting public interest, and reviving the regulatory function. Whether one is an enthusiast or a skeptic, recent U.S. policies have been adjusting to a more cooperative global posture, emphasizing dialogue, diplomacy, and multilateralism in resolving global problems. A transformation of the global system into a more active, orderly, and cooperative system is now an official policy, as President Obama declared recently:

> All of us share this world for but a brief moment in time. The question is whether we spend that time focused on what pushes us apart, or whether we commit ourselves to an effort—a sustained effort—to find common grounds, to focus on the future ... to respect the dignity of all human beings.[7]

Clearly, many countries seem unable to master the rules of the game in the era of globalization. To be an equal player, not a mere subject of the new global order, effective governance is a condition for cultivating the benefits. Current scholarship on governance is struggling to free its coverage from traditional and parochial literature in comparative politics and comparative political theory that only infrequently ventured outside the cultural boundaries of Europe and the United States. Traditional scholarship has also been less interested in institutional reforms and conditions of political thought outside Western democratic models (Macridis and Brown 1990: 2–3). Thus, when information is conveyed about governance in developing societies, most likely it is shaped by images of their failures or formed according to the predispositions of the observers.

Globalism and Public Administration

Global interdependence is forcing reconsideration of the traditional assumptions, propositions, and principles of public administration. "Globalization has an impact on most dimensions of public administration in most countries, and constrains the ability of national governments to act independently" (Schiavo-Campo and McFerson 2008: 4). Comparative Public Administration, New Public Management, and recent International Public Administration are essentially attempts to reevaluate existing assumptions, and to discover and apply best practices. The discourse on the improvement of global public management capacity has not resolved issues of how to institutionalize appropriate organizational structures and processes within diverse cultural, economic, and political conditions. To what extent organizational structures and processes are culturally determined is not definitively established yet, nor do we know how the norms and conventions of the culture, within which an organization is embedded, influence rules of conduct for the organization and its employees. Because success of reform initiatives largely depends on the degree of coherence between proposed change and preferences and priorities of the political leaders, public managers need to "apply political skills in the process of managing performance and change" (Milner and Joyce 2005: 1). Actually, many countries have a long way to go before building effective institutional frameworks of governance and of management, notwithstanding external and internal pressures for improvement. The following conclusions are derived from the practice of public administration over the years as well as from the literature:

- The rulers and managers of the state, in particular, have to take charge of reform strategies. They have the authority and the responsibility, they know their own work, they control the resources, and they are accountable for the final outcomes.
- Comparative analysis of the human experience in management over the past century confirms the utility and value of many administrative concepts and practices such as accountability, transparency, management by facts, ethics, performance measurement, participatory management, and capacity building. How to advance these concepts of management and to incorporate them into reform strategies is a responsibility of governance.
- The practices of governance and administration require continuous adaptation of structures and processes to deliver policies and services according to society's needs and demands. Good governance and effective management in the global context are not endowed or ordained hierarchically; they evolve, adapt, and continually improve in response to society's changing needs, and reflective of learning from gained knowledge and experience.
- The most appropriate and reliable indicator of the efficacy of a public institution is its performance. Failures of the state, particularly those of the developing countries, to implement effective reforms that aim at achieving acceptable

rate of economic growth, improve accountability and openness, build political and administrative institutional capacities, and develop civil society foundations have profoundly undermined confidence and trust in the contemporary state and its leadership. Such failures provided a rationale for the growing role of the marketplace as an alternative to the berated performance of public institutions, regardless of the common realization that the market is not and cannot be a substitute for public policy.

■ Public administration operates in a multifaceted context as it delivers basic services to society. As a profession, it encompasses leadership, institutions, management, politics, and culture. It is not easy to integrate and to utilize these various dimensions to achieve common objectives. Rules and processes of governance are not neutral in practice and can distort outcomes of a governance system. Thus, independent evaluation, audit, investigation, legislative oversight, and similar instruments are regular features of responsible governance. The distinction between governance as an analytical concept and governance as operational processes separates the form from the practice of public authority.

■ The pressures on the contemporary state for adapting traditional systems of public management have created frequent reassessment of premises, tenets, and future directions of the field. Donald Klingner suggests that if U.S. public administrators are to respond effectively to the need to rebuild the country's international reputation, public administration "should be directed toward global development in ways that meet specified criteria: Data-driven, performance-oriented, sustainable, utilizing smart practices" (2009: 21). A new global reality is that an "increasing number of policy decisions are now being made by global institutions instead of individual countries" (Welch and Wong 1998: 45). This new global reality, in addition to recent technological developments and other contextual challenges, necessitate that public administration examine and reevaluate many of its assumptions and practices to provide effective responses to these internal and external realities.

It is possible to define some lessons learned during the recent past from trends and prospects of change within the public administration profession that have been stimulated or instigated by global necessities. Some of these changes remain in the process of being accepted and confirmed on a larger scale. Public administration as a field of study is in a transformation mode to remain responsive to larger needs and demands. These are summaries of important adaptations that have been made or need to be made.

Decisions by Negotiation and Collaboration

The impact of globalization and regional integration in Europe, Asia, the Americas, and the Arab world is that national governance as well as international organizations have come to "rely more than ever before on reaching decisions through multilateral negotiations" (Metcalfe and Metcalfe 2002: 267). Increasingly decisions of one country have impacts on other countries. Invariably, reactions and feedback of some countries are inputs into the decisions of other countries. This is more reason for increasing reliance on negotiations in many areas of public policy with effects extending beyond national boundaries of one country. Global interdependence is a reality in economics and finance, environment, travel, defense, security, and healthcare. Globalization trends have underscored the necessity for effective communication as economic integration increases and the financial, political, social, and cultural lives of countries become more intertwined (Thomas 1999; Kettl 2000: 490). The new reality requires free interactions among nations seeking to promote their self-interest within the rules of the game.

Negotiation is also a managerial process requiring capacity and skills to produce agreement and joint action. Improvement of capacity requires "overcoming old attitudes and oversimplified assumptions and models of the negotiating process" (Metcalfe and Metcalfe 2002: 269). Within public administration, collaborative public management is gaining thrust from growing research on collaborative management and from emerging collaborative organizational structures and processes (McGuire 2006: 33). Among institutions of state and local governments as well as among nations, increasing reliance on negotiation and search for agreements to resolve problems and settle policy issues is indisputable. Negotiation may not be embraced in an empire-building approach with imperial authority to put down challenges rather than to persuade and negotiate agreements. Nor does the negotiation stance fully answer the question of distribution of power within a society.

Nevertheless, from different starting points, all societies have experienced profound shifts in authority relationships. The concentration of powers has been challenged everywhere. Absolutist, authoritarian regimes have been undermined by forces of democratic values, competition, new means of communication, education, and the far-reaching global interactions (OECD 2001: 9–10). Thus, the character of governance and the methods of exercising power have been changed significantly. Students and practitioners of public administration and politics are gradually shifting their behaviors and methods of managing as they develop better understanding of what is being changed and why. In the end, a more humanizing environment is infusing governance in its internal and external relationships.

Adapting the traditional, hierarchical, and legal structures to a decentralized, less hierarchical, and more collaborative models of management is not easy. The apparent failure of governance in many countries, and the trend of allocating a greater role for the private sector in national development, provided the impetus for those who prefer shifting the responsibility of public bureaucracy from "managing" to "facilitating" economic activities (Kaboolian 1998). Neoliberal globalism has inspired persistent attacks on public bureaucracy and renewed attempts to discredit the traditional administrative systems without advancing viable, workable alternatives (Jreisat 2001b). Despite fads and fashions in the field of public administration, a growing emphasis is on improving traditional administrative knowledge, skills, and attitudes, not supplanting them with alternative notions, described as "more than a little vague" (Considine and Lewis 2003: 133) such as "reinventing" governance or the New Public Management.

The hierarchical "command and control" paradigms have been undermined or modified by processes and systems emphasizing cooperation, quality, team-building, networking, motivation, performance measurement, accountability, ethics, and empowerment of employees. These concepts have contributed significantly to a meaningful transformation of contemporary governance. Although the applications of these new organizational and managerial changes are not uniform, one finds many demonstrations of their effects on development and institutional learning worldwide.

Performance Culture

Governance is more attentive to results of its policies and actions than any time before. Assessing performance is a universal organizational and managerial culture that stresses results-oriented management. "Governments around the globe adopted management reforms to squeeze extra efficiency out of the public sector" (Kettl 1997: 446). Performance measurement is a management tool used to monitor and report results of programs and policies and to ensure accountability of public officials. Other means are employed in establishing evidence of good performance such as performance audit, management audit, external reviews, and independent general inspection. The most visible tool and the most widely practices method of performance measurement, however, has been performance budgeting.

Effective practice of performance measurement is demanding and requires management adaptability, cooperation, and creativity in the utilization of this tool. In recent years, public administration invariably emphasized performance and development of new administrative capacities to offset its proclivities and tendencies to drift into a hierarchical "command and control" mode, producing rule-driven rigidities. The New Public Management (NPM) movement was one response that endeavored to address some of the needs and changes prompted by globalization. But, NPM has not received uncritical endorsement from the profession. Among many criticisms leveled against NPM is that it remains grounded in instrumental rationality that, ultimately, could erode fundamental values of representative governance and commitment to public service. Actually, not all the effects of globalization on public administration have been sorted out in terms of significance and magnitude (Lynn 2001; Riccucci 2001), but the need for managerial adaptation is unmistakable.

Role of Leadership

Public administration education has been making serious strides in responding to distinct demands for effective managerial leadership in the global context.

Organizational leaders are critical for governance because of the many crucial functions they perform. Leaders are responsible for negotiations, mediation, and sensitivity to human rights and diversity. Also, leaders are involved in conflict resolution, intercultural communications, contracting, and problem-solving techniques, beyond what traditional concepts of public service provide. Beyond the technical competence, a leader has to be politically astute and skilled in building consensus and partnerships while maintaining the highest standards of integrity. Studies of leadership offer a variety of perspectives and theories: traits approach, contingency theory, situational approach, transformational leadership, behavioral approach, and others. All models of governance systems include some mechanisms for developing leadership: selection, recruitment, training, and institutional teamwork. Improvement and intensification of such development processes are central to development and implementation of the strategic objectives of the organization and the society in a highly complex and competitive international environment.[8] A comprehensive, skills-based model of leadership attracted the attention of researchers for a long time (Northouse 2004). Briefly, the "skills-approach" is more concerned with what leaders can accomplish than who they are. It is the "ability to use one's knowledge and competencies to accomplish a set of goals or objectives" (Northouse 2004: 36).

E-Government

It is realistic to assume that all countries "have been executing major initiatives in order to tap the vast potential of the Internet for the distinct purpose of improving and perfecting the governing process" (UNDPP-ASPA 2002: 1). Broadly defined, e-government refers to various information and communication technologies in use by the public sector. A more specific view of e-government defines it as "utilizing the internet and the world-wide web for delivering government information and services to citizens" (UNDPP-ASPA 2002: 1). In a report published by the UN Division for Public Administration in cooperation with the American Society for Public Administration (UNDPP-ASPA 2002: 7), countries are classified into "high e-gov capacity" such as the United States, Australia, South Korea, New Zealand, Norway, Canada, UK, France; "medium e-gov capacity" such as Poland, Venezuela, Russian Federation, Saudi Arabia, Turkey; "minimal e-gov capacity" such as Armenia, South Africa, Cuba, Jamaica; and, "deficient e-gov capacity" such as Cameron, Ghana, Thailand, Tanzania. The same UN-ASPA report that compares the world's reliance on the information technology found, also, that e-government profiles of the UN member states are at extremely different phases of development. The stages of e-government are described as follows:

Emerging: An official government online presence is established.
Enhanced: Government sites increase, information becomes more dynamic.
Interactive: Users can download forms, e-mail officials, and interact through the Web.

Transactional: Users can actually pay for services and other transactions online.
Seamless: Full integration of e-services across administrative boundaries.

Accordingly, a compelling questions on the issue of capacity is what environmental factors help promote building societal capacity in information technology? Clear evidence links wealth, government policies, access, training opportunities, and education in general to high capacity e-government. The opposite is also true (i.e., lack of these factors leads to capacity deficit). Another important question relates to application of this capacity. To what extent is information technology used by public administrators for interfacing with citizens as well as for improving public services and enhancing performance? Although the answers vary from one country to another, no doubt that enormous worldwide progress has been made in the more recent years. Using electronic government to deliver public services reached new heights in countries like Australia, Belgium, Canada, South Korea, the United States, the UK, New Zealand, and others. Communication technology enhances the culture of openness in government and counteracts the traditional rigidities of a centralized bureaucracy.

It is important to underline the real as well as the potential in the use of e-government. The global interdependence of countries created a sort of resurgence of interest in knowledge-based, information-based, or data-based public policy decisions. The so-called information revolution facilitated this reliance on data, in all countries, more than was possible just few years ago. At the same time, data-based management thrives in a knowledge-based society where information is used, produced, maintained, transformed, and disseminated locally and globally. Information builds overall qualitative improvement in management capacity and professional expertise. To be sure, Information Communication Technology (ICT) facilitates use of and access to information, but investment in research and development, flourishing scholarship, and availability of quality education are the foundation for developing a genuine knowledge-based society.

Finally, setting standards for the ICT can have long range public policy implications to national capacity for innovation and competition and the ability of governments to efficiently and cost effectively perform services such as national security, disaster response, and e-Health administration. Standards are set in ways that serve as a form of regulation and decision making such as the extent of user privacy on the Internet (DeNardis 2010). Because of these possible policy implications, governments have a vested interest in promoting open technical standards adhering to principles of transparency, cost efficiency, and interoperability. Various possibilities for governments to engage with information and communication technology standardization (development, regulation, funding, adoption)—and, ultimately, to exert market influence and provide efficient e-Governance functions through procurement policies that promote open standards—require interoperability frameworks and specific information technology standards for e-Governance infrastructures (DeNardis 2010).

A serious dimension that is less explored in the literature is the negative effects of the use of electronic technology to commit crimes, fraud, and identity theft and to endanger national security. This is the downside of this new reality. Cyber warfare is not theoretical anymore. Malicious software and evil creativity proved to be a serious threat not only to personal use of this technology, but, also, its use to inflict serious damage to manufacturing plants, energy, water supplies, and banking systems as well as to nuclear plants, military targets, and national computer systems. This is a global challenge and may soon require universal standards of regulations and conventions.

The Comparative Perspective

The global context is consistent with the basic mission and premises of a cross-cultural comparative approach for learning and practicing public administration. In response to the new global reality, public administration has to utilize more effectively a comparative perspective that incorporates Western and non-Western systems for developing generalizations and discovering the best practices. A major challenge to researchers in constructing comparative studies is "resolving issues of purpose and method" (Lynn 1998: 233). Comparative analysis of the future has to demonstrate openness to incorporate indigenous models and native patterns of study and application along with Western concepts and models (Jreisat 2002; Henderson 1995; Welch and Wong 1998). Properly construed and executed comparative research provides needed assessments of competing explanatory frameworks, tests models across time, space, cultures, organizations, and contexts (Lynn 1998: 233). Resolutions of various pending issues would be judged by criteria based on relevance to practice and linkage with the main field of public administration. Defining common patterns of administration from multicultural experiences would improve applicability, temper the archaic "institutional ethnicities," and increase responsiveness to new needs and demands of a changing context.

Conclusion

As a strategic partner in governance, public administration has to acquire accurate knowledge of the total setting of governance, its assets, capabilities, and priorities. As a crucial structure in modern society, in fact in all societies at all times, governance has attracted a great deal of studies and analysis as well as myths and ideological twists and curves. This is why in this analysis, an effort is made to delineate, define, and compare to develop a clear view of what constitutes governance. The quality of governance is inseparable from the quality of public management.

The dramatic changes in economics, technology, education, and politics have increased interdependence and interconnections among all countries of today's world. This is the phenomenon of globalization that affected so many aspects of current living. Certainly, globalization influenced governance and public administration within it. Globalization has become of the essence for modern economics and politics. Discussions, analysis, and prognostications of globalization are abundant, and the search for instruments of adaptation and adjustment are continuing. The bottom line, globalization introduced advantages and benefits but also risks and perils. The choices for public policies are more clear, and the pressures in both directions of benefits and risks require new competence and knowledge by public servants.

Thus, development of special capacities in critical thinking and creative analysis to deal with issues of governance is compelling. The challenges demand intellectual integrity and fidelity to genuine empirical learning by public employees rather than the stultifying fixation of preconceived ideologies. Good solutions of public issues emerge when approached openly, empirically, and with broad participation. Critical thinking involves skills in questioning assumptions and in utilizing imaginative and multi-disciplinary perspectives in the analysis. Public administration reform has to be comprehensive and rooted in a cultural commitment to multiple perspectives and a broad vision that integrates rather than compartmentalizes knowledge and information. For public administration learning and doing, concepts and application, each contributes to the improvement of the other.

References

Ahrens, J. 2002. *Governance and Economic Development*. Northampton, MA: Edward Elger.

Beinecke, R. H. 2009. *The Innovation Journal: The Public Sector Innovation Journal*. (Electronic Journal) Vol. 14(1): 1–17.

Berle, A., and G. Means. 1932. *The Modern Corporation and Private Property*. NY: Macmillan.

Berle, A., and G. Means. 1968. *The Modern Corporation and Private Property*. NY: Harcourt, Brace & World.

Chapman, R. A., ed. 2000. *Ethics in Public Service for the New Millennium*. Burlington, VT: Ashgate Publishing Co.

Cocker, D. A. 2002. Development Ethics and Globalization. *Philosophy & Public Policy Quarterly*. 22, (4): 13–20.

Considine, M., and J. M. Lewis. 2003. Bureaucracy, Network, or Enterprise? Comparing Models of Governance in Australia, Britain, the Netherlands, and New Zealand. *Public Administration Review*, 63 (2): 131–140.

DeNardis, Laura. 2010. E-Governance Policies for Interoperability and Open Standards. *Policy & Internet*. Vol. 2: Iss. 3, Article 6. *DOI*: 10.2202/1944-2866.1060. Available at: http://www.psocommons.org/policyandinternet/vol2/iss3/art6

Donahue, J. D., and J. S. Nye, Jr., eds. 2003. *Visions of Governance in the 21st Century*. Washington, D.C.: Brookings Institution Press.

Dunham, R. S. 2003. A Grass-Roots Revolt against Information Age Intruders. *Business Week* (August 4).

Falk, R. 1999. *Predatory Globalization: A Critique*. Cambridge, UK: Polity Press.

Farazmand, A. 2002. Administrative Ethics and Professional Competence: Accountability and Performance Under Globalization. *International Review of Administrative Sciences.* Vol. 68 (2002): 127–143.

_____. 1999. Globalization and Public Administration. *Public Administration Review.* Vol. 59 (6): 509–522.

Gawthrop, L. 1998. *Public Service and Democracy: Ethical Perspectives for the 21st Century.* Newark, NJ: Chattham House.

Greider, W. 2009. The Future of the American Dream. *The Nation.* (May 25): 11–16.

Henderson, K.1995. Reinventing Comparative Public Administration: Indigenous Models of Study and Application. *The International Journal of Public Sector Management,* 8 (4).

Hyden, G. 2002. Operationalizing Governance for Sustainable Development. In J. E. Jreisat, ed. *Governance and Developing Countries.* Boston and Leiden, the Netherlands: Brill.

Jaffe, G. 2010. Gates: Cuts in Pentagon Bureaucracy Needed to Help Maintain Military Force. *Washington Post* (Sunday, May 9: A03).

Jain, R. B. 2002. Globalization, Liberalization, and Human Security in India: Challenges for Governance. In J. E. Jreisat, ed. *Governance and Developing Countries.* Boston and Leiden, The Netherlands, Brill.

Jreisat, J. E. 2006. The Arab World: Reform or Stalemate. *Journal of Asian and African Studies.* 41 (5/6): 411–439.

_____. 2004. Governance in a Globalizing World. *International Journal of Public Administration.* 27 (13 & 14): 1003–1029.

_____. 2002. *Comparative Public Administration and Policy.* Boulder, CO: Westview Press:

_____. 2001a. Governance and Developing Countries. *Journal of Developing Societies.* XVII (2).

_____. 2001b. The New Public Management and Reform. In K. T. Liou, ed., *Handbook of Public Management Practice and Reform,* New York: Marcel Dekker: 539–560.

_____. 1997. *Public Organization Management: The Development of Theory and Process.* Westport, CT: Greenwood Publishing.

Kaboolian, L. 1998. The New Public Management: Challenging the Boundaries of the Management vs. Administration Debate. *Public Administration Review, 58* (3): 189–193.

Keohane, R. and J. S. Nye. (2000). Introduction, in Nye and Donahue (eds.) *Governance in a Globalizing World.* Washington, D.C: The Brookings Institution Press.

Kettl, D. 2000. The Transformation of Governance: Globalization, Devolution, and the Role of Government. *Public Administration Review, 60* (6): 488–497.

Kettl, D. 1997. The Global Revolution in Public Management: Driving Themes, Missing Links. *Journal of Policy Analysis and Management,* 16 (3): 446 462.

Kettl, D., and J. Fesler. 1991. *The Politics of the Administrative Process.* Newark, NJ: Chatham House.

Klingner, D. E. 2009. Using US Public Administration to Support Global Development. *Journal of Regional Studies and Development* 18 (2): 1–29.

Klingner, D. 2006. Building Global Public Management Governance Capacity: The Road Not Taken. *Public Administration Review* 66 (5): 775–779.

Korten, D. 1995. *When Corporations Rule the World.* West Hartford, CT: Kumarian Press.

Locker, K. O. and D. Kienzler 2008. *Business Administration Communication.* 8th ed. NY: McGraw-Hill.

Lonti, Z., and M. Woods. 2008. Towards Government at a Glance: Identification of Core Data and Issues Related to Public Sector Efficiency. OECD Working Papers on Public Governance, No. &, OECD Publishing. doi:10.1787/245570167540.

Lynn, L. E. 2001. The Myth of the Bureaucratic Paradigm. *Public Administration Review.* 61 (2): 144–160.

Lynn, L. E. 1998. The New Public Management: How to Transform a Theme into a Legacy. *Public Administration Review, 58* (3): 231–238

Macridis, R. C., and B. E. Brown, eds. 1990. Comparative Analysis: Method and Concept. In *Comparative Politics: Notes and Readings*, ed. Macridis, R. C. and B. E. Brown, 1–16. 7th ed. Belmont, CA: Wadsworth.

Mahon, R., and S. McBride 2009. Standardizing and Disseminating Knowledge: The Role of the OECD in Global Governance. *European Political Science Review.* 1 (1): 83–101.

Mahoney, J., and K. Thelen. 2010. Preface. In *Explaining Institutional Change*, J. Mahoney and K. Thelen, eds. xi–xiii. Cambridge University Press.

Manning, N., and N. Parison. 2004. *International Public Administration Reform.* Washington, D.C.: The World Bank.

Margolick, D. 2010. The Return of the Neocons. *Newsweek.* (February 1): 33–39.

Marx, M. F. 1957. *The Administrative State.* Chicago, IL: The University of Chicago Press.

McGuire, M. 2006. Collaborative Public Management: Assessing What We Know and How We Know It. *Public Administration Review.* (Special Issue, Supplement to Volume 66): 33–43.

Metcalfe, L., and D. Metcalfe. 2002. Tools for Good Governance: An Assessment of Multiparty Negotiation Analysis. *International Review of Administrative Sciences.* Vol. 68 (2): 267–286.

Michalski, W., R. Miller, and B. Stevens (2001). Power in the Global Knowledge Economy and Society. In Secretary-General, OECD, ed. *Governance in the 21st Century.* OECD: Paris.

Milner, E., and P. Joyce. 2005. *Lessons in Leadership: Meeting the Challenges of Public Services Management.* London, UK: Routledge.

Myerson, H. 2007. Labor Unions go for Global. *The Washington Post*, reprinted in *St. Petersburg Times.* April 28: 16A.

Northouse, P. G. *Leadership: Theory and Practice.* 3rd ed. 2004; Sage: Thousand Oaks, CA.

Nye, J. S., and Donahue, eds. 2000. *Governance in a Globalizing World.* Washington, D.C: The Brookings Institution Press.

OECD. 2000. *Trust in Government: Ethics Measures in OECD Countries.* Paris, France.

OECD. 2001. Governance in the 21st Century Secretary-General, ed. Paris, France.

Peters, G. B. 2000. Governance and comparative politics. In J. Pierre, ed. *Debating Governance.* 36–53. NY: Oxford University Press.

Pierre, J. 2000. Introduction. In J. Pierre, ed. *Debating Governance.* 1–10. NY: Oxford University Press.

Presthus, R. 1978. *The Organizational Society.* Revised ed. NY: St. Martin's Press.

Prestowitz, C. 2003. *Rogue Nation: American Unilateralism and the Failure of Good Intentions.* New York: Basic Books. (in Books, Review by Rossant, J. *Business Week.* June 16: 22.

Rahm, D. 1999. The Role of Information Technology in Building Public Administration Theory. *Knowledge, Technology, and Policy.* 12 (1): 74–83.

Redford, E. 1969. *Democracy and the Administrative State.* Oxford University Press.

Rhodes, R. A. W. 2000. Governance and Public Administration. In J. Pierre, ed. *Debating Governance.* 54–90. NY: Oxford University Press.

Riccucci, N.M. 2001. The "Old" Public Management Versus the "New" Public Management. *Public Administration Review.* 61 (2): 172–175.

Rohr, J. A. 2000. Ethics, Governance, and Constitutions. In Chapman, R. A, ed. *Ethics in Public Service for the New Millennium.* 203–216. Burlington, VT: Ashgate Publishing.

Rohr, John. 1986. *To Run a Constitution: The Legitimacy of the Administrative State.* University Press of Kansas.

Rosell, S. A. 1999. *Renewing Governance.* Ontario, Canada: NY: Oxford University Press.

Schiavo-Campo, Salvatore and Hazel M. McFerson, 2008. *Public Management in Global Perspective.* Armonk, NY: M.E. Sharpe.

Shalala, D. E. 2004. The Buck Starts Here: Managing Large Organizations with Honesty and Integrity. *Public Integrity.* 6 (4): 349–356.

Stiglitz, J. E. 2009. A Real Cure for the Global Economic Crackup. *The Nation.* (July 13): 11–14.

Thomas, V. 1999. Globalization: Implications for Development Learning. *Public Administration and Development.* 19 (5): 5–17.

UNDP. 2007. *Governance Indicators: A User's Guide.* 2nd ed. UNDP Oslo Governance Center. http://www.undp-pogar.org/resources/publications.aspx?t=0&y=3&p=0 (July 11, 2009).

UNDP. 1997. *Decentralized Government Program.* (Management Development and Governance Division, UNDP, September).

UNDPP-ASPA (United Nations Division for Public Economics and Public Administration and American Society for Public Administration). 2002. *Benchmarking E-Government: A Global Perspective. A Report.* New York, (May).

Waldo, D. 1948. *The Administrative State.* New York: Ronald Press Co.

Welch, E., and W. Wong. 1998. Public Administration in a Global Context: Bridging the Gaps of Theory and Practice between Western and Non-Western Nations. *Public Administration Review* 58 (1): 40–50.

Werlin, H. H. 2003. Poor Nations, Rich Nations: A Theory of Governance. *Public Administration Review.* 63 (3): 329–342.

Endnotes

1. Inaugural address by Andrew Cuomo, newly elected governor of New York, *St. Petersburg Times* (January 8, 2010): 10A.
2. The World Bank Institute Web site: http://info.worldbank.org/governance/wgi/index.asp.
3. http://www.undp-pogar.org/resources/publications.aspx?t=0&y=3&p=0 (July 11, 2009).
4. POGAR's activities, which include providing policy advice, engaging in institutional capacity building, and testing policy options through pilot projects, revolve around the main concepts of participation, rule of law, and transparency and accountability. Web site: http:/www.pogar.org/.
5. Transparency International: http://www.transparency.org/policy_research/surveys_indices/cpi.
6. http://www.undp.org/governance/about.htm accessed July 6, 2009.
7. From President Obama's Speech in Cairo, Egypt, (June 4, 2009). *Text-NYTimes.com.*
8. Unpublished report by Group of Experts on the United Nations Program in Public Administration and Finance (fifteenth session), May 12, 2000. P. 3.

Chapter 2

Comparative Public Administration

Of ourselves, so long as we know only ourselves, we know nothing.
Woodrow Wilson (1887)

Introduction

Comparative public administration (CPA) is the study of administrative institutions, processes, and behaviors across organizational, national, and cultural boundaries. The CPA is a method of investigation and analysis that compares attributes and performance of administrative systems and subsystems as well as individuals or groups in positions of decision making to generate knowledge and enhance understanding of public management. Comparison recognizes similarities and differences and underscores successful practices, thus, expanding options and alternative strategies for improving the performance of public institutions.

The context (environment) of public administration consists of various external factors that exert significant influences on management action and behavior through different means and channels. External factors include societal values, legal norms, politics, international-global accords, culture, and the state of the economy. Together, these diverse external factors have considerable impact on public management, stimulating or stifling systemic traits and performance. In democratic governance, however, the political environment "determines the scope and objectives of the public services; it is the political environment which determines the values to be applied when delivering these services; ... and [the political environment] is the most important factor in the differences between public administration and management or administration in other contexts" (Chapman 2000: 219). These external influences on public administration are often loosely grouped together under the terms *environment, context,* or even *culture* (Almond and Verba 1989).

The comparative approach has been an important thrust within the field of public administration, committed to human learning and to discovery through comparison. The CPA seeks to advance administrative knowledge by focusing on administrative structures, functions, behaviors, and performance across organizational and cultural boundaries to improve reliability and applicability of administrative concepts and practices. As Bannister (2007: 171) notes, "The human urge to compare one's performance with that of others seems to be an intrinsic part of our psychological make-up." Comparison is more prevalent in our expressions and formal judgments than commonly acknowledged. We often compare performance to previous years, to other people, to other organizations, to cost, to benchmarks, and to similar functions and activities across jurisdictions and across national boundaries.

Consistently, the CPA seeks discovery of patterns and regularities of administrative action and behavior to produce new knowledge and insights and to affirm and refine existing information. The outcome, whether comparative research discovers new knowledge or validates existing information, is that public administration scholars and practitioners are better able to sort out and to adopt most worthy practices. "Comparison is so central to good analysis that the scientific method is unavoidably comparative" (Collier 1991: 7). Similarly, social scientists regard the comparative approach as "the methodological core of the humanistic and scientific methods" (Almond et al. 2000: 33). As a requirement of the scientific investigative process, the comparative approach has frequently been noted and emphasized in public administration literature since Woodrow Wilson's famous article in 1887. After many decades, Dahl's (1947: 8) widely quoted declaration remains true. Namely, as long as the study of public administration is not comparative, "claims of a science of public administration" sound rather hollow. Dahl concluded that the development of an American, British, or French science of public administration is feasible. But he also inquired: can there be "a science of public administration" in the sense of a body of generalized principles, independent of their peculiar national setting?

Comparative studies of organizations and institutions also reinforce understanding of global influences while expanding the domain of intellectual inquiry beyond traditional, parochial tendencies. Credible comparison of any aspect of governance cannot be confined to culture-bound practices any more for certain reasons: (1) The impact of globalization and regional integration in Europe, the Americas, and the rest of the world, points out that many decisions are made through multilateral negotiations and agreements that are binding to participating countries and beyond. Also, a large number of international organizations are frequently setting rules and policies that moderate the notion of unfettered authority of the nation state. (2) The examination of administrative practices of other societies permits us to see a wider range of administrative actions and choices, beyond the horizon of our own experiences. Rephrasing Woodrow Wilson, if we study only ourselves we know only about ourselves and remain isolated in an interconnected world. The CPA scholarship, at various phases of its evolution, devoted much attention to learning about unfamiliar, non-Western countries and their aspirations to transform and to modernize their administrative systems.

Comparative research broadens knowledge of conditions conducive to strong or weak administrative performance by focusing on a range of patterns of administrative activities and characteristics of the systems performing them. Much learning is achieved from practices that worked well and from those that did not. Not surprising, therefore, that administrative reform and capacity building are major concerns in the comparative literature. To learn from the best practices is to encourage the recognition and the utilization of the most appropriate organizational structures and processes. In many countries, irrespective of the results of reform plans for improving performance of public organizations, the contents of such plans have largely been based on lessons learned through cross-cultural comparative investigations (Manning and Parison 2004). While explanatory research is essential for the advancement of scholarship, it also benefits practitioners by expanding their horizons of choice and their capacity to observe, learn, and improve performance. Certainly, the practitioner gains deeper understanding of institutions, and the political processes that influence them, by comparing experiences across boundaries and across institutions.

Critical External Influences

Public administration is subject to significant formal and informal influences from its environment. Because public administration is increasingly influenced by these external variables, public management is far more informed when research findings are based on examination of the practices in more than one context or one country. Comparing few cases is preferable to a single case analysis for evaluating hypotheses or verifying conclusions. Utilizing a manageable number of cases in the analysis can be a more productive research effort than statistical or experimental approaches with their almost unlimited scope for accumulating data and manipulating variables. By comparing a limited number of administrative issues and questions, researchers are able to provide improved descriptions of conditions, sharper definitions of variables, and greater focus on the subject and its most crucial aspects (Pollitt and Bouckaert 2004; Manning and Parison 2004).

The ongoing dramatic change in information communication technology (ICT), introduced many tools of management research and learning that were not available a few years ago. These advanced tools of communication and information gathering make the processes of cross-cultural learning easier and more manageable. For many years, most developing countries have been seeking to build the knowledge and skills of their public employees through various forms of training tailored to the needs of their organizations. One form of learning has been the meetings of managers from developed and developing countries, joining in a variety of seminars and training activities in the United States, Europe, or in developing countries to discuss and learn about administrative problems and solutions in many contexts. Utilizing new information technologies, made the flow of information on administrative successes and failures constant and in all directions.

To cultivate the advantages of the comparative approach, one has to face the invariable need for constructing a framework that would allow systematic comparison of administrative systems of different countries with different levels of development. A broadly accepted framework has to meet the test of utility. Specifically, a proficient framework for comparative studies has to manifest the following general characteristics:

- Capacity for synthesis of current comparative administrative knowledge
- Balance between conceptual and practical concerns of the field
- Emphasis on constant and variable factors that matter in administering public services
- Accounting for contextual variations of conditions on the ground

While scholarly productivity is continuous in comparative studies of public and private administrations within single countries, much less research has been conducted at the cross-cultural levels. Reasons for less cross-cultural research output are many, including feasibility, language barriers, funding, lack of existing empirical data, and less than desirable levels of transparency in many countries. Nevertheless, a growing interest in contextual constraints has inspired reexamination of many organizational actions and relationships, especially those related to political, economic, and social factors. We are told, for example, that a "number of cross-national comparative analysis studies have been done ... several of which show that structure differs across cultures regardless of technology" (Roberts and Grabowski 1996: 415). Conceptual insights derived from comparing international experiences are a major source of guidance for a variety of organizational restructuring initiatives.

Currently, comparative and development administration is undergoing major shifts of focus in responding to the challenge of globalism. The CPA has to provide evidenced and practical knowledge of the real conditions on the ground. Administrative knowledge generated through cross-cultural studies, particularly in relation to reducing cost, improving quality of public services, and managing national development has to demonstrate greater understanding of the operational dimension of management. As a result of a growing commitment to what Ryan (1994) called "anti-parochial, anti-ethnocentric drive," the CPA has to construct dependable models of administrative application and practice, derived through worldwide effective descriptive and empirical comparisons. Diverse comparative administration perspectives promise greater relevance and research versatility. Two illustrations underscore the inherent adaptability of the comparative approach and the constant search for valid explanatory and prescriptive generalizations. These perspectives do not claim "reinventing" the comparative administration, and do not represent all such endeavors, but they are serious attempts to redirect and to invigorate the analysis:

1. *The primacy of the immediate context.* A main premise of this perspective is that improving the administrative function is linked to understanding the attributes of the immediate political and administrative context. In a comparative study of management reform in twelve developed countries (Australia, Belgium, Canada, Finland, France, Germany, Italy, Netherlands, New Zealand, Sweden, UK, and the United States), Pollitt and Bouckaert (2004: 39) "laid considerable stress on the characteristics of existing political and administrative systems in influencing processes of management change." These political-administrative systems, they point out; provide "the existing terrain—the topography over which reformers must travel ... different countries display different topographical features and therefore different challenges to those who wish to carry through reform" (2004: 39). Similarly, Manning and Parison (2004: xiii–xiv) analyzed public administrative reform experiences in fourteen countries in their attempts to find out what reform initiatives could serve to reduce public expenditures, improve policy responsiveness, improve government as an employer, and improve service delivery. Many of these fourteen countries are in Pollitt and Bouckaert's list of countries with additions of Brazil, Chile, South Korea, and the Russian Federation. No African or Arab country was included in either list. The reform model applied by Pollitt and Bouckaert (2004: 40) relies on comparative literature in developing the "key features" of their model:
   - The state structure, including the constitution
   - The nature of the central executive government, including the type of political system
   - Functional elements, including relationships between political leaders and top civil servants
   - The dominant administrative culture
   - Diversity of channels through which ideas come to stimulate public management reform

2. The *globalist* or *internationalist* perspective prompts the CPA to accommodate growing global needs and intensifying international necessity. Globalization of our world, Riggs (1991a: 473) noted, "compels us to rethink the context of what we call Public Administration." Public administration cannot remain unaffected as globalization processes dramatically undermined geographical distance and deepened economic interdependence. Notwithstanding the contributions of the early comparative administration, development

administration, and the "new public management," the future of public administration, Klingner (2009) concludes, is in being "international purposive praxis," serving what he calls the "Millennium Goals." This public administration is essentially purposive, data-driven, performance-oriented, and sustaining smart practices (Klingner 2009: 8). "Administrators are coming to view the world as a vast organizational matrix which can be tapped for solutions to economic development or environmental problems" (Ryan 1994: 24).

Whether the determiner of administrative reform is anchored in the state context (Pollitt and Bouckaert 2004; Manning and Parison 2004) or in the global interdependence (Klingner 2009; Farazmand 1999; Ryan 1994; Riggs 1991a), comparative analysis cannot do well without either perspective, and will continue to rely on both dimensions. The primacy of internal reality versus external interdependence is a question that can only be fulfilled empirically. A methodology of comparative administration based on several cases or on global processes should enhance reliability of results and improve evaluation of performance. Specific information (descriptive and quantitative) on multiple cases, including global management practices allows students and practitioners to be more confident in considering evidence, verifying information, and evaluating cause and effect of management actions and behaviors (Jreisat, 2005).

Moreover, an effective reform strategy to enhance institutional capacities has to realize and to appreciate the importance of the civil service performance, and be deeply mindful of the need for support of the political leadership for any reform strategy. Civil service systems play critical roles, even if basic knowledge of civil service systems in many countries is usually inadequate (Bekke, Perry, and Toonen, 1996: vii). Public personnel management has been studied extensively, from at least four perspectives, according to Klingner and Nalbandian: (1) the functions needed to manage human resources in public agencies; (2) the process by which public jobs are allocated; (3) the interaction among fundamental societal values that often conflict over who gets public jobs and how they are allocated; and, (4) public personnel management is personnel systems—the laws, rules, organizations, and procedures used to express these abstract values in fulfilling personnel functions (1998: 1).

To meet its aims and to fill a knowledge gap, comparative research has to establish and define good practices in various settings. During the 1980s, conservative leaders in the United States, United Kingdom, Canada, and Australia blamed civil service for many problems in the society. The civil service stood accused of "being bloated, expensive, unresponsive, a creation of routine deliberately resistant to change, and largely incapable of dealing with new challenges" (Peters and Savoie 1994: 419). The corrective measures taken by the political leaders of these countries were mainly reducing the size of civil service, privatizing many of their functions, and politicizing senior administrative appointment to increase political control. The stated purpose of these policies was to introduce competitiveness in government operations, "debureaucratise" the system, and restructure governance (Peters and Savoie 1994: 419). Ultimately, these measures did not produce what was promised. On the contrary, implementation of public policies and the usual public services got worse. The conclusion: "the political leadership not only misdiagnosed the patient but also applied the wrong medicine" (Peters and Savoie 1994: 418). Subsequently, many of the civil service alterations in these countries were reversed or modified after change of the political leaders.

Learning from studies across national boundaries and analysis of multicultural experiences would free public management from current "institutional ethnicities" and advance a valuable learning process to include all countries. At the macro level of administration, however, overall characteristics that affect the performance of traditional public services often overlap with comparative politics (Rowat 1988). Comparative politics has been preoccupied with reflection on political institutions in a handful of Western countries and a scattering of developing countries (Heady 2001). The emergence of many developing countries since World War II brought forward issues and problems of management and nation building that were either neglected or unfamiliar terrain to scholars of Western comparative politics.

Distinctive Management for National Development

Comparative public administration has been at the front of social sciences, identifying and studying administrative problems and practices of developing societies soon after World War II. A consequence of this emphasis is the evolution of a special compilation of concepts and applications which, subsequently, became known as *development administration*. "The term 'development administration' came into use in the 1950s to represent those aspects of public administration and those changes in public administration which are needed to carry out policies, projects, and programs to improve social and economic conditions" (Gant 1979: 3). Independence from the imperial rule created strong expectations by the people looking for improved standards of living, correction of inequities and injustices of the past colonial era, and governance that guides social and economic development by planning, funding, and managing large investments in public enterprises (Esman 1988). An important factor adding to the administrative workload in the newly freed countries was the weakness of the private sector. Consequently, it was essential, even urgent, for the incumbent regimes to fulfill the aspirations of their people by being involved and supportive of economic and social development initiatives (Esman 1974; Gant 1979).

Developing countries quickly discovered that classic administrative concepts and methods were most appropriate for managing public services that have clearly defined goals, employ simple methods, and have predictable and specific outcomes such as building roads and other public work projects, collecting taxes, delivering standard services, and maintaining law and order. The rationalistic focus of Western precepts of public administration, as Esman (1974: 7) pointed out, produced emphasis on written rules, precedents, predictability, consistency, equity, routine, efficiency, and techniques. Western administrative conceptualizations depoliticized administration, deemphasized program outputs, and relegated public administration mission to attaining progressive efficiency. "Promoting social change brings public service into different patterns of relationships that classic western administrative theories have not accounted for" (Esman 1974: 7).

While governments of developing countries were facing intense demands from their people for public services, these newly decolonized regimes did not enjoy secure political base, nor had the needed managerial and professional skills. Their developing administrative systems were in a dire need for programmatic commitment, managerial flexibility, and creative leadership, characteristics hindered by existing rigid bureaucratic and hierarchical structures. "The pervasiveness of social conflict in developing countries and the weak institutions and procedures for mediating conflict place these polities in constant jeopardy. Economic growth and political development tend to generate conflicts among social, economic, regional, and ethnic groups faster than they produce methods and institutions for conflict management" (Esman 1974: 14).

Development administration promised continuous attention to formulation, evaluation, and implementation of projects to serve objectives of national socioeconomic development. Countries that emphasized such development strongly utilized two major instruments to prepare their management and institutions to handle the new responsibilities:

1. Expand and cultivate a suitable workforce through *education* and *training* that transform human resources into a public service possessing the necessary skills, attitudes, and commitment to national development. A combination of internal and external training initiatives were devised and implemented in many countries that involved large numbers of public managers and employees. Development plans included building universities, schools, and training institutions committed to education, research, and advisory services in development administration were established. Many emerging countries contracted many consultants from outside to provide advice and technical skills.

2. *Central planning* was adopted as the instrument of rationalizing developmental policies. During the two decades after World War II, government-sponsored national development plans were regarded as key instruments for expanding the economy, improving justice and equity in the society, and achieving the welfare state. The Keynesian economics provided the backdrop to the welfare state and to mixed economies, assuring that big government is compatible with freedom, welfare, and efficiency. Public policies of developing countries embraced the notion of state sponsorship of development projects, investment in the economy, and managing a variety of public

enterprises. The ascendency of Keynesian economics and the dominance of the modernization paradigm "reinforced the notion of big government and the salience of development administration as a moral and intellectual vocation" (Esman 1988: 126).

Still, the overall results of central planning were largely disappointing. In general, central plans lacked clarity and specificity of execution procedures and suffered many other shortcomings such as weak commitment to projects, rigid and routine management, no participation by citizens and private institutions from outside the bureaucratic setting, and lack of information and expert knowledge about planned projects. The accumulation of such problems and shortcomings resulted in serious deviations from preconceived plans. Formal requirements of project preparation, analysis, and management changed in the course of implementation (Rondinelli 1982: 46). Central ministries and departments assigned major development duties failed to reorient and strengthen existing or newly created structures for managing development plans and projects. They simply presided over modestly effective operations with dismal records of accomplishments.

Today, comparative and development administration occasionally appear together as in the *Handbook of Comparative and Development Administration* (Farazmand 2001). Others may routinely juxtapose the two terms in the literature, implying a particular practical or conceptual association. By the end of the 1980s, however, development administration is infrequently the subject of scholarly attention, even if the need for the knowledge, skills, and values represented in the development administration perspective remain salient and compelling. An important part of the explanation for the modest contribution by the development administration approach is that big government, statist involvement in the economy, and the whole notion of central control through planning were widely disparaged after the collapse of communist systems and the ascendance of the neoconservative movement in the United States (the Washington Consensus) that sought to relegate most functions of governance to the private sector. The New Public Management was one alternative offered for a minimum state and maximum privatization. Moreover, "donor agencies, both bilateral and multilateral, have attempted to transfer to a development context theories and practices adopted at various times in developed countries" (Bertucci 2008: 1002).

During the early years of the emerging countries, the limited available knowledge of administrative systems was mainly derived from comparative administration studies of newly independent nations such as India, Pakistan, Egypt, and Thailand. To be sure, this knowledge was insufficient in content and relevance, but the CPA itself was also at an embryonic phase of conceptual articulation. Emphasis on the administrative problems of developing countries in the early comparative literature resulted in (1) forcing administrative reform to the top of the agenda for action in many countries, (2) recognizing the significance of institutions with capacity to act as foundations for developmental policies, and (3) breaking out of the parochial mode and gradually developing shared experiences with a global outlook on governance. Not surprising, therefore, that during the early years of the comparative movement, the conventional practices for building administrative capacity were preoccupied by the need to create instruments that can define and champion administrative improvements (Riggs 1964).

Subsequently, development administration focused on the question of institution building as a sure path for developing administrative capacity in the new nations. Building viable, capable, and innovative institutions to lead in development efforts was advocated and promoted in education, training, and internationally through the efforts of the U.S. Agency for International Development. The institutions that received the endorsement of consultants and financial support by AID include national planning councils or boards, institutes of public administration, development-oriented universities, and research institutes. Foreign consultants followed the trail, also peddling all sorts of "development-oriented training programs" for public employees in developing countries.

The *institution-building framework* appeared to have high promise in the 1960s. It was developed by a consortium of scholars of development from universities of Pittsburgh, Michigan, Indiana, and Syracuse with significant efforts from people like Fred Riggs, Milton Esman, William Siffin, and others. An *institution* was described and analyzed through three categories of variables:

- A category that attempts to explain organizational behavior through the examination and measurement of five major variables: leadership, doctrine, program, resources, and structure.
- A category of variables deals with linkages or interdependencies that exist between an institution and relevant parts of the society: enabling linkages, functional linkages, normative linkages, and diffused linkages.
- The concept of transactions denotes the exchange of goods and services, power, and influence between the institutions and other social organizations that interact with it. The content of these exchanges vary from seeking support to overcoming resistance, exchanging resources to transferring norms and values (Jreisat 1975).

Despite variation, institutional analysis reveals similarities of assumptions and goals, and appeals to practitioners. Also, institutional analysis received earlier endorsement of many academicians, consultants, and foreign aid technicians. Increasing global interdependence, however, requires comparative and development administration to revive and to renew initial premises and concepts to deal with change in economics, technology, management, travel, and cultural values. The political boundaries of all countries are facing the pressure for free access and for competent management that is able to make the necessary adjustments.

The issue of *national culture* is another conceptual and practical challenge to comparative administrative analysis. How much of the variation in organizational management is caused by attributes of the national culture? Research findings are often conveyed in terms of the impact of culture on managerial attitudes, beliefs, and behavior (Graves 1972; Hofstede 1980) with the other organizational variables either implied or ignored. A likely inconsistency is that "in both single-culture and comparative studies, nation and culture have been used as if they were synonymous, with national boundaries separating one cultural group from another" (Adler, Doktor, and Redding 1986: 298). The difficulty in equating nation and culture is readily demonstrable in many developing countries where cultural homogeneity is lacking. In these countries, frequently boundaries were drawn arbitrarily by the colonial rulers for political reasons or after a military conquest as evident in Africa, the Middle East, and the Indian subcontinent.

Despite variation and complexity, comparative cultural studies of management have not produced anything close to consensus on the importance or the magnitude of cultural influences on public management. Methods of measurement of cultural influences on organization and management remain basic, often contradictory. One view argues that culture determines managerial practices because culture is "the collective programming of the mind which distinguishes the members of one human group from another" (Hofstede 1980: 25). A different perspective concludes that organizational variance is less dependent on culture than on other contingencies such as technological development, interdependence with other organizations, market considerations (Child and Tayeb 1983), and type of political context. Cross-cultural studies of human behavior and psychology, for example, have no adequate explanation to the finding that people behave in one way with members of their own culture, and differently with members of foreign cultures.

Still, a basic premise of the comparative perspective is that functional patterns of organization and management are determinable and transferrable from one system to another. For this reason, comparative public administration is always searching to discover regular patterns and main practices throughout the human experience, irrespective of place and time. As Riggs (1991a: 473) argued, scholars can no longer afford to base their theories on the truly exceptional American experience and to limit CPA to the study of "foreign" governments. Essentially, the processes of generating reliable administrative knowledge and developing trusted administrative principles are inherently comparative. Comparative research continues to promote intercultural studies across national boundaries and to investigate multicultural experiences that emerge out of "institutional ethnicities" within a country.

Demand for Relevance

Comparative studies have been conducted for centuries, producing broad comparative surveys leading to broad generalizations. Most of these cross-state comparisons have been cross-disciplinary (Deutsch 1987: 7). Perhaps the most prominent early user of such comparisons is Aristotle, who combined the Platonic methods of abstraction with the study of concrete cases. Aristotle sent his assistants around the Mediterranean to collect the constitutions of 128 city-states. The result was Aristotle's *Politics*, a valuable piece of theory which has endured over the centuries, and generating many important cross-disciplinary generalizations (Deutsch 1987: 7).

Although students of comparative administration may consider their subject a product of the post WW II era, actually a strong call for a comparative orientation of public administration goes back to much earlier time. Woodrow Wilson's famous article, often referred to as the first articulation of public administration as a field of study, repeatedly emphasized the comparative approach as the foundation of developing administrative principles. Wilson believed that it is possible, indeed desirable, that we find the regularities and the principles of public administration through comparisons. In 1887, Wilson wrote that "nowhere else in the whole field of politics, it would seem, can we make use of the historical, comparative method more safely than in this province of administration" (Wilson in Shafritz and Hyde 1997: 25).

Profusion of systematic comparative public administration is a fairly recent activity, imprecisely linked to the downfall of colonialism. Scholars who bridged the interests of administration and politics took the lead in the early phase. In 1953, the American Political Science Association had a committee on comparative administration, before the American Society for Public Administration created the Comparative Administration Group (CAG). During the 1960s, the CAG expanded its activities and attracted over 500 members that included academicians, students, management consultants, and operatives of technical assistance programs to developing countries. Subsequently, the CAG was merged to become the first section of ASPA that subsequently was named Section on International and Comparative Administration (SICA). Fred W. Riggs provided intellectual and organizational leadership to the CAG during its early days. He managed the group, attracted more members, and contributed significant writings that set new directions in comparative studies. Other names that have been prominently involved during the early years of the comparative enterprise include Dwight Waldo, Milton Esman, Ferrel Heady, Frank Sherwood, Ralph Braibanti, John Montgomery, William Siffin, and others.

In a report to the annual meeting of ASPA, April 1961, Fred Riggs specified three emerging trends in the comparative study of public administration: (1) a trend from normative toward more empirical approaches, (2) a shift from idiographic (distinct cases) toward nomothetic approaches (studies that seek explicitly to formulate and test propositions), and (3) a shift from predominantly non-ecological to an ecological basis of comparative study (Heady 1962: 2). Another perspective attempted to articulate the early "concerns and priorities" that Ferrel

Heady (1962: 3) referred to as the "motivating concerns" of the comparative public administration:

■ Search for theory and for reforming administrative practices
■ Contribution to comparative administration of advances in the study of comparative politics generally
■ The interest of scholars trained in the continental administrative law tradition
■ The intensified analysis on a comparative basis of perennial problems of public administration

After the demise of the colonial order and the end of the Cold War period, a growing interest in internationalization of public administration was stimulated by a growing emphasis on conditions and factors such as democratic values, economic development, international cooperation, and egalitarianism. Such objectives and values, with advances in communication technologies, are increasingly becoming central commitment to current scholarship in comparative public administration and governance. The challenge is that scholarly productivity focusing on the administrative context (culture, politics, economic development, even history) has not been matched with appropriate insights of the inner, operational working of organizations. This is particularly true of organizations operating in developing societies, which remained without sufficient comparative information on organizational and managerial performance. For a long time, public organizations in many developing countries have been operating without adequate facts and information to support their decision-making processes, particularly in budgetary allocations and in managing civil service reforms. Worse, with shaded transparency, it is difficult to determine who benefitted from public policy outputs and who did not, or to ascertain how accountable government actions have been.

More relevant comparative administration research serves a critical need. Improvements of relevance and better synthesis of comparative studies continue to depend on the ability to develop generalizations from aggregates of particular facts that have been reliably established without ignoring the concreteness and distinctiveness of the cases being investigated (Jreisat 1997: 17). Part of the problem is that early comparative knowledge was mainly derived from single case analysis that often served as the empirical base for developing tentative generalizations. To extrapolate from a thin, particular knowledge base of the operating attributes of the system involves obvious risks and challenges: Are the rules of evidence adequately served to warrant deriving general conclusions from the case at hand? How to ensure that the relationship between the particular (the operating system) and the general (the context) is complimentary and coherent? Concentrating on one of these two dimensions to the exclusion of the other is tantamount to maintaining the diffuseness and irrelevance that has been afflicting many consultant reports as well as scholarly comparisons.

Contextual analysis brings to the forefront the important relationship between comparative public administration and comparative politics. Comparative politics promoted and gave representation to comparative administration in its own early intellectual concerns. Subsequently, the organized interest of each group spurred distinct institutional pursuits. Comparative politics concentrated on the political system as if it consists only of political objectives and processes. And comparative administration viewed politics as influence to be reckoned with, but essentially distinct from administration, regarded as an interdisciplinary field with a horizon that extends to financial, technological, sociological, and political domains.

Comparative politics recognizes the political system as a "set of institutions, such as parliaments, bureaucracies, and courts, which formulate and implement the collective goals of a society or of groups within it" (Almond et al. 2000: 13). But scholars of comparative politics often discuss bureaucracy or public administration as tangential rather than as "the cutting edge" of governance. Yet, comparative administrative research is continually attempting to empirically define the vital links with the political order and to specify conditions and variables that determine relationships with its political context through empirical evidence.

With the end of the 1970s, cross-cultural studies have achieved preeminence in university teaching and research, in both public and business administration curricula. Although the *Journal of Comparative Administration* was transformed into *Administration and Society*, in search of a wider scope and larger readership, other journals welcomed articles of comparative and development content. *Public Administration and Development, International Review of Administrative Science,* the *International Journal of Public Administration,* and *the International Public Management Journal* are among many public administration periodicals that have been particularly receptive. Mark Huddleston (1984) accounted for 628 references in comparative public administration selected from a much larger pool of publications, which led him to conclude that those who ring the death knell of the comparative approach are misreading the evidence.

During the last two decades, however, the CPA seems to have lost the momentum of the 1960s and 1970s. At the dawn of the twenty-first century, comparative and development administration continue to search for a new focus and a new vision. Suggested prescriptions for revitalization are many. One approach favors a reexamination of objectives, appraisal of research methods, and evaluation of linkages with the main field of public administration. Other perspectives raise issues of relevance to practice and the need for better synthesis of previous research findings. As expected, opinions and conclusions vary greatly. Some have already declared the demise of comparative administration because it lacks "clear identity" and it remains "ambiguous" (Henry 2001: 38; Van Wart and Cayer 1990). Nonetheless, as Aberbach and Rockman (1988: 437) point out, the "comparative study ... propels us to a level of conceptual methodological self-consciousness and clarity rarely found in noncomparative studies of public administration." Granted, the CPA may have not fulfilled all its potential; it remains, however, a significant and a compelling channel for improving the viability and relevance of the field of public administration.

Comparative Administration in a Globalizing World

Cross-national administrative analysis is increasingly associated with the pervasive phenomenon of *globalism*. Public administration today is at the center of the human endeavor to restructure and reshape contemporary societies. To be sure, globalism is not new but its intensity, complexity, and effects on human societies are progressively more conspicuous. Some aspects of globalism began as early as human societies exchanged economic and social benefits through travel and trade as well as through war, conquest, and domination. The new reality of globalization and governance requires adaptation of public administration practices and improvement in its research, teaching, training, and professional commitments. Comparative research today is earnestly looking for appropriate management concepts, policies, and practices that are valid across organizational and national boundaries to meet the global demands in areas such as security, environment, immigration, technology, health care, finance, and economics. Critical assessments and comparisons of the utility of different approaches and practices, therefore, are essential for integrating the most valid into the education and the practice of public management.

Again, globalism represents the "growing integration of the economic, financial, social and cultural lives of countries" (Thomas 1999: 5). Although views often differ on whether globalization is promoted by market forces, creation of the multinational corporate labyrinth, or a by-product of the information-scientific-technological revolution, its effect on the profession of public administration is indisputable. What really matters at this time is to be able to accurately assess the consequences, define the specific impact on management of public affairs, and devise appropriate actions and adjustments to the new context. Quickly, however, one finds out that evaluating results of globalism is difficult to disentangle because of a complex mixture of elements and a continually shifting emphasis. A complete assessment of the benefits of modern globalization can be lengthy and difficult to determine with a measure of finality. Still, the advocates list these effects:

- Rise of market capitalism around the world, which creates jobs, transfers money and investments, and makes products available to consumers who did not have them before.
- Value neutral and universally disseminated scientific and technological inventions have been facilitating and accelerating the processes of interdependence without coercion.
- New technologies of communication, particularly the Internet, made information freely available to once sheltered and closed societies.

■ Increasing interdependence among nations promotes collaborative and cooperative endeavors among countries and governments with benefits to all.

For the opposite view, however, globalization is a colonial ploy by big powers, including multinational corporations, to perpetuate their domination of the rest of the world. Sometimes, criticism and opposition to global economic consequences took violent expressions by demonstrators as during international meetings from Seattle and Québec (Canada) to Prague and Davos in Europe. Also, the 2001 World Economic Forum's annual celebration of globalization turned out to be a forum for its critics. Opponents derided the elite gathering as the unacceptable face of global capitalism. Leaders and ministers from several developing countries unleashed a barrage of scathing criticisms, complaining about inequities in trade rules and import barriers in industrialized countries to a shortage of aid and capital flows that were denying developing countries many of potential benefits of globalization.[1] At Davos, Brazil's agriculture minister criticized farm subsidies by industrial countries that undermine competition. India complained that it is required to lift all import restrictions in April 2001, but developed countries were not scheduled to lift their restrictions on textile imports until 2005. The south is not looking for charity, declared the Indian Minister of Finance: "We are looking for equal opportunity."[2] At the Summit of the Americas meeting (April 21, 2001) in Quebec City, Canada, heads of state claimed that free trade is the best way to ease poverty and inequality in the hemisphere. But the critics and protesters complained that free trade has to benefit all citizens, not just corporations. More than 30,000 free trade opponents, many of them union members, activists, human rights advocates, and environmentalists protested that globalization has deepened problems, even destroyed the lives of others.[3]

Specifically, the critics of globalization repeat these reservations:

■ Global capitalism advanced by leaps in technology, failure of communism, and few spectacular economic successes in East Asia, but did not benefit everybody. The benefits of information technology have not been widely shared. By the end of the twentieth century, statistics support this contention indicated that 88 percent of the world's Internet users live in the industrial countries, only 0.3 percent in the poorest countries of the world.[4]

■ In some developing countries, "multinationals have contributed to labor, environmental, and human-rights abuses"[5] and caused damages to these societies far greater than the benefits. Thus, it is not surprising that many developing societies view with concern the growth of globalism linked to unrestrained behavior of multinational corporations during this post Cold War time.

■ Poor countries find global capitalism disruptive to their lives and societies. Yet, they have been unable to enact safeguards and regulations to protect their environments and workers as the industrial countries have done decades ago.

- Global capitalism and free trade have not only introduced free commerce in ordinary goods but also stimulated free commerce in money. For small countries, this often resulted in destabilizing their economies and even holding them hostages to whims of financial speculators, as demonstrated during the financial meltdown of the market in 2008–9.
- Current global capitalism perpetuates economic dominance of few industrial regions: Europe, Japan, and the United States. Of the 1,000 largest global corporations, the United States and Europe own over 75 percent. No African, Arab, or Latin American country is among the owners of any of these 1,000 giant corporations.

Thus, public administration finds itself operating within a different global context that is still evolving, but, simultaneously, causing novel and hard challenges. What is happening does not seem as if an old system is passing away and a new global system is being born. Rather, the change is in progress but is expected to profoundly alter the order of things. In this transitional global mode, students of comparative administration find it easier to discuss what is being changed more than what is emerging as the final, new global system. It is not clear yet how globalization is affecting performance of public organizations. What is certain, globalization introduces new opportunities as well as new tensions and flurry for public administration to deal with. Consider the following:

1. The trend of allocating greater role for the private sector in national development has resulted in shifting the responsibility of public administration in the new economy from *production and management* of goods and services to *facilitating* and *regulating* economic activities. Accordingly, public administration has to renegotiate its relationships with the political and economic sectors of the society while developing new capacities and skills of its human resources. Public managers need capacities in coordination, managing conflict, contracting, and in initiating and enforcing legal and regulatory frameworks. Unable to cope with their daily public service obligations and responsibilities, most administrative systems of developing countries are caught ill-prepared for the new responsibilities foisted by globalism.
2. Globalization appears to encourage and to accelerate a shift from the centralized traditional bureaucratic organization to a managerial model with diluted central authority and greater emphasis on inter-organizational and cooperative management. The changing global situation changed expectations from governance, calling for deeper commitments by managers to professional values and behaviors in the conduct of public affairs.
3. A decisive aspect of current and future management is the greater accent on an organizational culture that highly values performance. Within results-oriented organizational culture, managerial skills in demand are flexibility, adaptability, cooperation, and creativity. In the new global context, performance

and accomplishments of objectives are indispensable accounts of successful management.

4. The emphasis on a new managerial model and a culture of organizational performance refocuses attention on the role of leadership. Thus, reexamination of methods of recruitment and development of skills among administrative and political leaders has become a necessity. More than "entrepreneurial qualities" is involved here. Realizing that today's leaders operate in a complex and more competitive global environment, emphasis on knowledge of other systems and cultures, skills, and attitudes has become quite apparent. Modern organizations exhibit democratic norms and employment conditions that comply with principles of merit and managerial competence in areas such as negotiations, mediation, human rights, diversity, equality, and problem-solving techniques. In a study sponsored by the United Nations Public Administration Program, "the most relevant competencies for the manager of the future" consist of the following aptitudes and skills: integrity, vision, capacity for policy analysis, judgment and capacity for decision-making, people empowerment, managing performance, building trust, and accountability.[6]

These challenges indicate that administrative reform is becoming the common response to the new demands of societies. To accelerate such reform, particularly in developing countries, training and personnel development have been the indispensable prescriptions for closing the gap between current and desired conditions. Thus, a variety of training methods have been in use, including education at all levels, training-on-the-job, coaching, mentoring, distance learning, and many other tailormade training activities. Assessments on the ground in many developing countries, however, indicate that consultant reports and their recommended training have not been sufficient ingredients to bring about the desired transformation.

No more public managers should assume their comparative preeminence or correctness. Business executives have earlier start in dealing with diverse cultures and intercultural communication for a simple fact: to sell products and manage international plants or work in a country where a multinational company office is located, you need to know as much as possible about such country. McDonald's has restaurants in over 100 countries and earns 66 percent of its income outside the United States (Locker and Kienzler 2008: 433). Thus, numerous business managers in the private sector have had experiences in many cultures. Not so with public managers unless they were in the U.S. foreign service.

In brief, the impact of globalism on public administration has been considerable. Globalism altered the context of administration and necessitated reexamination of the ability of public management to change, apply information, use new technologies, and implement new patterns of management. The global context diffuses rather than concentrates power and authority. It alters the structural patterns of decision making and requires managers to transform their methods by learning how to deal with networks and to negotiate in the context of multiorganizational and multicultural settings. In the past, globalism has been associated with policies of downsizing governments and privatizing many of their traditional functions. Today, recruitment of public managers, development of employees' skills, and retention of competent managerial leadership have acquired different emphasis. Assessing the impact of globalization on public administration, however, is different from assuming that a "new paradigm" is on the way towards a universal application. Using the case of civil service reforms, adopted by the government of Zimbabwe in 1991, Mavima and Chackerian pointed out that "the adoption and implementation of these global norms and standards was constrained by local institutions that are associated with the country's unique history" (2002: 91). They conclude that, conceptually, their "finding challenges the simplistic notions about global integration and transcendence in public administration." As to practice, this study underlines "the need for reform prescriptions to achieve synergistic support between international standards and norms and local institutions" (Mavima and Chackerian 2002: 91).

Only through a systematic comparative analysis of several cases can public administration respond, authoritatively, to these concerns. Today's globalism expands the domain, and reconfirms the role of CPA research agenda. To be sure, failures of many developing countries to attain a sustainable development seem to bring about skepticism not only over the role of administration but also about many assumptions that have not materialized. Weak institutional capacities have been blamed for poor performance. But, many other factors have been indicated in explaining the slow progress of change such as lack of rule of law, absence of democratic values, recruitments of senior managers on non-merit criteria, and failure of the budgetary and fiscal public policies. While the comparative administration movement is credited with a pioneering recognition of the importance of global influences, and with attempts to induce greater interest in developmental initiatives, satisfying these objectives has been anything but methodical or uniform.

The struggle for policy accomplishments and for administrative change continues among nations, but the results remain uneven. Still, most reform programs seem to embrace these common goals:

- Ensuring *accountability* of public management.
- *Measuring and evaluating performance of governance systems.*
- *Developing human resources*, particularly by ensuring effective compliance with the merit system in personnel policies and by adapting training and education of public servants to suit the new global reality.
- Instituting dependable measures of audit and evaluation to promote *ethics in public service* and to convincingly battle corruption with reliable means of scrutiny and adjudication of misconduct.
- Employing *cost reduction* measures and develop consciousness of the need to rely on more efficient techniques, based on reliable information, in the conduct of public affairs.

■ Enforcing *quality criteria* throughout public service that also have clear elements of incentives, empowerment of management, and stronger mandate for citizen-friendly services.

Legacy of the Comparative Approach

The legacy of the CPA, criticism notwithstanding, is most notable in its contributions to administrative theory and practice. Comparative research expanded our understanding of the role of public administration in modern society, and underlined the importance of relationships between administration and other dimensions of governance. A vital contribution of comparative administration is its concentrated attention to building administrative capacities and reforming public management. Scholarship and comparative administration research urged the field out of its narrow ethnocentric perspectives into a wider horizon of global scope. Outcomes associated with or promoted by comparative studies are described in the following sections.

Construction of Administrative Typologies

Creating a typology is an attempt at classifying massive political and administrative data according to some basic criteria or distinctive feature of the systems under study. This practice is not new in the fields of administration or politics. In fact, one of the most famous and frequently discussed in the literature is Max Weber's ideal types that construct certain elements of reality into a logically consistent conception. Weber used these generalized types of polities, "authority systems," to understand society as a subject of lawful regularities. Historically, Weber noted three types of authority systems, each with a distinct pattern of staffing and employment: traditional, charismatic, and legal-rational (see Chapter 3).

Types of administrative systems have always been influenced by earlier works in comparative politics that compiled, classified, and correlated data involving large number of variables on a large number of countries (Banks and Textor 1963; Taylor and Hudson 1983). Several typologies and classifications have been conceived with an eye on emerging nations, seeking workable models of governance in the post-independence period. Cross-national classification of polities as in *A Cross-Polity Survey*, compiled by Banks and Textor (1963), included 115 nation-states organized according to fifty-seven characteristics such as area, size, population, urbanization, Gross National Product, literacy rate, freedom of the press, religious configuration, political modernization, and character of bureaucracy.

Milton Esman's classification scheme focused on the ability of the emerging countries to create, and effectively deploy, a variety of instruments of action to successfully carry out the burdens of socioeconomic development. Esman's typology consists of five political regime types with significant implications to public administration: (1) conservative oligarchies, (2) authoritarian military reformers, (3) competitive interest-oriented party systems, (4) dominant mass party systems, and (5) communist totalitarian systems (Esman 1966). Similarly, Merle Fainsod (1963) provided a typology that focused on the relationship between bureaucracy and political authority. Accordingly, he identified five different types: (1) ruler-dominated bureaucracies, (2) military-dominated bureaucracies, (3) ruling bureaucracies, (4) representative bureaucracies, and (5) party-state bureaucracies. Initially, these types and the ensuing cross-national comparative analysis stimulate thinking about choices and values maximized within each choice.

No doubt, typologies serve useful purposes of data gathering and analysis. As analytical constructs, they provide frameworks for research and help organize descriptive and explanatory characteristics and interrelatedness among a number of features that constitute a type or another. But typologies have their limitations, too. They can distort reality or set ideal type models that differ from the real world in significant aspects. Any classification system, attempting to organize massive data, ends up sacrificing some detailed information by grouping together aspects that are not exactly the same to establish generalizations. Still, classification is necessary in defining and underlining differences and similarities and in the development of explanatory concepts and generalizations.

Defining Functional Patterns

The contribution of the CPA in comparing critical administrative functions across nations has considerable benefits. An illustration is Aaron Wildavsky's (1985) *Budgeting: A Comparative Theory of Budgetary Processes.* He explicitly utilized a comparative perspective in examination of dominant variables that characterize forms of budgetary behavior in rich countries (Britain, France, Japan, and the United States) and in poor countries. Similarly, a study by A. Premchand and Jesse Burkhead (1984), *Comparative International Budgeting and Finance*, compared financial management and budgeting in thirteen developed and developing countries. In search of developing an administrative reform model, Pollitt and Bouckaert (2004) relied on comparative literature to construct the "key features" of their model that was applied in assessing administrative reform efforts in twelve countries. Many other comparative works can be found in journal articles: Allen Schick (1990), for example, compares budget results in five industrial countries. R. J. Stillman attempted a more comprehensive review of European administrative systems.

Among administrative functions that attracted the interest of comparative research at an early stage has been civil service in all its phases and processes. Civil service systems, as Bekke, Perry, and Toonen (1996: vii) point out, play critical roles throughout the world, but our basic knowledge of civil service systems remains inadequate. The authors determine that much of theory and empirical research on civil service systems dates from the comparative administration movement of the 1960s. Actually comparative knowledge about how civil service systems function or how any other particular administrative structure might be managed is either unavailable or tentative. This indicates that there has been little joining or follow-up to the early comparativists' efforts.

Language and Terminology

Clearly defined terms are essential for the scientific advancement of any field of knowledge, and for developing commonly understood meanings. Despite progress made over the years in public administration scholarship, ambiguity and occasional confusion of terminology remain. For illustration, consider *development adminis-tration, development management, comparative administration,* and *comparative management.* Although *comparative public administration* and *comparative public management* are often used interchangeably, it is possible to draw a fine distinction. *Administration* calls to mind institutional linkages and comprehensiveness of the sub-ject. The term *management* is often used to stress the "applied and practical nature" of the field (Baker 1994: 7). *Administration* stands next to and interacts with politics or economics as a field with its own internal and external dimensions. *Management,* on the other hand, evokes techniques and skills that are viewed as components of administration. The differentiation is not a clear-cut but a more-or-less type where *administration* denotes the field of study, the academic certification, and the profes-sional association and *management* refers mainly to the operational processes.

A distinction between *management* and *administration* based on the premise that *management* is the more recent or more valid and *administration* is outmoded or outdated (Lane 2000: 20) is rejected as faddish and gratuitous. The choice of the term *public management* to reflect the view that governments are adopting the techniques of the marketplace or the private sector while using *administration,* therefore, to denote antiquated processes that are less efficient and less effective (Chandler 2000: 5) is also unacceptable. A distinction by Riggs (1998: 29) suggests that emphasis on *development management* points to parallels in business adminis-tration where politics is viewed as irrelevant. This focus, Riggs contends, "enables us, in our schools and departments of Public Administration, to assume that we have some kind of universally relevant and valuable expertise that can be applied everywhere, in many systems of governance" (1998: 23).

Knowledge Generation

The most durable legacy of the CPA, in an epistemological sense, is its contribu-tions to knowledge generation about administrative systems that were unknown to most scholars and to the literature, particularly in the West. The CPA enriched theory construction, improved the overall understanding of administrative functions, and expanded the horizon of administrative research to include many emerging countries that previously were ignored. As pointed out above, the comparative perspective is credited with being a major force in launching the field of "development administration" and consistently focusing on relationships between administration and its context (Riggs 1989). Nevertheless, a pressing question remains why has scholarly productivity of comparative research declined in recent years? The familiar explanation refers to the inability of the comparative perspective to overcome its conceptual diffusion, improve its utility, and secure more funding for continuing field research. These factors alone have been sufficient to abort the momentum of the intellectual development of the 1960s. Today, as Kickert and Stillman (1996: 66) point out, the comparative administration literature is dated and in need of new insights and fresh empirical information to be revitalized and equipped to face realities of the twenty-first century.

Other less direct explanations for the state of affairs, perhaps, have to include impact of international events. During the post–Vietnam War era, the U.S. government and Foundations went through a period of introspection and decline of interest in affairs of other countries. As a result, funding of research on other societies decreased, particularly those dealing with developing countries. Also, the collapse of the communist systems and failure of the Soviet bureaucratic edifice to produce the promised visions for the society refocused attention on overall failures of the state everywhere. Presumed or real failures of the public sector and its various contraptions led to retrenchment; many of its functions were shifted to the marketplace. Adding to the disillusion is the political distortion of relationships between citizens and their governments that undermined traditional notions of "public service." All this reinforced the trend of limiting the role of government, particularly administration, through downsizing and privatizing.

Attempts to revive scholarly interests in the subject met with limited visibility, with few exceptions such as F. Heady's *Public Administration: A Comparative Perspective*, in its sixth edition. Other examples are *Handbook of Comparative and Development Administration* (2nd ed. 2001), edited by A. Farazmand; *Public Administration in Developed Democracies* (1990), edited by D. Rowat; *Comparative Public Management*, edited by R. Baker (1994); *Comparative Public Administration* (2002), edited by J. A. Chandler; *Comparative Bureaucratic Systems* (2003), edited by K. Tummala; *Comparative Public Administration: the Essential Readings* (2006), edited by E. Otenyo and N. S. Lind; and *Comparative Public Administration and Policy* (2002), by this author.

Except for Heady and Jreisat's studies, the other six volumes (Farazmand, Rowat, Baker, Chandler, Tummala, and Otenyo and Lind) are readers by multiple authors. Contributions in professional journals are a major source of continuity in comparative administration scholarship. Among journals that regularly publish on the subject are *Public Administration and Development, International Review of Administrative Sciences, Public Administration Review, International Journal of Public Administration*, and *International Public Management Journal*.

In terms of application, it seems that developing countries have not performed as instructed by international consultants or in accordance with foreign aid blueprints.

These countries have not lumbered their way faithfully through Western-designed schemes of administrative reform. Despite all earnest efforts, researchers find administrative reform increasingly intractable. This is not to say, however, that no societal change has occurred. In developing societies, dynamic forces have been at work, altering every aspect of life in these systems and not always in the preferred way or direction. Thus, describing and interpreting what is happening in these countries is a compelling task for comparative administration research, if to retain its relevance and viability. The future challenge is how to utilize the wide-ranging human experience in advancing knowledge of theory and practice of public administration to build essential institutional capacity. Comparative public administration research will continue to have a key role in this regard.

Conclusion

Current global trends require cross-national knowledge and information on managing public policies. Public administration has neither sufficiently responded to the new reality, nor demonstrated special capacity to manage it. Public administration education at the present is facing a need for comparative, non-ethnic-centered administrative education. For various reasons, the education establishment of public administration has not responded effectively to the knowledge deficit. A comment in a symposium on the future of public administration, in a supplement of the *Public Administration Review,* is indicative. "A number of authors speak explicitly to the issue of internationalization and the changing environment of public administration. This is not surprising. But, speaking about these issues is one thing—moving beyond the status quo is another" (O'Leary and Slyke 2010: 5). Recognizing the difficulties and challenges, however, is not a sufficient reason to justify lack of progress.

Relevance, responsiveness, and adaptation to global conditions require that public administration research and education emphasize the critical aspects with an eye on the worldwide experiences. Focus on the imperatives of public administration is a start. Professional public management is intrinsically dependent on progress in improving certain critical dimensions of public management that I refer to as the imperatives of administrative theory and practice. They are: (1) competent and ethical leadership; (2) commitment to institutional reform; (3) willingness and ability to adapt and to adopt good management practices irrespective of national origin; and, (4) reliance on factual data and modern technology in the conduct of public affairs. To expand its knowledge base on all these dimensions, beyond the confines of national boundaries, public administration institutions have to cultivate the comparative method to partake in the total human experiences.

For effective utilization of the comparative method, scholars and researchers have to change their outlook towards the main field of public administration, and to develop the abilities to employ comparison for knowledge creation. Cross-cultural comparisons require motivated scholars and researchers who are also understanding of the culture, history, and language of other societies to conceive their inherent characteristics and to appreciate the significance of their institutionalized relationships. Managers continually compare current with past performance; they compare with standards and benchmarks to gauge progress and to recognize where and when achievements are made. By comparing, a researcher identifies the constants and the variables of management, underlines the range and the sequence of variations, determines the influences behind the structures, and perceives the level of support for change (Thompson, et al. 1959). Through comparison, public managers are better able to account for consequences of performance and variation across organizations and across countries.

In all this, research has to acquire more empirical comparative information on various systems and cultures. Another track for improvement is through employing appropriate investigation tools such as middle-range concepts that can be verified and ultimately integrated in a meaningful framework. Finally, education in universities and practical training in its variety need to integrate comparative administration information in teaching students and in training practitioners. The incredible changes in information communication technology (ICT) promise a profound change in reaching out to other experiences and practices worldwide. The amount of information students are able to access today through the Internet in a graduate seminar on comparative administration is overwhelming. The challenge for education is to provide conceptual and practical couching for students to be able to apply appropriate interpretation, integration, comparison, and analysis to be able to draw generalizations from data, improve understanding, and have new and meaningful learning.

References

Aberback, J. D., and B. A. Rockman. 1988. Problems of cross-national comparison. In *Public Administration in Developed Democracies: A Comparative Study,* ed. D. C. Rowat, 419–440, New York: Marcel Dekker.

Adler, N. J., R. Doktor, and S. G. Redding. 1986. From the Atlantic to the Pacific Century: Cross-cultural management reviewed. *Yearly Review of Management of the Journal of Management,* 12 (2): 295–318.

Almond, G. A., et al. 2000. *Comparative Politics Today.* 7th ed. New York: Longman.

Almond, G. A., and S. Verba, eds. 1989. *The Civic Culture Revisited.* Sage.

Baker, R., ed. 1994. *Comparative Public Management.* Westport, CT: Praeger.

Banks, A., and R. Textor 1963. *A Cross-Polity Survey.* Cambridge, M.I.T. Press.

Bannister, F. 2007. The curse of the benchmark: An assessment of the validity and values of e-government comparisons. *International Review of Administrative Sciences* 73 (2): 171–188.

Bekke, H., J. Perry, and T. Toonen, eds. 1996. *Civil Service Systems in Comparative Perspective.* Bloomington, IN: Indiana University Press.

Bertucci, G. 2008. The state of international development management. *Public Administration Review*. 68 (6): 1002–1003.

Chandler, J. A., ed. 2000. *Comparative Public Administration*. London: Routledge.

Chapman, R. A. ed. 2000. *Ethics in Public Service for the Millennium*. Burlington, VT: Ashgate.

Child, J., and Tayeb, M. 1983. Theoretical perspectives in cross-national organizational research. *International Studies of Management and Organization*, 7 (1): 3–34.

Collier, D. 1991. The comparative method: Two decades of change. In *Comparative Political Dynamics*. D. A. Rustow and K. P. Erickson, eds. New York: Harper Collins.

Dahl, R. A. 1947. The science of public administration: Three problems. *Public Administration Review* 7 (1): 1–11.

Deutsch, K. W. 1987. Prologue: Achievements and challenges in 2000 years of comparative research. In *Comparative Policy Research: Learning from Experience*, eds. M. Dierkes, H. N. Weiler, and A. B. Antal, 5–25. New York: St. Martin's Press.

Esman, M. J. 1988. The maturing of development administration. *Public Administration and Development*. 8: 125–134.

_____. 1974. Administrative doctrine and developmental needs. In *The Administration of Change in Africa*, E. P. Morgan, ed. 3–26, New York: Dunellen.

_____. 1966. The politics of development administration. In *Approaches to Development: Politics, Administration, and Change*. Eds. J D. Montgomery and W. J. Siffin, 59–112. New York: McGraw-Hill.

Fainsod, M. 1963. Bureaucracy and modernization: The Russian and Soviet case. In *Bureaucracy and Political Development*, ed. J. La Palombara, Princeton, NJ: Princeton University Press.

Farazmand, A. ed. 2001. *Handbook of Comparative and Development Administration*. 2nd ed. New York: Marcel Dekker.

Farazmand, A. 1999. Globalization and public administration. *Public Administration Review* 59 (6): 509–522.

Gant, G. F. 1979. *Development Administration: Concepts, Goals, Methods*. Madison, WI: The University of Wisconsin Press.

Graves, D. 1972. The impact of culture upon managerial attitudes, beliefs and behavior in England and France, *Journal of Management Studies* 10, 1.

Heady, F. 2001. *Public Administration: A Comparative Perspective*, 6th ed. New York: Marcel Dekker.

Heady, F., and S. L. Stokes, eds. 1962. *Papers in Comparative Public Administration*. Ann Arbor, MI: Institute of Public Administration, University of Michigan.

Henry, N. 2001. *Public Administration and Public Affairs*. 8th ed. Upper Saddle River, NJ: Prentice Hall.

Hofstede, G., 1980. *Culture's Consequences: International Differences in Work-Related Values*. Beverly Hills, CA: Sage.

Huddleston, M. W. 1984. *Comparative Public Administration: An Annotated Bibliography*. New York: Garland.

Jreisat, J. E. 2005. Comparative public administration is back in, prudently. *Public Administration Review* 65 (2): 211–222.

_____. 1997. *Politics without Process: Administering Development in the Arab World*. Boulder, CO: Lynne Rienner Publishers.

_____. 1975. Synthesis and relevance in comparative public administration, *Public Administration Review*. 35, 6 (November/ December).

Kickert, W. J. M., and R. J. Stillman. 1996. Changing European state, changing public administration. *Public Administration Review* 56 (1): 65–67.

Klingner, D. E., and J. Nalbandian. 1998. *Public Personnel Management.* 4th ed. Upper Saddle River, NJ: Prentice Hall.

Lane, J. E. 2000. *New Public Management.* London: Routledge.

Locker, O. L., and D. Kienzler. 2008. *Business and Administrative Communication.* 8th ed. New York: McGraw-Hill.

Manning, N., and Parison, N. 2004. *International Public Administration Reform: Implications for the Russian Federation.* Washington, D.C: The World Bank.

March, J. G., and H. A. Simon. 1958. *Organizations.* New York: John Wiley.

Mavima, P., and R. Chackerian. 2002. Administrative reform adoption and implementation: The influence of global and local institutional forces. In *Governance and Developing Countries,* ed. J. E. Jreisat, 91–110, Leiden, the Netherlands: Brill.

O'Leary, R. and DMV. Styke. 2010. *Introduction to Symposium on the Future of Public Administration in 2020.* Public Administration Review. Supplement to Vol.70 (1): S5–S11.

Otenyo, E. E., and N. S. Lind, eds. 2006. *Comparative Public Administration: The Essential Readings.* New York: Elsevier.

Peters, B. G., and D. J. Savoie. 1994. Civil service reform: Misdiagnosing the patient. *Public Administration Review* 54 (5): 418–424.

Premchand, A., and J. Burkhead. 1984. *Comparative International Budgeting and Finance.* Piscataway, NJ: Transaction Publishers.

Pollitt, C., and G. Bouckaert. 2004. *Public Management Reform: A Comparative Analysis,* 2nd ed. Oxford, UK: Oxford University Press.

Roberts, K. H., and M. Grabowski. 1996. Organizations, technology and structuring. In *Handbook of Organization Studies,* ed. S. R. Clegg, C. Hardy, and W. R. Nord, 409–423. Thousand Oaks, CA: Sage.

Rondinelli, D. A. 1982. The dilemma of development administration: Complexity and Uncertainty in control-oriented bureaucracies. *World Politics.* Vol. XXXV (1): 43–72.

Rowat, D. C. ed. 1988. *Public Administration in Developed Democracies:* A comparative study NY: Marcel Dekker.

Riggs, F. W. 1998. Public administration in America: Why our uniqueness is exceptional and important. *Public Administration Review* 58 (1): 22–31.

———. 1991a. Public administration: A comparativist framework. *Public Administration Review.* 51 (6): 473–477.

———. 1991b. Bureaucratic links between administration and politics. In *Handbook of Comparative and Development Administration.* 2nd ed. A. Farazmand, ed.: 485–510. New York: Marcel Dekker.

———. 1989. The political ecology of American public administration," *International Journal of Public Administration.* 12 (3): 355–384.

———. 1964. *Administration of Developing Countries.* Boston: Houghton Mifflin.

Ryan, R. W. 1994. The importance of comparative study in educating the U.S. public service. In *Comparative Public Management,* ed. R. Baker, 23–35, Westport, CT: Praeger.

Schick, A. 1990. Budgeting for results: Recent developments in five industrialized countries. *Public Administration Review* 50 (1), 26–33.

Taylor, C. L., and M. C. Hudson. 1983. *World Handbook of Political and Social Indicators.* 3rd ed. New Haven: Yale University Press.

Thomas, V. 1959. Globalization: Implications for Development Learning, *Public Administration and Development* 19 (1): 5–17.

Thompson, J. D., et al. 1959. *Comparative Studies in Administration*. Pittsburgh, PA: University of Pittsburgh Press.

Tummala, K. K., ed. 2003. *Comparative Bureaucratic Systems*. Lanham, MD: Lexington Books.

Van Wart, M., and C. J. Cayer 1990. Comparative public administration: Defunct, dispersed, or redefined?. *Public Administration Review* 50 (2): 238–248.

Wildavsky, A. 1985. *Budgeting: A Comparative Theory of Budgetary Processes*. Piscataway, NJ: Transaction Publishers.

Wilson, W. 1887. The study of administration. In *Classics of Public Administration*. eds. J. M. Shafritz and A. C. Hyde, 1997, 4th ed. New York: Harcourt Brace College Publications.

Endnotes

1. Buerkle, Tom, and Alan Friedman. *International Herald Tribune*, January 27, 2001.
2. *St. Petersburg Times*. April 22, 2001. P. A1.
3. *St. Petersburg Times*. April 22, 2001. P. A1.
4. According to the Minister of Economic Development and Cooperation of Germany, Heide Wieczorek-Zeul, addressing the UN summit conference (June 2000).
5. *Business Week*. November 6, 2000, p. 74.
6. "Managerial Response to Globalization," draft of a report by a Group of Experts on the United Nations Program in Public Administration and Finance, 15th session (May 8–12, 2000), p. 5.

Chapter 3

Bureaucracy

> The true test of a good government is its aptitude and tendency to produce a good administration.
>
> **Alexander Hamilton (*The Federalist*)**

Bureaucracy and Comparative Analysis

The administrative system of a country or its national bureaucracy refers to agencies, bureaus, units, organizations, departments, ministries, or appointed committees of the public sector. In large governments, these units employ thousands and, collectively, millions of public employees. They initiate, influence, interpret, and implement the authoritative policies and laws of the state and its political subunits. Bureaucracy is regarded as a system because its parts and units are interrelated in serving the policies and goals of the state. While agencies and similar units constitute subsystems of bureaucracy, each of these units and organizations by itself may also be considered a system. Viewing bureaucracy as a large system with many subsystems enables analysts to define and to measure its input of resources, goals, and public demands as well as its output of goods, services, and regulatory actions. Studying and analyzing bureaucracy as a system emphasizes functional and complex relationships among and between actors, offices, and their environment.

Focusing on the national administrative system in comparative studies places the institution of bureaucracy at the center of analysis. At the outset, it is important to point out that the national administrative system is conceived flexibly to incorporate various subsequent theoretical and practical modifications, extensions, and adaptations to the classic model of bureaucracy. At this macro level, one is able to delineate overall administrative characteristics and their significance to the function of governance. A close examination of the national bureaucracy also helps to bring out and to define crucial relations with the political order. Interdependence of the administrative and the political systems largely shapes the structure and defines the formal functions of bureaucracy. It is not surprising, therefore, that studies of comparative national bureaucracy and comparative politics converge or overlap on various aspects.

Early comparative studies were preoccupied with attributes and functions of political institutions in a handful of Western countries and a scattering of developing countries (Heady 2001). The emergence of many Third World countries in the post–World War II era brought forward issues and problems of management and nation building that heretofore were neglected or unfamiliar to scholars of Western comparative politics. Today, a major purpose of CPA is to improve understanding of national administrative systems across countries by studying institutions that are central to governance and, at the same time, constitute suitable units for comparative research. The focus, therefore, is genuinely international rather than confined to a select few systems. Generally, the term *bureaucracy* is used to denote national administration, as in the classic conceptions, and subsequent changes and adaptations that followed. A country's bureaucracy is its national administrative system in its present form and function. What a bureaucracy does in a particular country, and how it is doing it, are not assumptions to be made but empirical questions to be answered through empirical investigation and research.

Classic Bureaucratic Model

Bureaucracy is a specific institutional structure that has received its initial designation and its characterization from the German sociologist Max Weber (1864–1920) in the early part of the twentieth century. Classic bureaucratic theory is linked to Max Weber's name as Scientific Management is to Frederick Taylor's. Although Max Weber devoted his studies to areas other than bureaucracy, his brief discussion of bureaucracy—as the form of administration functioning in a legal-rational system of authority—became the most widely recognized statement on the subject. Weber (translated by Gerth and Mills, 1946) outlines the basic features of bureaucracy as the following:

1. Fixed and *official jurisdictional areas* are generally ordered by rules and laws.
2. Principles of *office hierarchy* and of levels of graded authority mean a firmly ordered system of superior-subordinate authority.

3. Management of the modern office is based on *written records* and *documents* (files).
4. Management usually presupposes thorough and expert *training.*
5. Official activity demands the *full working capacity* of officials (career employees).
6. Management follows general *rules*, which are more or less stable and exhaustive, and can be learned.

The core elements of the model are specialization, hierarchy of authority, impersonality, system of rules, written records, and recruitment process based on merit (education, training, and skills). Weber's emphasis on generalizable properties of bureaucracy tends to challenge the claim that Western civilization and systems are distinct, thus superior. By accentuating the similarities among bureaucratic systems in the West and between these and other earlier and contemporary cultures, Weber's drive to make his theory of bureaucratic universal dictated that he play down the cultural differences while emphasizing the process, its rationality, and the need for its institutionalization. The political context, however, is a different issue altogether. The authority system dictates fundamental properties of the administrative system. After a review of history and effective use of the comparative approach, Weber identified three types of authority systems:

In the first, the *legal-rational system of authority,* bureaucracy operates within carefully prescribed rules and processes. A main feature of this system is that obedience is based on legal and impersonal order. Offices, rather than persons, are the basis of authority. These offices are organized in a hierarchy, occupied by staff paid on a scale tied to their positions in this hierarchy, and according to their levels of competence and expert knowledge. "The persons who exercise the power of command are typically *superiors* who are appointed or elected by legally sanctioned procedures and are themselves oriented toward the maintenance of the legal order. The persons subject to the commands are *legal equals* who obey 'the law' rather than the persons implementing it" (Bendix 1962: 294).

The second, the *traditional authority system,* bases legitimacy on the "sanctity of order." Obedience is not to enacted rules, but to persons, who govern by tradition and inherited status. "The persons subject to the command of the master are *followers* or *subjects* in the literal sense—they obey out of personal loyalty to the master or a pious regard for his time-honored status" (Bendix 1962: 295). The administrative staff is usually recruited from among the favorites of the chief and from those tied to him by purely personal loyalties. Kinship, wealth, and family origin play an important role in the selection of the staff. Consequently, in contrast to the legal rational model, the staff of traditional administrative systems lacks defined spheres of competence, rational ordering of offices, and technical training as a regular requirement.

The third, the *charismatic authority system,* is legitimized by the superhuman qualities of the leader in power. Followers do not elect this leader; their duty is to recognize the charisma and respond to it. The administrative staff consists of followers and disciples chosen not in accordance with rules but, mainly, on the basis of political loyalties. To be more than transitory, a system built on the charisma of its leader has to routinize the line of succession (Diamant 1962).

Weber realized that in the "real world," a mixture of the three patterns of authority exists. However, usually one of the three designations—traditional, charismatic, or legal-rational—predominates. During the past six decades, Weber's work attracted extraordinary attention by social scientists in the United States and in Europe. Earlier American scholars such as C. Wright Mills, Philip Selznick, Robert Merton, Reinhard Bendix, Peter Blau, Alvin Gouldner, Talcot Parson, and others invested considerable energies in interpreting, evaluating, extending, and examining what Weber said and meant. Weber's impact on American sociology is deep and lasting; sociologists regard Weber as "the founder of systematic study of bureaucracy" (Merton 1952: 17). Weber's formulations are considered the fountainhead for much theoretical and empirical inquiry into bureaucracy.

It is true that Weber constructed an "ideal type" model designed to be logically precise and consistent, and never to be found fully manifested in a concrete reality. An ideal conception, however, can help us think systematically and assess the existing reality. In fact, some aspects of Weber's ideal theory of bureaucracy exist in all large-scale organizations—public or private. "The rational-legal form of bureaucracy," wrote Charles Perrow, "is the most efficient form of administration known" (1984: 5). Perrow regarded the bureaucratic model as "superior to all others we know or can hope to afford in the near and middle future." The fact remains that few administrative models excite as much debate and controversy as the subject of bureaucracy. Volumes have been dedicated to the subject without exhausting all salient issues. Thus, in this work, I discuss only selected issues to represent general features and questions related to the role of bureaucracy in modern society. Particularly, I seek to develop better understanding of the bureaucratic model and its suitability for comparative analysis.

The bureaucratic model proved to be a paradox to administrative theory and practice in many ways. Michel Crozier pointed out that Weber had furnished a brilliant description of the ideal type of a bureaucratic organization and a suggestive analysis of its historical development that apparently paved the way for a positive, value-free sociological analysis. "Yet the discussion about bureaucracy is still, to a large extent, the domain of the myths and pathos of ideology" (Crozier 1964: 175).

To examine Weber's bureaucratic model only as an instrument of managerial efficiency and effectiveness is to lose sight of its larger significance. Weber's "particular genius," Brian Fry noted, "was to place administration in a broad historical context and to associate the processes of bureaucratization with the processes of rationalization in the Western world" (1989: 42). The bureaucratic model was to emphasize technical skills, knowledge, merit, justice, due process, and all those values featured in modern professional management. Thus, Weber applied the comparative approach successfully over time and space in the search for regularities and common threads.

Assessments and Criticisms of Bureaucracy

Despite its significant role in modern society, bureaucracy rarely enjoys a positive public image. Bureaucracy has been fending off bitter attacks from without and an erosion of confidence, if not disillusionment, from within. But, even if bureaucracy is unappreciated or reviled, it is a fact of contemporary life and of governance everywhere. The "American government, the society, and its citizens are now dependent upon vast, interconnecting web of complicated administrative systems, processes, and procedures" (Stillman 1998: xvii). Critics of bureaucracy are diverse; their rationales also vary. "Policies, organizations, and public officials have failed, all with consequences ranging from unfortunate on a local level to egregious on a global level" (Hill and Lynn 2009: xiii). At the same time, administrative accomplishments and successes are no less numerous and compelling. "As a matter of fact, the daily business of government at all levels is performed with commendable competence by officials committed to public service" (Hill and Lynn 2009: viii). In popular views and in scholarly literature, bureaucracy has been linked to various good and bad attributes. It is possible to define and classify two clusters of negative views of bureaucracy:

One set of criticisms may be called the *colloquial view*, which equates bureaucracy with inefficiency, red tape, lengthy forms, lust for power, domination, incompetence, and a host of similar scathing characterizations (Stillman 1998: 4; Goodsell 1994). Such images are often nurtured in popular stories, prejudicial journalistic writings, and conservative political views that continually portray bureaucracy as a pathological problem of modern society. Also, bureaucracy is a convenient scapegoat, which can be blamed with impunity by political leaders for public policy shortcomings and failures. Such accusations are rarely based on dispassionate evaluation and analysis but often are politically motivated.[1] Criticisms are usually based on personal beliefs, anecdotes, ideological preferences, political expediency, or simply conformity with a trend. Such negative views, even if widely spread, are not a central concern of this study. Useful analysis of bureaucracy has to be a value-neutral approach, accepting bureaucracy as a structure that may perform well or poorly, and this to be ascertained by evidence. Determining the characteristics of a particular bureaucracy remains essentially an empirical question.

A second set of criticisms relies on theoretical analyses and empirical appraisals of bureaucracy and its role in modern society. This type of criticism is rooted in inductive and deductive analysis, utilizing reliable social science methods. One finds in such studies some influential arguments that actually reach beyond the structure or formal functions of bureaucracy. These discussions often indicate a wider scope of concerns, particularly on the question of impact on society and relationships with the political system. The significant concerns that dominated discussions on the subject of bureaucratic defects and pathologies may be divided into four major clusters of issues:

1. The power concern
2. Political development and bureaucratic influence
3. Change and innovation
4. The "ideal-type" concept

The Power Issue

Bureaucracy is a powerful institution of modern society. Its performance can drastically assist or hinder the state's capacity for effective governance. Max Weber himself acknowledged that the position of a fully developed bureaucracy is always overpowering. Ralph Hummel explained that Weber believed bureaucracy converts "man's social relations into "control relations." "His norms and beliefs concerning human ends are torn from him and replaced with skills affirming the ascendency of technical means, whether of administration or production" (Hummel 1977: 2). But Weber repeatedly indicated that his model is an "ideal type" that does not exist in a pure form but as a mixture of various characteristics. In practice, however, a principal basis of this power is expertise, elevated by good training and superior technical skills of those who join the bureaucracy (Gerth and Mills 1946: 228). A high degree of specialization creates a need for coordination at a higher level of authority as well as through processes of work. The purpose of such structural articulation is to reach higher efficiency of performance. But the combination of the bureaucratic processes often generates excessive power in the hands of such a disciplined institution. Because the source of this bureaucratic power is not the will of citizens, and the method of granting it is not through representation, even if bureaucratic authority is answerable to duly elected representatives, bureaucracy is almost always suspect or publicly charged on ideological grounds.

Critics contend that concentration of power in the hands of bureaucrats has the potential of destroying the democratic process and weakening democratic institutions. The problem of efficiency versus democracy is relevant to all formal organizations. One clarification is offered by Blau and Meyer (1971: 13) based on distinguishing three types of association:

- If an association is established for manufacturing a product or winning a war then considerations of efficiency are of primary importance.
- If an association is established for the purpose of finding intrinsic satisfaction in common activities, say religious worship, then considerations of efficiency are less relevant.

■ Finally, if an association is established for the purpose of deciding upon common goals and courses of action to implement them, which is the function of democratic government, the free expression of opinion must be safeguarded against other considerations, including those of efficiency.

Thus, Blau and Meyer conclude that organizations of the first type (industrial and services) would always be bureaucratized, but those of the third type (public policy making) never would. The authors' thesis, however, does not resolve the problem in mixed situations. Also, for policy-making organizations, it is commonly accepted (and Weber himself has recognized) that setting national goals and policies in a democratic system is a function of elected people rather than appointed bureaucrats.

Although the issue of bureaucracy versus democracy is not new, it has been the subject of a continuing debate that has changed in form and in substance over time. From the right, as early as 1940s and before, conservatives saw a "danger that our impatience for quick results may lead us to choose instruments which, though perhaps more efficient for achieving the particular ends, are not compatible with the preservation of a free society" (Hayek 1944: x). Accordingly, bureaucracy is incompatible with democracy. This line of thinking perceives a historical pattern. In *The Road to Serfdom*, Friedrich A. Hayek (1944: vii) took the position that increasing government control over the economy would ultimately lead to nation-wide socialism, which requires that a central plan to replace the market. He offered this illustration: In 1934, Germany, Italy, Russia, and Japan applied central planning; ten years later, they had all become totalitarian states. Such overdrawn conclusion is tenuous for two reasons: First, several other countries employed central planning, even considerable measures of socialism—for example, the United Kingdom and India—but were not transformed into totalitarian states. Second, the evidence of cause and effect relationship between planning and totalitarianism is flimsy at best.

Similarly, some recent criticisms of the state regard the growth of bureaucracy as incursion by the government, beyond what they perceive as its "acceptable" and limited boundaries. The expansion of the role of public policy in the economies of the U.S and other countries, after the economic disaster of the 2008–9, has also been labeled socialism and communism by ideologues and extreme political groups. Although state activism was often the result of weakened regulatory processes and abuse of the market mechanisms that required state intervention, the assertive regulatory process and the use of public expenditure as a stimulus have faced rigorous negative reactions not unlike those attacks of earlier times.

From the left, bureaucracy is also considered an obstacle to the functioning of a democratic society. For radical political left, bureaucracy is a problem that stands in the way of creating a democratic society. According to the radical left, rules, regulations, hierarchy, standardization, and impersonality of organizational decisions, essential elements of the Weberian bureaucracy, are manifestations of authoritarianism and oppression of the individual. Views of the left are not unanimous or even harmonious. The following statement, even if exaggerated, is illustrative:

> A bureaucratic system is hierarchical in nature...in all bureaucratic organizations authority rests on the ability to apply coercion. The authority to apply coercion is delegated to subordinates by those at the top. In a bureaucratic system it is assumed that there must be one person or group of persons who can finally be held responsible for system's operation. The bureaucratic system fits exactly the description...of the Stalinist system: It consists of a Stalin at the top and little Stalins all the way down the line. (Mcgill 1970: 100)

Bureaucracy and Political Development

This issue is also a derivative of the democracy-versus-bureaucracy discourse. Comparative public administration has always been concerned about the impact of political authority and political culture on administrative performance. A major debate among scholars, applying the comparative approach in the early 1960s, has been focused on factors of power, efficacy, and the politics of bureaucracy. The capacity developed by a truly bureaucratic organization presumably creates or intensifies the issue of control in democratic governance. Such concern often seems to reach a dead end or turn into abstracts and deductions of what Heady calls the "imbalance thesis" (Heady 2001: 439–443). The well-known advocate of the "imbalance thesis" is Fred W. Riggs, who had always maintained this position. Namely, in developing countries, bureaucratic power and efficiency contribute to lack of political development. Bureaucracy, as perceived by Riggs, constitutes a ruling class with its own self-interest; thus, bureaucratic dominance has adverse effect on the future of political institutions (Riggs 2000). The antithesis of Riggs' proposition has been restated by many authors over the years, including Ferrel Heady, Milton Esman, Ralph Braibanti, and others.

Ralph Braibanti's edited volume *Political and Administrative Development* (1969) attracted contributions from prominent scholars in political science and comparative public administration such as Carl Friedrich, Giovanni Sartori, Martin Landau, Harold Lasswell, Fred Riggs, John Montgomery, and others. Braibanti's view on the "imbalance thesis" was clearly stated. He pointed out that competent bureaucracy is a prerequisite for national development. Thus, strengthening the administrative structures must proceed irrespective of the rate of maturation of the political process. "Nevertheless," Braibanti pointed out, "in recognition of the stress involved in rapid bureaucratic development occurring simultaneously with expanded mass participation in political life, we seek here to explore means of increasing the capability of other institutions not only to stimulate bureaucratic innovation but also to moderate bureaucratic discretion, to enhance the symmetry of political growth, and to improve the quality of participation" (1969: 1). The message is that developing administrative capability should not be impeded and should not be at the expense of political development. Administrative development should sustain political development rather than undermine it.

Despite contrary claims, effective political systems and effective administrative systems often coexist in mutually reinforcing capacities rather than in a zero sum game of competition. The primacy of political control over administration is not in doubt, irrespective of the level of effectiveness in exercising it. Evidence from the Arab states, for example, indicates that political leaders have kept very tight rein on all powers of the state, particularly those related to public funds and military control. In reality, the political features of the state allowed the administrative process many of its current attributes: highly centralized, beset by nepotism and political patronage, and burdened by its own weight of swelled ranks of poorly trained public employees (Jreisat 1997: 227). Under these political forms and processes, professional management with neutral competence is hard to sustain. Similarly, programs of administrative reform falter primarily for lack of political support and incongruities with political regime values. Thus, the capacity for action by both of the political and the administrative systems is weakened as is common in many developing countries.

The challenge for comparative research, then, is to define links with the political order that really matter, regardless whether such links strengthen or hinder opportunities for administrative reform. The objective is to specify conditions and variables that determine relationships through empirical evidence gathered from case studies and refined middle-range propositions at the organizational level. Political authority and political values not only determine the boundaries of administrative change but also shape bureaucratic attitudes in the conduct of state affairs, particularly towards citizens. For too long, consultants and researchers on reform have focused on issues of centralization, technical skills, civil service procedures, and bureaucratic behavior. While these are important elements of the administrative capacity building of any system, they must not overshadow crucial considerations such as the form and the behavior of the political regime.

In developing countries, administrative change questions are linked to attitudes of the political leaders. To what limit does the political authority support reform? What elements of the bureaucracy may be changed? How much citizens' participation is allowed in public decision making, and how different opinions are dealt with? Who is to benefit by the change? Beyond studying regime types, it is essential to define under what conditions regime's support is possible. If not, the alternative could be a waste of huge budgets and extensive efforts to a change that is incompatible with existing political authority, hence with little chance of implementation.

Similarly, a frequently expressed theme equates big government with big and rigid bureaucracy that wields excessive powers, potentially threatening to citizens' free living. Instead of being the instrument of public policy implementation, the critics argue, bureaucracy is becoming the master dictating the policy. The important question, then, who has the power of control and on what grounds? Max

Weber's formulation describes the three types of authority system (presented earlier) each with a distinct foundation of authority. In the traditional system, legitimate power comes from the tradition and the inherited status of family and wealth. Consequently, when the political order is not representative of citizens, it would be unrealistic to expect bureaucracy to be. Also, such system is not fully bureaucratized (rules, technical competence of the staff, hierarchical responsibilities, etc.) and so remains highly inefficient. In the charismatic system, the legitimacy of power is tied to the exceptional qualities of the leader. Thus, again, it is not representation that governs political or administrative authority. And in the legal-rational system, legitimacy of power emanates from the belief in the rightness of the law and the respect for it (Gerth and Mills 1946). Americans, for example, habitually describe their political order as a "system of laws'" and they like to justify many public decisions with the ultimate defense by pointing out that "it is the law."

How can bureaucracy be made to conform with citizens' views, preferences, and values? If bureaucracy were always neutral in its values, obedient to the elected superiors, and limiting its activities to enforcement of public laws and rules, then most controversies surrounding bureaucracy would melt away. But size of bureaucracy, its continuity in office, its expert knowledge, and its effective channels of communication with the public tipped the balance of power-structure in some societies in favor of bureaucracy. This is more noticeable in societies that experience high turnover in the political and executive leadership such as frequent resignations of the cabinet or the chief executive. Bureaucracy's performance under these conditions tends to fill in the gap created by the political vacuum rather than usurping power, as the critics charge.

Certainly, performance seems to concern the public far more than the issue of whether bureaucracy is an impediment to democracy, an issue relayed often in an exaggerated form. Charles Goodsell, in *The Case for Bureaucracy* (1994), accumulated "hard" data on citizens' opinions of public bureaucracy, beginning with a survey by Leonard White in 1929 to public polls in the 1990s. He concluded that the "hard" data on bureaucracy are "overwhelmingly favorable." "Bureaucracy works. To claim otherwise is either to ignore the evidence or to assert that we are being totally fooled by the paradigm of rationality, with only a few critical theorists able to escape the charade" (Goodsell 1994: 46).

Thus, fears of bureaucratic despotism in democratic societies are magnified for ideological and political reasons. But this should not mean a defense of a perfect situation. Administrative reform is a continual objective of public policy and strengthening tools of monitoring and control is a constant challenge. Generally, combinations of control and monitoring mechanisms over bureaucratic powers are found to varying degrees of effectiveness in all systems of governance:

- The power of "oversight" in the hands of elected officials is a versatile tool when fairly and competently employed. "Oversight" is an instrument that offers elected officials various channels to check, monitor, approve, and evaluate bureaucratic performance. One such instrument is budget approval, which is a responsibility of elected representatives, in almost all systems that have such election, at the national as well as the local levels of government. The failure of the political system to perform its budgetary responsibilities often adds to the problem rather than restrains it. Investigative powers as well as the enactment of laws by representatives of the people are also effective methods of oversight when and if properly executed.

■ Various personnel policies such as recruitment, promotion, transfers, and training when based on merit and transparency of decision making tend to produce values essential for the functioning of democracy. Even if not in office through citizens' votes, one assumes that today's bureaucracy is representative of the society in its various economic and social strata and not some novel or strange implant in the body politic of a society. It is not a far-fetched thesis that the U.S. bureaucracy is more representative of the people than the elected U.S. Senate, occasionally referred to as the "millionaires club." Moreover, conscious efforts have been made in many countries to improve representation and equity concerns within the institution of bureaucracy. Acknowledging the considerable progress made in the United States, Frederickson (2000: 5) proposes a theory of social equity as the "third pillar" of public administration, "with the same status as economy and efficiency as values or principles to which public administration should adhere." Also, "the concept of representative bureaucracy has now occupied an important place in the literature of public administration and political science for some three decades," as Nachmias and Reosenbloom (2000: 39) point out. Thus, harmony between bureaucratic values and preferences and those of citizens is attainable; important advancements in this direction have already been made. To be effective as an organization of high capacity and efficient methods of operation, bureaucracy has to be in tune with its larger environment, and not to exist as a xenophobic organ implanted by invisible forces within the institutions of governance.

Change and Innovation

Critics assume that bureaucracy as a systems is rigid, unable to change, and cannot be innovative. Conventional wisdom has it that bureaucracy is conformist, seeks standardization and routinization of work, therefore, causes inflexibility and resistance to change in managing public organizations. Even training in administrative skills, considered appropriate under most conditions, may result in serious maladjustments such as greater standardization and rigidities in the application of newly acquired skills.

In a bureaucratic system, change must be universalistic, encompassing the entire organization, Crozier (1964: 196) argues. In fact, change may even lead to further centralization and further safeguarding of impersonality of the system. "Because of the necessary long delays, because of the amplitude of the scope it must attain, and because of the resistance it must overcome, change in bureaucratic organizations is a deeply felt crisis" (Crozier 1964: 196). Various theoretical constructs and derivative techniques evolved to modify early parochial assumptions of public administration. Indeed, cross-cultural comparisons and the subsequent advent of development administration are among the vigorous responses in this respect. Development administration, in its early conception, has been viewed as an integral part of societal development, as well as profoundly influenced by overall societal attributes. In other terms, while development administration is to disconnect with the known anomalies of traditional administration, it is, also, to associate with overall change and development in the new nations. In the industrial countries, however, responses to bureaucratic rigidities, over-conformance to rules and regulations, and unsatisfactory responsiveness to community needs and to policy objectives, took different shapes and offered different alternatives:

- Promises of a free form of organizational setting and a relativist entrepreneurial leadership seem to offer options other than the known bureaucratic hierarchical structure. Thus, what was really envisioned or assumed by those seeking answers in managerialism and free marketing is the purge of the classic bureaucratic edifice that dominating management accepted wisdom for many decades. Team building, Total Quality Management (TQM), reinvention, and reengineering are some of the examples suggested as substitutes or alternatives to the bureaucratic model. Total Quality Management in particular gained wide support as a theory and as a practice for its appealing attributes. Some of these crucial attributes are its commitment to customer-driven quality, employee participation in quality improvement, commitment to continuous improvement and to actions based on facts and analysis (Berman 1997: 282). A general assumption in a large segment of contemporary management literature is that the attributed rigidity, and other negative characteristics of the bureaucratic model, justify or require abandonment of the model and expediting search for discovery of a better alternative.
- Political motives foster continual search by political leaders to escape from the responsibility for budget deficits, incurring huge public debts, and retreating on the front of social welfare policies. These political attitudes find bureaucracy an irresistible target for redirecting citizens' dissatisfaction or rationalizing failures of their policies. Big government is the explanation for this camp, even when the ratio of public employees to citizens is in decline. Increasing poverty, rising crime levels, and deteriorating social conditions are connected to bureaucratic mismanagement or poor administrative performance. Rarely, we encounter political leaders who would consider their policies and their lack of support to professional public management as a contributing factor to governance problems. When faced with evidence, politicians have perfected methods of ducking issues altogether.

One suggestion for promoting change is by decoupling of public administration and bureaucracy. "An ingrained and narrowly focused pattern of thought, a 'bureaucratic paradigm,' is routinely attributed to public administration's traditional literature" (Lynn 2001: 144). In attempting to disassociate the two, Lynn (2001: 144) suggests that a "careful reading of that literature reveals, however, that the 'bureaucratic paradigm' is, at best, a caricature and, at worst, a demonstrable distortion of traditional thought that exhibited far more respect for law, politics, citizens, and values than the new, customer-oriented managerialism and its variant." Interestingly enough, it seems that a mixture of caricature approximation, with a measure of distortion, provided the backdrop for Osborne and Gaebler's (1992) characterization of bureaucracy to justify their "reinvention of government." A less subtle but still depreciating bureaucracy is the claim that the traditional public administration is superseded by "a new approach to public sector governance, i.e. contractualism" (Lane 2000: 3).

The common assumption is that bureaucracy, preoccupied with standardization, setting rules and routine, tends to turn into a rigid, nonchanging, noncreative edifice impeding effective governance. Less recognized, however, are the conditions that induce the occurrence of such tendencies. Misunderstood also is the fact that lack of rules and standards could create far more damaging conditions in managing public or private organizations. The issue, then, is excessiveness in reliance on rules and standards, notion sociologists refer to as "ritualism" in applying rules that they become the end rather than the means. In this context the following concepts are germane: (1) Compliance with rules and regulations is a common phenomenon encountered in managing organizations of all types. Rules are tools for ensuring accountable behaviors and preventing chaos. (2) Excessive compliance often results from an organizational culture that punishes mistakes by employees, fosters distrust among various echelons of positions, and centralizes decision-making powers in the hands of the few at the top of the organization. (3) Over-compliance could follow overall management incompetence that employees use rules to cover lack of wits and inability to exercise judgment.

Over and over, accountability and responsiveness to citizens' needs and demands by public employees come to the forefront of discussion. But accountability involves various relationships, types of incentives, degree of control, and behavioral expectations (Romzek 1997: 35). Organization theory faces a real dilemma on this feature. To improve administrative responsiveness and effectiveness, critics and reformers seek deregulation and removal of layers of rules, regulations, and constraints. This means also decentralization and more discretion and flexibility at lower levels of authority. Problem is the result may be loss of control and even loss of accountability. As Romzek (1997: 36) points out, the trends correspond to a pendulum that swings between two extremes: one is the direction of control, red tape, and rigidity and the other is towards greater discretion and flexibility. Recent calls for eliminating red tape, streamlining procedures, adopting customer service orientation, engaging entrepreneurial management, and similar acts of managerialism are another swing of the pendulum in the opposite direction of the bureaucratic rigidity.

Fearing for their jobs in societies with high unemployment levels, and dreading unrestrained political and administrative powers at the top, public employees seek safety through compliance and by avoiding risk. "Following the rules" usually means minimizing the chances of making punishable mistakes. Under these conditions, changing organizational culture, empowering employees, and training and personnel development usually go a long way to remedy some of these symptoms and to stimulate creativity and change. Addressing the issue of costly bureaucracy in the Pentagon, Secretary of Defense Robert Gates pointed out that a simple request for a dog-handling team in Afghanistan must be reviewed and assessed at multiple high-level headquarters before it can be deployed to the war zone. The secretary continued to say, "Can you believe it takes five four-star headquarters to get a decision on a guy and a dog up to me?" (Jaffe 2010: A03).

The "Ideal-Type" Concept

Ideal or perfect bureaucracy is never achieved. Yet, ideal-type theoretical construct serves useful analytical purposes such as guiding research, specifying relationships, and clarifying basic characteristics. The critics contend that idealizing a condition defies testing or verification in a systematic research and, therefore, cannot be elevated to the standing of a scientific knowledge. This is a major criticism of the classic bureaucratic model. Concurring with this notion should not mean accepting a derivative issue that a pure model is to be considered an idiosyncratic or a mere aberration. Actually, the real world of organization and management often is an approximation of ideal-type conceptions. Determination of such variation is a major obligation of comparative analysis in the search for effective administrative measures.

In doing their jobs, administrators will always have a measure of discretionary power that allows a varying latitude in modifying the form and the process necessary to reach their objectives. Of course, this discretion or latitude may be narrowly or broadly defined, depending on many administrative and contextual factors. Administrative literature, for instance, since Chester Barnard's *The Functions of the Executive*, and with the advent of the Human Relations School of management, has accepted the idea of an informal organization often coexisting along with the formal one. In contrast to the image of bureaucracy as a pure form, considerable evidence suggests that to maintain its claims of efficiency, the bureaucratic model allows for variation and flexibility in application. Indeed, informal relations and unofficial practices often contribute to efficient operations (Blau and Meyer 1971: 26). Moreover, as Diamant (1962: 82) points out, "much of the misunderstanding of the Weberian bureaucratic ideal-type stems from the failure to relate the type of administrative staff and organization to the appropriate form of authority." Diamant emphasizes that Weber had no doubt that the kind of administrative staff one might expect to find in a given political system would vary with the form of legitimate authority claimed and accepted in the society.

In sum, despite tendencies to discredit bureaucracy and to associate with it various negative images, the merit of focusing on bureaucracy in the analysis remains overriding. Anti-bureaucratic sentiments and the numerous myths and distortions surrounding the subject often prevent objective assessments of the matter (Goodsell 1994). Unfavorable images have been internalized, particularly in the American culture and to a lesser extent universally, that a balanced consideration of the issues is becoming hard to reach. The negative conception of bureaucracy is misleading as it is discouraging to students of the public administration. The negative perspectives seem to accumulate the dysfunctions and unanticipated consequences of the Weberian formulation of bureaucracy to construct a straw man rather than to provide a realistic analysis of organizational and managerial issues. This is like a case of mistaken identity where a growing distrust of governance for failure and for corruption of politics has been misdirected to blame bureaucracy and civil service. "Diminished trust and confidence in government brought with it an onslaught of attacks on civil servants that called into question the motivations of civil servants and the control systems that direct them" (Perry and Hondeghem 2008: 2). Such notions simply detract from realizing the full benefits of the analysis and hinder neutral judgments on bureaucracy and its considerable role as an institution performing essential functions for governance of modern society.

Another powerful source of the boisterous criticism is business mass media, which are not totally altruistic or entirely motivated by concerns for the public interest. Privatization usually opens up new opportunities for private profits; but privatization is difficult to attain if public management is performing well. Thus, although privatization did not always result in improvements in public service, myths are perpetuated about efficiencies of the private sector that are unrealistic and even contrived. In fact, government can never tolerate the waste and the high cost of the incentive systems of the private sector. Imagine government competing with the private sector and paying the U.S. secretary of defense or any public official the same as the CEO of Disney Corporation, for example, or as the nearly 100 large companies that awarded each of their top executives options mega grants worth over $12 million annually.[2] Nor can the public sector offer the other benefits available to corporate managers, let alone justify the cost of huge failures such as in the case of savings and loan associations, steel industry, Enron, AIG, and many other businesses that lost out to foreign competitors, or were victimized by gigantic schemes of fraud and mismanagement.

In the final analysis, the bureaucratic model in the Weberian sense is an ideal model that rarely exists in practice. On the other hand, public administration has incorporated enormous changes and modifications since Max Weber pronounced his framework. Today's public administration is an interdisciplinary field that consists of clusters of frameworks; each derives its content from a variety of intellectual roots. Whether in managing human resources, budgets, or whole organizations, public administration regularly utilizes concepts from behavioral sciences, economics, sociology, political science, accounting, and anthropology to serve its objectives. The assumed separation of politics and administration in the classic management frameworks is considered inadequate.and unrealistic, as Waldo (1984) and many other scholars have repeatedly stated. Administrative theory and processes have been seasoned with behavioral concepts that deal with people's motivations, incentives, and human developmental needs. Economics and accounting supply information that improves our knowledge of public sector cost-utility, measurement of output, and improved accountability practices. Laws implemented faithfully by public administration institutions prohibit discrimination on basis of gender, race, ethnicity, religion, or age. Public administration administers international agreements and continually initiates actions to strengthen global linkages. The list of interactions and mutual adjustments can be lengthy; many of the current activities could not be foreseen or even contemplated by the Weber's construction of the bureaucratic model. The point is that the use of the term national bureaucracy is tantamount to contemporary public administration rather than the Weberian formulation. Because some features of the classic bureaucratic model are present in all organizations, the term bureaucracy remains in use, but in a value-neutral sense.

Regardless, a "big question" facing public administration as a field of study is how to sustain a genuine interdisciplinary status while adapting to progressively more evident global concerns. At one level, public administration should be free to adapt and to be influenced by insights from any field of knowledge that may enhance its function and improve its processes of action. As Frank Thompson pointed out, "The health of public administration as a field depends on its ability to bring together the contributions of multiple disciplines in ways that foster balance, synthesis, and synergy" (1999: 119). There is also the perennial charge that public administration is identified with having "inferior methodology," possessing a "weak scientific base," "having no theory-building tradition," and suffering from a "reputation for low quality scholarship" (Thompson 1999; Lynn 1996; Kettle 1999). Perhaps, part of the reason for such bleak assessment is the mediocrity of education and training in some universities as well as to migration to public administration by scholars who have only thin understanding of public administration. This latter group are generally trained in related fields such as political science and economics but shifted their careers to public administration mainly due to job market considerations. These scholars continue to expect disciplinary clarity and deterministic conceptions in a professional, interdisciplinary field as public administration with overwhelmingly relativistic and eclectic concepts and practices. Certainly, the contributions, commitment, and potential of public administration cannot be evaluated by disciplinary criteria. Public administration is substantively connected to more than one discipline. Moreover, the ultimate value of public administration is in shaping the structure of government and in efficiently and effectively managing its functions. Of course, we agree that "the advancement of public administration as a field requires it to shed any vestige of its reputation for doing work of limited quality focused on a narrow domain" (Thompson 1999: 120). What area of social science would not benefit by such advice? But this is a different matter altogether.

The ultimate test of public administration, particularly the comparative aspect, is inseparable from its ability to cultivate concepts and practices that produce significant quantitative and qualitative improvements in the performance of public organizations. This objective is well-served by (1) continued refinements of administrative theory in relation to application; and (2) by systematic monitoring of managerial practices to identify complementary measures that create substantive effects, thus enabling us to know, with a measure of confidence, "what really works." Indeed, as Donald Kettl points out, public administration does have important things to say to public officials. "Public administration has a rich theory and even richer tradition of analyzing what is truly public about government management, and this is the piece most prominently missing from the public reform debate" (Kettl 1999: 131).

Conclusion

Bureaucracy is a key institution of national as well as local governance. Today's bureaucracy, however, has largely been customized and profoundly adapted to fit the conditions of its context. Also, within the national bureaucracy (administration), each organization is distinct in its practices and proficiency. Much advancement in knowledge of human behavior over the past several decades has resulted in modifications of Weber's classic formulations. The impact of change in managerial concepts and practices as a result of new approaches such as Human Relations School, Team Building, and Total Quality Management has been profoundly manifested. The rationale for the CPA in focusing on bureaucracy in its modern reality is based on these factors:

1. Bureaucracy provides a framework that focuses on the administrative system in a realistic way. It is more practical to observe, investigate, and evaluate bureaucratic performance than to attempt managing grand abstract models, seeking to incorporate prominent visions and characterizations with low operational applicability. This is a contrast to critics' views that assume all comparative public administration studies are preoccupied with abstract grand modeling, which would squeeze the universe to fit its mold. Incidentally, the choice of the national bureaucracy as the unit of analysis is not a determination of the ultimate merit but a choice of the most appropriate level of analysis for the CPA.
2. Bureaucracy is a prevalent institution, operating in almost all countries, albeit with different competencies and accomplishments. It is hard to imagine governance of the state without the institution of bureaucracy that brings

necessary insights and knowledge not only for delivery of public services, but also for the greater domain of policy making and policy implementation. Thus, more information is usually available on bureaucracy in different contexts because of institutional visibility, concrete structures and actions, and having identifiable membership, definable objectives, and measurable levels of performance (Heady 2001).

3. The study of national bureaucracy lends itself to a single case method as well as to a multiple case analysis and comparison. To be sure, bureaucracy may be a small or a large institution, depending on the size of the country and the type of government. But bureaucracy has always been a manageable unit for study and analysis. Utilizing bureaucracy as the unit of analysis, therefore, means improved ability to generate middle-range hypotheses for testing within one or more countries.

4. Most of the sins attributed to bureaucracy are either magnified misdeeds or consequences of misapplication. A basic question is whether bureaucracy indeed exerts a hobbling effect on political development. Although bureaucracy can accumulate excessive powers, more often than not, it remains subservient to the political order. Bureaucratic power is the result of attributes that make bureaucracy imperative in the first place such as expertise and continuity in office. But, an effective political system has the oversight means to check bureaucratic deviations, maintain reliability of the processes of performance, and continually stimulate administrative improvement to counterbalance any excess of bureaucratic influence. To bypass some traditional shortcomings of bureaucracy in developing countries, development administration was prescribed with features that promise to serve better the objectives of national development. The comparativists seem to have confidence in development administration as a unique set of structures and functions unencumbered by traditional bureaucratic anomalies of legendry rigidity and resistance to change. But even such conceived development administration cannot be detached from the political context.

5. National bureaucracy operates within a web of relations and shares in the stewardship for public policy. But bureaucracy is only one part of governance, an inclusive concept that involves many structures and functions. In complex processes of interactions, each of the legislative, executive, and judicial powers maintains autonomy but also shares responsibilities and powers. Thus, the functioning of national bureaucracy has to be viewed in a broader understanding of governance. A balanced consideration of all institutions and processes of decision making and their consequences is essential for effective conduct of comparative analysis. As the classic model of bureaucracy stipulates, the proper functioning of bureaucracy is not separate from its legal-rational political context or in today's terms a civil society with supremacy of the law.

Undeniably, powerless public institutions, often controlled by corrupt and authoritarian leaders, have been at the root of the myriad of economic, political, administrative, and social problems afflicting a large number of developing countries. In numerous cases, processes of public policy formulation and implementation—major vehicles of the governance processes—have been rendered almost inoperable. The catalog of failures and deficiencies of governance in these situations can be quite lengthy. Political leaders regularly decline the opportunity to develop reliable methods of succession that evoke citizens' confidence and trust. They fail to advance sustainable and equitable political and economic policies that are institutionally rather than personally based. From Latin America, to Asia, and to Africa, the similarities of issues and problems of governance are truly remarkable: issues of leadership succession, poor results of developmental policies, and lack of enforceable legal rights of citizens within a civil society.

Finally, the evolving complex global reality requires compliance or participation by all countries to share in its promised benefits and to minimize any potential negative consequences. Such involvement is not fruitful without developing competent and ethical institution of national bureaucracy. To be sure, developing countries are truly displeased with the rules of the game, but they are not against globalization itself. To be equal players, not mere subjects of a new imperialist capitalism, these countries must recognize that good governance is no less important than the free markets. Moreover, in preparing globally competent administrators and organizations, as Donald Klingner points out, "the ability to manage diverse, multi-disciplinary and multi-organizational work teams is critical" (2009: 19). Effective governance and a properly functioning legal system and regulatory process, supported by an accountable, legitimate political authority are also important for professional bureaucratic performance in diverse global context. However, team building, networking, and developing cooperative systems are increasingly becoming central elements in global administration.

This review chapter is an attempt to convey the complexity and the diversity of views on the subject of bureaucracy. Many of the assessments of bureaucracy are directed at its dysfunctions rather than addressing its wide range of features and functions with detachment. This is not to ignore the dysfunctions and unanticipated consequences of the model, but to state that they are neither intended nor inevitable. Certainly, applying the bureaucratic model in its value neutral sense would make it a functional framework for comparative analysis until we are able to devise a more appropriate research model. In the meantime, while comparative analysis is deliberating its own limitations and how to revive its research commitment, the comparative study of bureaucracy raises additional questions and challenges. The resolution of most of these issues and concerns is possible only through more empirical research and field observations. Effective application of comparative methods of research is the most likely venue to resolve many pressing practical issues and concerns as it is the certain path for the advancement of theory and practice of public administration.

References

Bendix, R. 1962. *Max Weber: An Intellectual Portrait*. New York: Anchor Books.

Berman, E. 1997. The challenge of total quality management. In *Public Personnel Management*, 2nd ed., eds. C. Ban and N. M. Riccucci: 281–294. White Plains, NY: Longman.

Blau, P. M., and M. W. Meyer 1971. *Bureaucracy in Modern Society*. 2nd ed. New York: Random House.

Braibanti, R. 1969. *Political Administrative Development*. Durham, N.C: Duke University Press.

Crozier, M. 1964. *The Bureaucratic Phenomenon*. Chicago: The University of Chicago Press.

Diamant, A. 1962. The bureaucratic model: Max Weber rejected, rediscovered, reformed. In *Papers in Comparative Public Administration*, eds. F. Heady and S. L. Stokes, 59–96. Ann Arbor, MN: Institute of Public Administration. Univ. of Michigan.

Frederickson, H. G. 2000. Public administration and social equity. In *Diversity and Affirmative Action in Public Service*, ed. W. D. Broadnax, 5–22. Boulder, CO: Westview Press.

Fry, B. R. 1989. *Mastering Public Administration: From Max Weber to Dwight Waldo*. Chatham, NJ: Chatham House.

Gerth, H. H., and C. W. Mills 1946. *From Max Weber: Essays in Sociology*. New York: Oxford University Press.

Goodsell, C. T. 1994. *The Case for Bureaucracy*. 3rd ed. Chatham, NJ: Chatham House.

Hayek, F. A. 1944. *The Road to Serfdom*. Chicago: University of Chicago Press.

Heady, F. 2001. *Public Administration: A Comparative Perspective*, 6th ed. New York: Marcel Dekker.

Hill, C. H., and L. E. Lynn Jr. 2009. *Public Management: A Three-Dimensional Approach*. Washington D.C.: CQ Press.

Hummel, R. P. 1977. *The Bureaucratic Experience*. NY: St. Martin's Press.

Jaffe, Greg (2010) Gates: Cuts in Pentagon bureaucracy needed to help maintain military force. *Washington Post*. (Sunday May 9: A03).

Jreisat, J. E. 1997. *Politics without Process: Administering Development in the Arab World*. Boulder, CO: Lynne Rienner Publishers.

Kettl, D. F. 1999. The Future of Public Administration. Journal of Public Affairs Education. 5(2): 127–134.

Klingner, D. C. 2009. Using US public administration to support global development. *Journal of Regional Studies and Development*, vol. 18, (2): 1–29.

Lane, J. E. 2000. *New Public Management*. London: Routledge

Lynn, L. E., Jr. 2001. The myth of the bureaucratic paradigm: What traditional public administration really stood for. *Public Administration Review* 61 (2): 144–160 (March/April).

Megill, Kenneth A. 1970. *The New Democratic Theory*. New York: The Free Press.

Merton, R. K. 1957. *Social Theory and Social Structure*, rev. ed., New York: Free Press.

———. 1952. Bureaucracy: Theoretical conceptions. In *Reader in Bureaucracy*, eds. R. K. Merton et al. New York: The Free Press.

Nachmias, D., and D. Rosenbloom 2000. Measuring bureaucratic representation and integration. In *Diversity and Affirmative Action in Public Service*, ed. W. D. Broadnax, 39–50. Boulder, CO: Westview Press.

Osborne, D., and T. Gaebler 1992. *Reinventing Government*. Reading, MA: Addison-Wesley.

Perrow, C. 1984. *Complex Organizations: A Critical Essay*. 3rd ed. Glenview, IL: Scott, Foresman.

Perry, J. L., and A. Hondeghem, eds. 2008. *Motivation in Public Management*. New York: Oxford University Press.

Riggs, F. W. 2001. Bureaucratic links between administration and politics. In *Handbook of Comparative and Development Administration*, ed. A. Farazmand, 815–838. New York: Marcel Dekker.

Romzek, B. S. 1997. Accountability challenges of deregulation. In *Public Personnel Management*, eds. Ban, C. and N. M. Riccucci, 35–54. White Plains, NY: Longman.

Stillman II, R. 1998. *The American Bureaucracy.* 2nd ed. Chicago: Nelson-Hall Publishing.

Thompson, F. 1999. Symposium on the Advancement of Public Administration: Introduction. *Journal of Public Affairs Education.* 5(2): 119–126.

Thompson, J. D. et al. 1953. *Comparative Studies in Administration.* Pittsburgh, PA: University of Pittsburgh Press.

Waldo, D. 1984. *The Administrative State.* 2nd ed. New York: Holmes and Meier.

Endnotes

1. A report by T. Yokota and Y. Nagaoka in *Newsweek* June 21, 2010, titled "Japan's Not-So-Prime Minister," is telling. They say that Japan's new prime minister [Naoto Kan] "has a reputation as a flip-flopper." He used to slam Tokyo's powerful bureaucrats as "a bunch of idiots." But when he was sworn in as prime minister in June 2010, he promised to consult "their knowledge and expertise." P. 5.

2. In 1998, the CEO of Disney was paid a total of $575.6 million, according to *Business Week*. April 19, 1999. P. 72. (Over 70% of employees at Disney were making a little more than minimum wage.) Annually business journals publish these figures and show how they continue to grow. In 2010, *USA Today* (April 2: 2B) published the names of the twenty-five most highly paid corporate chief executives in 2009. The pay per person ranged between 5 and 50 million dollars annually.

Chapter 4

Comparative Research and Methods

Comparison is fundamental to all human thoughts. ... It is the methodological core of the humanistic and scientific method as well.

Almond et al. (2000)

Introduction

It is axiomatic to say that a great deal of what we know about public administration is a matter of agreement among researchers, observers, and practitioners. Administrative knowledge is largely experiential and evolutionary—seldom based on a sudden, dramatic discovery. Agreements evolve from observation, tradition (the way things have been done), expert opinion, and aggregate descriptive and illustrative data on the subject. Administrative information generated from these various sources are synthesized through qualitative and quantitative tools of analysis to establish patterns, regularities, and conclusions as well as to confirm, modify, or nullify existing assumptions and propositions. To establish generalizations, effective research strategies employ methods and techniques that address some basic questions such as the following:

1. Clear objective. What do we want to know through comparison?
2. Significance and relevance of the comparison. Why do we want to know it?

3. Existing knowledge about the objective. What do we already know?
4. Methods and processes for achieving objectives. What tools do we need to know?

The execution of a research project requires skillful consideration of these and similar questions that affect research design such as selection of cases, descriptive data, explanatory statements, choice of appropriate techniques, and how to effectively obtain and apply the information needed. Generally, these measures are taken prior to commencing the actual comparison and benchmarking. At the end, comparative research defines its findings including any general patterns, similarities, and differences established. Conceptually, comparative administration research findings are presented in various forms and styles: descriptive, prescriptive, normative, concrete, and quantifiable results.

Utilizing wide-ranging human experiences over time, comparative public administration produced considerable administrative knowledge and information about many systems of governance. Such information was put to good use in building administrative institutional capacity within many countries. Also, findings and prescriptions of comparative studies were largely employed by unilateral and multilateral aid programs to developing countries. Additionally, the comparative literature enriched public administration teaching and training. Without such groundwork, it would not be feasible to establish realistic generalizations or expand the comparative research momentum across systems. But, an effective framework is a necessary tool for dealing with various research challenges, including "how to distinguish the conditions under which there is greater variation across than within systems" (Aberback and Rockman 1988: 420).

Initial research strategies have often compared non-Western with Western systems. As a result, many of the most commonly known concepts, and often utilized variables in the comparative literature, have been products of such explorations. For example, well-known variables such as collective-individualistic, differentiated-undifferentiated, diffused-specific, universalistic-particularistic, and democratic-undemocratic or semi-democratic[1] have saturated early comparative literature often to underscore differences between social and political systems. Explicitly and implicitly, many suggested prescriptions assumed that to modernize is to move towards the side of the continuum taken by Western systems. It is not surprising then that by frequent use of the Western systems as benchmarks, modernization became repeatedly equated with Westernization.

These dualisms offer limited information and practical relevance to the growing emphasis on effective governance and effects of global interdependence. This is not to dismiss these contributions as mutually contradictory or insupportable. The dissatisfaction stems from the realization that these notions are anchored in preconceived modes, heavily rationalistic, deterministic, and of limited applicability to managing regular administrative tasks. Beyond the operational deficiency, these concepts, as Julian Laite (1988: 162) points out, assume that there is a unilinear development path, similar to that of Western systems. This view of development as a progression toward a universalistic and differentiated state disregards "the range and variability of the social systems encountered in the Third World" (Laite 1988: 162). Moreover, it has been argued (Wiarda 1991: 36) that the timing, sequences, and stages of development in the West may not be replicable in today's developing countries. Many changes in the global context contribute to this reality such as urbanization, modern information technologies, and unimpeded trade and capital transfers.

No matter how suggestive and descriptive the dual variables may have been, they did not measure vital administrative characteristics, nor did they offer guidance to internally or externally generated organizational change. To presuppose that modernization is ultimately a movement in a "Westerly" direction is to assume also that the only productive systems are those with specific structures and functions similar to Western systems. The ability to free information from preconceived ideas and ideals, and examine data on their own merit, requires awareness of what information we need and for what purpose.

Different research purposes require different information, which may be characterized as follows:

1. *Descriptive information.* At the ground level, comparative research requires descriptive information that defines relationships, designates critical factors, expands breadth of coverage, and increases accuracy of analysis. *Descriptive* work identifies the actual conditions as they are. Cross-cultural analysis often takes researchers into unfamiliar territories; thus, the need for descriptive information is inescapable. In determining what elements, factors, linkages, processes, and influences are relevant and what information is available or needed, normative concerns influence these choices. "There are no non-value-laden choices to make" (Bell 2010: 6). It is very difficult to analyze administration, or any other aspect of human activity, without bringing value judgment to bear—language and concepts we often use to study governance such as democracy, liberty, and security are themselves always value-laden (Bell 2010: 6). Cogent description requires an accounting as well as an assessment and evaluation of the facts and their implications. This evaluative level presents an excellent test of the observer's awareness, judgment, and ethics. What Barzelay (2001: 10) refers to as "case-oriented comparative research" has been a foundation work in comparative administration. Much of the emerging CPA approach during the 1950s and 1960s that set a path for expansion and development was in the form of case studies. These cases provided expert descriptive information of the administrative systems of many countries, thus expanded knowledge and stimulated far broader search coverage.

2. *Explanatory and analytical information* that is theoretically informed builds on accurate descriptive data to compare, relate, explain, and identify trends and patterns. This is an important research function because it defines policy choices as well. Quality of this process has the power of increasing confidence

in concepts and frameworks utilized in research. Explanatory information offers answers to why certain factors change from one case to another, finds out causes and consequences of certain administrative actions, or proposes interpretation and explanation of the *why* of the processes employed and the rationale of the structure and function of the unit or the system examined. To adequately serve such needs, the researcher has to have knowledge of the conceptual and the practical aspects of the issue with established ability to make reasoned judgments.

3. *Prescriptive and normative concepts* assume that certain choices and alternatives have been known and set on the task of choice and proposal. Although normative is the realm of value, normative theorizing always includes descriptive empirical assumptions. Prescription deals with solutions and recommendations that may emerge after the description and the analysis of issues, problems, deficiencies, and accomplishments are delineated. Prescriptions advance the analysis to the phase of change and solutions. Suggestions for improving service, achieving higher efficiency and effectiveness of the operation, restructuring organizations, developing the human resources, encouraging participatory management are examples of a prescriptive-normative phase of comparative research. A prescriptive concept is essentially a normative proposition that assumes knowledge of existing conditions that need change. To be effective, prescriptions and recommendations cannot be confined to instruments or tools of operational utility. They have to be mindful of the larger picture and vital impacts on the governance system as well as effect on ultimate outcomes of public decision making.

The mind-set of many scholars of public administration, and social sciences in general, who regard scholarship only as quantitative findings or qualitative explorations, had instigated many curious and self-defeating wars between the empiricist camp and the devotees of the normative approach. The literature is full of research utilizing sophisticated statistical tools that add nothing significant to theoretical or practical knowledge. Similarly, abundance of qualitative analysis dwells on simplistic and tangential issues of little epistemological value and adds nothing significant to administrative knowledge. As Robert Behn (1995: 315) correctly pointed out, "[A] reverence for methodology is not, however, what makes an endeavor scientific." Scientists do not start with data and methods, he noted. Scientists start with significant questions.

Comparative public administration scholarship is enriched by both good qualitative research and relevant quantitative analysis. To respond effectively to the real needs, the CPA literature will continue to rely on descriptive, explanatory, analytical, and prescriptive concepts and analysis as necessary. Still, the major purpose of a comparative research strategy is to develop knowledge, define general patterns, and identify smart practices across many cases, examined against a commitment to unequivocal specificity. The drive for universality is governed by political and cultural limits that often force variation. Although it is not always easy to free comparative administration from ethnocentric tendencies of the larger field of public administration (indeed all social sciences as well), it is important to underline these observations:

■ Debates in the literature over a full or a partial demise of comparative public administration are exercises in intellectual futility. As long as there is public administration, the comparative approach will be part of it, and the comparative method will be indispensable for the advancement of its theory and its practice.

■ As a substantive area of inquiry, the comparative administration approach has its own theoretical foundation and research methods. Whether comparison is made across systems or within systems, the conceptual foundation and the choice of method depend on the unit of analysis and the purpose of the comparison.

■ Cross-cultural studies of administration underline the significance of the context as a source of formidable influences that differentiate systems as well as instigate changing them. Identifying and evaluating these influences on public management is an objective of the comparative approach.

■ Comparative research cannot be limited to one technique or method of research in all situations. The literature reflects different approaches employed to identify and to explain managerial patterns and outcomes across many systems of governance. The utilization of diverse methods or a self-ordained single approach, empirical versus normative, are difficult dichotomies to avoid, but have to be recognized as endemic not only to public administration but also to social sciences in general. The comparative approach will not benefit by endorsing any rigid classification of methods whether scientific, rational, and quantitative on one side, or prescriptive, normative, qualitative, and value-laden on the other. One can find any of these perspectives in the comparative literature although at varying degrees of proficiency. Norma Riccucci (2001: 174) correctly points out that "there are many topics or issues in public administration and public management that do not appropriately lend themselves to empirical study; others do."

Useful research, then, requires careful preparation and planning, clear purpose, and assessment of what information is needed and how to use appropriate methods for getting such information. Assessment and understanding of the potential and the limitations of any method or framework is vital before embarking on a major comparative research project. The choice is not an isolated decision but the result of pondering many considerations, including the unit of analysis, contextual influences, objectives, and familiarity with alternative comparative methods.

Unit of Analysis

As a field of study, administration of public policies constantly adapts theory and practice to accommodate shifting relationships and changing objectives. Similarly, knowledge of social systems in general is hardly generated through sudden experimental discoveries; rather, it evolves cumulatively. Each stage of evolution is built on the preceding one. A framework or a model for administrative research provides a common ground, a takeoff point, and a map that guides research efforts, even if such model is challenged from time to time. Many of the earlier frameworks survived even when new ones seem more prevalent or in vogue. How, then, do we choose among theories and models may not have a rational reason beyond the fact that a large number of academics, practitioners, and consultants have already made the transition that made the new perspective (model, paradigm) dominant.

It is important, however, to emphasize that generalizations ignoring concreteness and distinctiveness of the cases being investigated would end up flawed. To ensure that the relationship between the particular and the general is complementary, generalizations must evolve from an aggregate of particular facts that have been reliably established. To illustrate, studying a certain office and the powers it assumes, examining how it implements decisions, describing hurdles it encounters, and exploring a variety of pertinent structural and behavioral elements—all are important parts in determining outcomes of reforms. Only after such analysis of specific aspects can overall patterns and processes be defined and changes credibly suggested (prescribed).

In the final analysis, the utility of a framework is judged by its command of basic assumptions about the nature of the field of public administration and the quality of the rules of evidence that orient research initiatives. Viewing management developmentally indicates that the apparent contradictions in public administration are not always intrinsic or "genetic" to the field. Often, public administration is required to serve states that were arbitrarily forged after some historical accident as in Africa or the Middle East. In many countries, concepts and applications of organization and management emerged with little prior designs or plans, but as a response to pressing needs and demands forcing contingent managerial actions. The early American administrative experience, for example, is a vivid illustration of the dynamic surge of public administration, generated in response to political and economic imperatives of the new state, and developed as a particularly American system of organization and management. Although the U.S. experience has been a success story, in its earliest days it was not entirely dissimilar to the experiences of many developing countries at the dawn of independence.

A significant initial step in administrative research is to determine, at least tentatively, the unit of analysis in the intended study. It makes a difference whether the investigation and comparisons are focused on (1) *individual* and *group* behaviors and performance, (2) the *organization* and its capacity, or (3) the overall characteristics and performance of a *national bureaucracy,* including the whole executive branch of government.

Of necessity, the national bureaucracy is the unit and the level I rely on in this work. Other long-standing comparative research traditions, however, have enriched administrative theory and practice over the years, particularly intra-national and cross-organizational comparisons. Meaningful comparisons are often made at the intra-national level, within the same culture. The individual, the organization, or other structures smaller than the nation-state have been widely utilized as units of analysis. In some works, the organization, actors (managers) and human behavior constitute the "analytic building blocks" of comparative research (Aberback and Rockman 1988: 423).

The study of the organization within or across political boundaries can be comprehensive and inclusive. The managerial practices of cities, districts, regions, and various public agencies have been compared within the same society. The literature actually is replete with comparisons of one administrative function—law enforcement, budgeting, recruitment, evaluation, and training—with another. These activities are often compared among organizations within the same political setting. In the United States, the Local Government Comparative Performance Measurement Consortium is an attempt by cities and counties nationwide to capture and report comparative data in several key service delivery areas (Kopczynski and Lombardo 1999: 124). The International City/County Management Association (ICMA) Center for Performance Measurement is dedicated to helping local governments measure, *compare*, and improve municipal service delivery. "ICMA's Comparative Performance Measurement Program currently assists approximately 130 cities and counties in the U.S. and Canada with collection, analysis, and application of performance information."[2]

Comparative organizational analysis consistently compares organizational characteristics and performance before and after the implementation of a fundamental change to determine the range of variation and its results. Local governments also routinely compare their own current performance with that in previous reporting periods. Systematic comparisons of carefully defined administrative processes, over a number of time periods, seek to establish the relevance of administrative questions to historical contexts. Actually, the historical orientation may aim at other broader concerns while explaining basic administrative developments.

Focus on the organization as the unit of analysis also lends credence to the notion that the most meaningful administrative actions take place in the context of formal organizations. Organizations coordinate and facilitate individual efforts, converting them into sustained collective actions that accomplish or serve goals, above and beyond the capacity of any individual. From a methodological perspective, the organization is a superior unit for comparative analysis because of its durable and measurable characteristics. Typically, organizations have specific purposes, concrete structures, determinable boundaries, established routines and technologies, defined communication channels, and central coordinative systems (March and Simon 1958: 2–9). No realistic view of the organization is possible without acknowledgment of its dependence on or interchanges with a larger system—the environment—for its input of resources and technology and for discharging its output of goods and services.

Almost five decades ago, James Thompson and his associates articulated a question of fundamental importance for the theoretical advancement of public administration. They noted that the dominant schools of administration have established curricula and research programs on the assumption that each field of administration (public, business, military, hospital, nonprofit, etc.) rests on unique elements, on constant and variables which are not merely different in degree from one field to another but are different in kind. The challenge to this position has come from those who assert that administration, in whatever context, is basically the same phenomenon. They have advanced a series of abstract models or theories of administration, management, organization, decision making, and communication to illustrate this notion (1959: 8–9). "The comparative approach seems to be the most promising way of settling this issue," according to Thompson and his associate (1959: 9). Also they noted that the cultural dimension "is essential to our understanding of administration," but "the comparative study of administration cannot be limited to cultural comparison alone" (Thompson, et. al. 1959: 9).

Still, the comparative approach has to contend with two basic limitations of the larger field of public administration: One is lack of reliable tools to evaluate the utility of its concepts. Students of management invariably have to contend with intractable anomalies by relying mainly on their own experiences and the educated judgments of their peers. The second limitation pertains to the unwillingness (or due to lack of professional qualifications) to cross over the cultural boundaries of North America and Europe and to carry out genuine comparative investigation. A truly cross-cultural comparison usually requires knowledge of culture, language, history, norms, and values as well as administrative institutions and processes of the system to be researched.

Thus, the choice is apparent in relying on a particular unit of analysis. Each alternative excels in answering certain questions but fades when dealing with others. The comparative organizational perspective, for example, is a powerful orientation to serve the many objectives of comparative analysis. It can build on a strong foundation of theoretical and applied knowledge about organizations, their structures, behavior, and performance. Also, organizational analysis provides language, variables, criteria of verification, systematic collection of data, and rigorously tested methodologies. But empirical cross-cultural findings at this level are hard to come by. Managing an extensive comparative organizational research cross-culturally can be an expensive, and hard to manage, enterprise. Moreover, such field research can be most effective when coupled with expert knowledge of the environment of the system under investigation.

Alternatively, focus on behavioral considerations of individuals and groups promises great payoffs only if complex computations and specification are met. At this level of specific micro-level managerial concerns, relevant and current aggregates are indispensable to serve the final research purposes. Actually, whatever the focus of comparative administration research, ultimately, it has to serve the needs and demands for theoretical integration and practical relevance. Satisfaction of these criteria requires informed application of conceptual frameworks to the real administrative processes and their effects on organizational performance.

Finally, conceptual frameworks of comparative administration have received considerable attention when they specified the variables or categories of variables used. So far, one finds a relatively high level of agreement on the main dependent variables such as organizational structure, leadership and power, internal processes, and goals. Environment is the independent variable. Environmental influences are subdivided into variables or categories of variables that encompass political, social, economic, and cultural elements. For the purpose of this study, national bureaucracy is the unit of choice for various reasons, as specified in the preceding chapter. Comparing national bureaucracies also is consistent with organizational analysis and the wealth of existing knowledge about organizational management over the past one hundred years.

The Context (Environment)

Comparative public administration made its most lasting intellectual mark in the area of cross-cultural analysis. The context is a source of variation and uncertainty for an administrative system because it is a basic source of influence and change of the system. Public administration development is intrinsically connected to the institutional development of the whole society: philosophical, political, technological, and economic. To be sure, various stages of this evolution have yielded some inconsistencies, but the overall thrust displays more continuity and coherence among the elements than generally recognized by most current relativistic conceptual creations. The analysis of administrative action, therefore, cannot be carried out in isolation. It has to be approached as a part of a whole, linking it to its historical, social, economic, and political environments. Because of these important linkages between administration and its context, a successful research strategy needs to resolve three particular sets of relationships that determine critical systemic organizational attributes:

- Linkages of the social context to administration.
- Linkages of the political context to administration.
- Effect of the internal operating system on the overall management.

Social Context

A more specific description of contextual relations is decisive for resolving questions surrounding administrative change, particularly the role of culture, which has been receiving increasing recognition in studies of organizational management

(Harris and Moran 1987; Schein 1985; Peters and Waterman 1982). Culture remains without a precise definition: "more than one hundred and fifty definitions are given, culled from the writings of anthropologists over three quarters of a century" (Foster 1962: 10). Even so, culture evokes shared values and patterns of interaction among social groups over long periods of time. Culture includes elements of language, religion, habits, morals, customs, and laws that are passed from older to younger members, and that shape behavior (Adler 1986).

In public administration, national culture broadly denotes all those ambiguous and indefinable factors in the environment that influence administrative practices (Goodsell 1994). National culture is distinguished from organizational culture, however, despite significant overlapping between them (Jreisat 1997a). More than five decades ago, Riggs (1961) suggested studying the "ecology" of public administration by encouraging culturally based investigations with the help of anthropologists. Today, "an understanding of the distinctive *environment* of an organization is the starting point of any successful diagnosis of the problems that exist and the strategies that are likely to work in any management context" (Yates 1991: 40).

Despite almost universal recognition of the impact of cultural environment on administrative behavior, information about this relationship continues to be basic but underdeveloped. A review of twenty-two studies of comparative management that employed culture as an independent variable to explain differences in management practices among nations found in most of these studies, *culture* was used as to mean "nation" (Nath 1988: 7). Many recent efforts sought to operationalize culture by isolating its dimensions or by differentiating its effects on administration from those of other environmental factors (Nath 1988: 7–8). To find out the extent to which culture determines administrative practice, Gert Hofstede (1980) relied on four dimensions to describe and to classify countries: *collectivism-individualism, power distance, uncertainty avoidance,* and *masculinity-femininity.* Hofstede devised scales to measure responses to issues dealing with the four dimensions found in a survey of 116,000 people in 50 countries (1980; 1984):

■ In *collectivist systems,* preference is for a tightly knit social framework in which individuals can expect their relatives, clan, or friends to look after them, in contrast with a loosely knit social framework wherein individuals must depend on themselves. In collectivist systems, public administration literature frequently evokes negative images, which leads to particularistic forms of decision making, a managerial euphemism for favoritism and nepotism in public organizations.

■ The dimension of *power distance* refers to the acceptance of power in institutions and organizations and how a society handles whatever inequalities occur. People in societies with large power distance accept a hierarchical order more readily than do those in a small power distances, who strive for equalization and demand justification for power inequalities.

- Societies with strong *uncertainty avoidance* maintain rigid codes of belief and behavior and are intolerant of deviant persons and ideas. This has consequences for the way people build their institutions and organizations as well as for the capacity for innovation within the bureaucratic apparatus of the state.
- The *masculinity* dimension is measured in terms of society's preference for achievement, heroism, assertiveness, and material success. The opposite, *femininity*, stands for preference of relationships, modesty, caring for the weak, and the quality of life. The implications of emphasis on one dimension of a culture or another are significant, particularly for recruitment, group dynamics, team building, communication, and the rest of the managerial processes.

While I do not question the validity of Hofstede's four dimensions of measurement, I do question his assumptions and conclusions. He views culture "as the collective mental programming of the people in any environment" (Hofstede 1980: 43). Such a conception leads to a sort of cultural determinism in which managerial decisions are the inevitable consequences of their cultural antecedents. Furthermore, since culture is difficult to change, administrative reform is consigned to failure unless the reformed structure is in the image of existing cultural patterns of the society (Farazmand 2001, Jreisat 2001: 667).

Certainly, societies consist of individuals who interact according to patterns shaped by cultural factors standardized and sanctioned by the society. Through socialization, these patterns become significant contributory elements to personality configurations. Such notions are foundational concepts in anthropology and psychology. However, to assume that individuals are "programmed" by their culture is to deny the dynamic characteristics of human personality and the processes of development, growth, and change. Individuals have the ability to learn, form new habits, forget old habits, recognize new situations, and develop new behaviors to deal with them (Linton 1945: 14). Even in the most integrated cultures, individuals retain distinctive characteristics and capacities for independent thought and feeling. Without such verifiable conceptual basis, administrative change would not be possible; training and development by outside technical assistance would be a futile effort. The theory that each culture develops its own administrative and organizational norms and processes, and, therefore, the transfer of knowledge and practices across boundaries is not possible, is rejected here for denying some basic human characteristics such as learning and developing. The information revolution, accommodated by contemporary technological breakthroughs, renders a powerful verdict on the validity of the notion of universality of knowledge in all human endeavors.

Many questions are raised about the idea of culture and its impact as "the collective programming of the mind which distinguishes the members of one human group from another" (Hofstede 1980: 43). Culture shapes how we view ourselves and how we view others, also it translates into a wide range of attitudes and behaviors. The impact of culture on individual attitudes and behaviors, and indirectly on institutions and society at large, is the most complex to demonstrate or assess. But, we have to be vigilant against stereotyping. Assessing cultural consequences with confidence requires measurement and procedures for assigning values and significance to cultures and to their impacts (Gross and Rayner 1985).

Investment in the development of appropriate research methods can facilitate the delineation and codification of the operating characteristics of social systems to determine those that impede and those that enhance administrative modernization. During this process, researchers must guard against the tendency to unnecessarily undermine societies' traditional values, in the sense of prejudging them as inherently inimical to change or inferior to other values. Western cultures themselves, often described as modern cultures, are actually mixtures of traditional and modern values and beliefs. The socioeconomic transformation of traditional societies cannot be achieved by destroying their identifying cultures and traditions. Instead, the transformation itself has to be a synthesis, somewhat similar to what Almond and Verba (1965: 12) refer to as an emergent "third culture, neither traditional nor modern but partaking of both." The process of synthesis is not simple as it varies according to numerous societal and more particular conditions.

Political Context: Type of Government

Comparative administration research has to face the issue of relationships between administration and the political order (type of government) within which administration operates. The effects of the political order on the development of public administration have been recognized but have not been sufficiently specified to have significant operational value. The influence of political culture on administrative behavior is perhaps the most widely recognized in the literature (Almond and Verba 1989 and 1965; Fitzpatrick and Hero 1988; Kincaid 1980; Johnson 1976). In their seminal study of "the civic culture," Almond and Verba (1965: 12) defined political culture in terms of political orientations, that is, attitudes toward the political system and its various parts, including bureaucracy, and attitudes toward the role of the self in the system. Viewed this way, *political culture* refers to a set of variables that may provide explanatory power to contextual as well as to internal structures and behaviors.

Type of governance, however, has a wider influence than just the influence of the political culture. It encompasses variables such as centralization and decentralization, citizens' participation in public policy formulation, and the whole notion of legitimacy and succession of leadership. George Sorensen (1990: 1) points out that some U.S. theorists of modernization (W. W. Rostow; Karl Deutch; Daniel Lerner; and others) share the conviction that economic development would go hand in hand with development towards democracy. (*Democracy* here means competitive politics, public participation in the appointment of leaders, and a measure of civil liberties). After examining six cases from Third World countries, Sorensen concludes that democracy has greater positive effects on welfare and equality of economic development than on economic growth itself, as in Costa Rica and India. Authoritarian rule, however, has greater positive effect on growth than democracy, as in Brazil under military government. Authoritarian rule may also involve a heavy human and social cost. A case that deviates from Sorensen's hypothesis is Zaire under Mobutu Sese Seko, where authoritarian rule resulted in negative growth, a decrease in welfare and equality, and high human and social cost. Other deviant cases are China and Taiwan, where an authoritarian rule has resulted in high growth, an increase in welfare and equality, and low human and social cost. The analysis gets more complicated with the introduction of the factor of stability over time and the variations of political forms, such as democratic, semi-democratic, authoritarian, and semi-authoritarian (Sorensen 1990: 16–17, 25).

Thus, because of the significance of the political impact, comparative public administrationists cannot escape the responsibility of *formulating hypotheses about relations between form of government and administrative processes*. Many critical questions still lack satisfactory answers: Is democratic, participatory government a prerequisite for administrative reform? Can substantive administrative reform encompassing participatory management processes take place under authoritarian rule? The central issue in such questions is defining administrative-political linkages. Some of these linkages matter more than others in terms of overall impact.

"In liberal democracies it is the political environment which determines the scope and objectives of the public services" (Chapman 2000: 217). The connections of public administration with its political context are most aptly manifested in the formulation, approval, and execution of the public budget. In her preface to Wildavsky's *The Politics of the Budgetary Process,* Naomi Caiden describes the relationship in these terms: "Budgeting was not just a technical realm for experts, but a critical manifestation of politics. For Aaron [Wildavsky], budgeting *was* politics" (Caiden 2001: xix). Politics-Administration relationships strengthen or hinder opportunities for administrative development. *Specifying conditions and variables that determine relationships has to be through empirical evidence, gathered from case studies and refined middle-range propositions.*

Information on experiences from many developing countries indicates that the political authority and political values not only determine the boundaries of general administrative action and behavior, but also shape bureaucratic attitudes toward citizens. "One of the essential characteristics and qualities of working in the public service within a modern democracy and one of the elements of the political environment is the emphasis on public accountability" (Chapman 2000: 225). This is also a difference between public administration and business management; accountability of public service includes requirements of being efficient and responsible consistent with values approved by the political environment (Chapman 2000: 226). Accountability in governance is hard to attain in the absence of effective checks and balances among the three branches of government.

Studies of developing countries illustrate the high quality of proposals and plans for change and reform. The problem is that few of such proposals get implemented, even after being formalized and approved for implementation. Appraisal of reform efforts in many countries discloses mediocre results, and implementation suffered from "incongruities of methods and objectives of reform" (Jreisat 1988: 85). Among such incongruities are the conventional limitations of bureaucracy, including copying Western administrative rationality in form rather than in substance and underestimating the impact of traditional values on public management. Invariably, the "real killer" of successful implementation, has been the political context, with its array of impediments such as excessive control, wobbly ethical standards, and over concern, if not obsession, with perpetuation of the rulers and their regimes in power.

Internal Operating System

The internal operating system is the management core, fundamentally affected by the external context even if distinct from it. Accumulating sufficient comparative information about operating management systems is essential to improve conceptual and empirical relevance of the analysis. It is a basic task for comparative analysis to appraise the structures and behaviors relevant to the performance of basic functions as civil service recruitment, budgeting, training, monitoring, and evaluation of public programs. Attitudes on decentralization, accountability of public servants, reform, and corruption are also determining factors in describing systems and defining their institutional capacities. Institutions do matter. Their abilities to cope with fiscal, developmental, and public service responsibilities are important means for researchers seeking realistic and relevant comparative information.

The internal politics of organization, for example, is rarely featured in the literature on organization management. This politics is an informal exercise of power, outside the defined lines of authority, and often engaged in by those who seek to get their way in the organization. Organizational politics can serve negative or positive purposes, employ legitimate or illegitimate methods. Negative politics denotes what French and Bell (1995: 307) characterize as extreme pursuit of self-interest, unsocialized needs to dominate others, and a tendency to view most situations in win-lose terms. The predominant tactics used often involve secrecy, surprise, holding hidden agendas and deception. Balanced politics, which serves positive purposes, on the other hand, is the pursuit of self-interest and the welfare of others. Those who practice positive politics, engage in open problem solving, and initiate actions that lead and influence (French and Bell 1995: 307). Negative internal politics are a pervasive influence, albeit subtle, surreptitious, and infrequently talked about openly. The rationalistic slant in management tends to overlook important segments of what takes place within the organization. Indeed, practices in all countries that we know anything about their management systems from universities to police departments, indicate that what is taking place is far more personal and subjective than most popular theories lead one to expect.

The problem is not limited to legitimate power that comes with formal authority, such as the power of a manager or supervisor over subordinates. This power (authority) allows managers and supervisors to reward or punish employees according to established procedures. Leaders or managers can buttress their legitimate powers with personal powers of expertise and mastery of inter-personal skills. The underhanded aspect of the personal power in the organization is when it becomes an instrument for personal gain, dishonesty, self-enrichment, and betrayal of the goals and objectives of the organization. This type of power usually develops behind the scenes, informally, through alliances and cliques, often through connections with similarly inclined persons in the organization. Individuals who have personal friendships with direct access to top leaders in the organization or to powerful political leaders are able to enhance their informal powers as a result. Cronyism and personal aggrandizement bring individuals and groups with similar motives to join ranks and to divert the outcomes of decisions in their favor. This is one root of corruption in organization management—public or private, in developed and in developing countries. Comparative studies have to contend with the problem that these powers are not easy to trace or to observe, nevertheless, their impact on reform outcomes is critical.

Fear of internal politics is the main reason most employees would resist change. The general feeling is that only individuals lacking political power will suffer the consequences of the financial cutbacks or downsizing, for example. Managers may offset general apprehension from change by emphasizing professional management and ethics, and by consciously inspiring trust among employees. Assuring staff that management is committed to fairness, equity, and collective interest may alleviate some of the anxiety over unfair practices and hidden political agendas.

Today, in nearly all countries, public management has to deal with budget cutbacks, shortfalls of revenues, budget deficits, and public resistance to higher taxes. Consequently, within this new reality, management of a public organization is expected to do more with less. Frequently, it has to account for what it does in defined, measurable outputs. The new climate of decline and retrenchment in the public sector is a reversal of the usual mode of growth. While public organizations are applying less familiar techniques and processes of downsizing, they are also given the responsibility of measuring their performances and justifying their costs. All these changes underline the demand for effective leaders to carry through the task of revitalizing the organization. This task includes defining the need for change, creating new visions, mobilizing commitment to those visions to transform the organization and its mission.

For comparative administration to be relevant, it has to emphasize the elements that shape internal dynamics of public organizations and professionalize their management. Improving performance is a fundamental goal and, at the same time, the hardest undertaking. Inescapably, the process requires developing indicators and methods of measurement, collecting data, and undertaking the analysis and interpretation of data on a continuous basis to determine the level of goal attainment.

Still, students of public management have to be regularly reminded of certain fundamentals:

- Public administration is theory and practice that are mutually enforcing and enriching.
- Core management strives to be in accord with societal values, shaped by its history, culture, economy, and politics.
- Understanding the operating system, and the actual managerial performance, as it happens and how it happens, is essential for developing a more realistic knowledge of applied management and for prescribing appropriate prerequisites of reform.

In sum, the external contexts of culture, type of governance, and attributes of the internal operational processes are critical for any effort to compare management systems. Each of these three dimensions is pertinent, even decisive in understanding as well as reforming the administrative system. Investigation of political and cultural components is essential for identifying basic influences on administrative structures and functions. The internal operating form and method has also a defining influence on what and how change takes effect. Ultimately, comparative analysis can render a valuable service by mapping administrative change strategies and defining political and cultural preconditions as well as internal features associated with successful or unsuccessful administrative reforms.

What Method for Research?

The right comparative method provides a vehicle for processing diverse, extensive information and distinguishing what is important and what is not. An appropriate comparative method is designated for specific reasons but remains merely an instrument for serving the overall research objectives. A research strategy may rely on more than one instrument or method in reaching its objectives. Invariably, a comprehensive research strategy promotes these initiatives:

- Mapping and establishing linkages between the social context and administration.
- Mapping and defining linkages with the political context.
- Understanding the internal operational process of the system.
- Comparing similarities and differences cross-culturally.

What and how political and cultural influences affect administrative action are critical research questions. The search for alternative political linkages that influence administrative performance has to provide evaluation of such alternatives before a choice is made. While various conceptual formulations have attempted to define the political and cultural impacts on administrative action, comparative public administration in general has not been very successful in articulating the issues. Nor has the comparative movement produced generally acceptable definitions of the variables or set in motion genuine and substantive research efforts in various social and political contexts, with few exceptions.[3] It is in these linkages and relationships between administrative systems and their contexts that we may be able to identify key factors that explain why there has been no great administrative reform accomplishments in many developing countries despite repeated attempts.

In addition to issues of feasibility, practicality, and concern for substance, a practicable comparative method provides an opportunity to bring together and integrate fragmented knowledge into a coherent, unified whole. Moreover, the choice of a method has to properly recognize the association and the pertinence of the operational dimension to systemic characteristics. Only a careful mapping of these diverse relationships and influences ensures the development of truly reliable generalizations. Two other objectives for an appropriate comparative method are, as C. E. Black (1966, 36) pointed out, (a) organization and classification of complex materials, and (b) explanation. The first is concerned with institutions, contexts, and political forms, while the second explanation is concerned with causes, functions, and relationships. Also, social scientific theory and research are fundamentally linked through two commonly applied methods of theory construction: *inductive* and the *deductive* methods.

The *inductive method* draws on practical experience and knowledge, extrapolating to create conceptual formulations. From a wide range of data and information, a generalization or a rule is developed. In arriving at a theoretical generalization, this approach relies on descriptive data about actual situations and behavior. The movement is from specific observations to a common feature, then, to explanation and interpretation. This process certainly provides for the development of generalizations that explain relationships between units observed. "Inductive reasoning," as Earl Babbie pointed out, "moves from the particular to the general, from a set of specific observations to the discovery of a pattern that represents some degree of order among all given events" (1998: 35).

The *deductive method* also draws conclusions from existing information and particulars, utilizing logically necessary consequences of given general assumptions. Neither the assumptions nor the conclusions need correspond to real-world conditions, but they help clarify logical relationships and thus help the investigator not only to understand the empirical coincidence of variables but also to derive logically related corollaries from relationships (Riggs and Weidner 1963: 12). In the deductive model, a particular fact is explained from a generalization; that is, the movement is from the general to the specific. It is possible to build deductive corollaries from propositions based on inductive models and evidence. While deductive models have been used far more in the natural sciences, the inductive method is a mainstay of public organization theory.

Deductive reasoning moves from a pattern that might be logically or theoretically expected to observations that test whether the expected pattern actually occurs (Babbie 1998: 36). Although deduction usually moves in the opposite direction of induction, these two different approaches are valid for development of a reliable theory. The relationship may be explained further by these statements: Studies of governance indicate that lobbyists' activities tend to concentrate on where the power of policy making is located (a generalization arrived at inductively). Thus, by deduction, we expect lobbyists to congregate and seek to influence the U.S. Congress (a deductive conclusion that may be verified or tested empirically—inductively).

In delineating a research strategy for comparative administration, one must decide whether the object of study will be the general processes and influences or the particular experiences of certain countries. The general processes can be examined by sharply limiting the number of variables, defining them rigorously, and specifying explicit relations among them. The particular experiences, however, are more suited for case studies that would provide detailed information unattainable through statistical surveys that isolate one or more functions for their measurements. Certainly, progress requires a variety of methods and techniques of research that enhance confidence in the results. Within the current emphasis on greater relevance and a more convincing conceptual convergence, comparative administration studies would profit from a careful consideration of these important instruments:

1. Middle-range models vs. grand models
2. Case studies
3. Models employing a structural-functional approach
4. Models with a behavioral focus.

Middle-Range vs. Grand Models

Research that investigate middle-range concepts across systems can produce more specific and reliable findings than those efforts invested in constructing traditional grand models. Grand theories seem to have exhausted their usefulness. Middle-range theories differ from grand theories and from summary statistical statements of empirically observed relationships. Middle-range models are efficient tools for applying evidence to few administrative aspects at a time, for linking concepts to each other, and for providing a balance between the abstract and the concrete in the formulation of hypotheses (Pinder and Moore 1980). In contrast, critics charge that the preoccupation of comparative public administration with building grand models became a "fixation" in its early self-directed choice of seeking a comprehensive theory or model in terms of which to define itself (Golembiewski in Henry 2001: 38).

Thus, relevance is much improved through employment of the middle-range research techniques that put forth specific and practical information. This information is usually reinforced by a special familiarity with the systemic and institutional features of the unit under study. When enough middle-range findings have been compiled, a far more practical and accurate investigation of national bureaucratic systems is achievable. As long as the national bureaucracy remains the main focus of most comparative research, information generated through middle-range concepts can serve as the building blocks for developing models of greater comprehensiveness and certitude.

To be sure, the most effective use of middle-range concepts has been at the organizational level and through case studies. Comparative organizational analysis provides crucial, well-defined variables for investigating administrative issues. Indeed, most meaningful additions to administrative knowledge since the 1960s have been at the organizational level, developed through middle-range theoretical and practical advancements (Jreisat 1997a: 116). If studies using this perspective are not cautiously executed, however, their potential can be severely reduced by challenges such as the need for specificity, dispersed evidence, and risks of fragmentation of results.

Case Studies

The case study method is a systematic research tool concerned with the context as well as the variables. Primarily, it seeks to discover rather than confirm or test hypotheses. The methodological characteristics of the case study method are particularistic, descriptive, heuristic, interpretive, and inductive (Merriam, 1988). Also, the case study method varies in content and approach. The most relevant case study is the one developed from observation and experience, but not all cases are based on such observation. "The facts in the case may be focused toward specific theories, but seemingly irrelevant material will also be included" (Buller and Schuler 2000, v). Ordinarily, cases are developed as synthesis of a variety of experiences. Others may be developed as hypothetical or abstract constructs, and may not represent concrete reality.

Case studies that are based on participant observations benefit comparative administration by enhancing its relevance. Close analysis of a manageable number of these observations within few real cases, is a preferable venue for improving reliability and utility of results. Moreover, case studies provide comprehensiveness (unless the focus is on a case component) that is hard to reach through other methods of research without sacrificing specificity and relevance. Well-written case studies serve as vehicles for organizing data and materials that allow establishing regularities and identifying recurrent themes. Properly executed and fairly specified case studies of administrative reform, for example, are valuable sources of information about a variety of related elements. They inform us about processes, practices, and behaviors as well as environmental influences (cultural, political, and historical). The patterns and regularities that may be found in comparing case materials are transformed into descriptive categories and characteristics that summarize experiences, integrate data, and synthesize conclusions. Abstractions often are unavoidable in the analysis of data collected by case study researchers. When such action takes place, however, most likely it is motivated by the need to connect and make sense of information gathered. From a practitioner's perspective, cases are enormously beneficial by providing rich details, for developing problem-solving skills, and for improving the ability to relate administrative practices to their conceptual foundations.

During the 1970s, under Dwight Waldo's leadership, the National Association of Schools of Public Affairs and Administration (NASPAA) received a grant from the U.S. Office of Education for developing case materials for classroom use in graduate programs in public administration. The project resulted in a bibliography of over 250 "Cases in Public Policy and Management." The cases were classified in categories corresponding to major curricular areas in schools and departments that offer courses on public policy and management. They include topics such as political and institutional analysis, economic and public finance, quantitative methods, ethical and moral issues, budgeting and financial management, organizational behavior and interpersonal relations, personnel, and general management (Waldo 1978).

Waldo's project mainly consisted of single-case studies that may be used for different purposes. Although comparison is not the central concern in compiling such cases, they presumably still may serve as useful material in comparative exercises. However, because the cases are based on observations mostly in the American context, they have limited utility for cross-cultural analysis.

Structural-Functional Models

To meet its obligations, government needs specialized institutions—agencies, and departments—to formulate and implement its policies. These administrative structures are often referred to as the bureaucracy. A government has other important structures such as the legislature, the judiciary, and political parties. Each of these structures performs specific functions. But one structure performing certain functions in a government does not mean that such structure will perform the same functions in all governments, nor will it perform with the same degree of competence and ethics across systems.

Structure is defined as patterned activities and patterned behaviors that become standard feature of a social system (Riggs 1964: 20). So, regularity and standardization are characteristics of structures. The processes of decision making in a bureaucracy, and how bureaucracy makes rules and regulations in an agency, are important parts of its structures—just as making laws by a parliament or a congress is indicative of the legislative institution's structural characteristics. Significantly, structure does not include all actions carried out by members of an organization; it includes only those that relate to its goals and purposes.

The structures of formal organizations, as Selznick pointed out, "represent rationally ordered instruments for the achievement of stated goals" (1948, 127). We know that structures vary in complexity, degree of formalization, functions served, and several other aspects. But in government, organizational structure has greater staying power than in a business corporation and, thus, exhibits different dynamism and distinct connection to performance. The point is that few public managers would really be "thriving on chaos" or on management relativism in implementing public policy, and fewer still would risk possible violation of laws that decree such policies. While high-tech, speculative industries may benefit by proposed revolutionary managerial techniques (if they do not fade away in the process), public organizations, in comparison, apply different rules of conduct, abide by different ethics, and serve different expectations (Jreisat 1997a).

Function is the consequence of actions or behaviors by members of an agency, bureau, department, or any other organization. The functions of administrative units range from education to maintaining orderly traffic on highways. Although structure is easier to define and has been more often studied, satisfying the functions of the unit is what ultimately matters most. More than any time before, today's public administration has been refocused on performance and consequences of administrative actions and behaviors. Political and administrative leaders in many countries—developed and developing—have been demanding that units of government practice result-oriented management. Indeed, many have concluded that this concern is also becoming a global shift in concepts and application, ushering in a "new public management."

To prevent misunderstanding, I emphasize a balanced approach for comparative public administration that considers both structure and function simultaneously. As a minimum, researchers need to relate structures to their legitimate goals in any thorough cross-cultural analysis. Many structures appear impressive but actually harbor very low capabilities. Consider administrative units of education or public health in a developing country, or even a legislative house, with their impressive buildings and huge staffs. The picture is incomplete without assessing the functions of education, public health, and legislation and to what degree and at what cost they meet society's needs. Appraising both of structure and function remains a very challenging task few comparative studies have adequately satisfied (Almond and Coleman 1960).

A major criticism of structural functional analysis is that it is conservative in its methodology. It focuses on the status quo, since it describes institutions as they are in a certain time; it provides a snapshot of the existing state. I agree with Almond and his associates, however, in their response to this criticism: "[T]o describe political institutions precisely and comprehensively at some particular time is not to praise or defend them but to try to comprehend them" (Almond et al. 2000: 36). In public administration, studies of institutions, almost always, are geared toward finding ways and means to change them, to improve their performance, and to make them more responsive to citizens' needs. To a large extent, all frameworks applied in comparative public administration are judged in terms of their advancement of such objectives.

Behavioral Focus

The human factor in administration is the most critical and, at the same time, the most elusive to study. It is less visible and less specific than structure. The behavioral perspective is useful for discovering patterns of administrative behavior and for explaining causes and influences that shape such behavior. This is the microlevel of administrative theory and process, presupposing a preference for small-scale phenomena—the human personality—before venturing into the larger ones.

The problem of "why people behave the way they do" is central to understanding a significant part of administration. "Traditionally, the domain of psychology has been the individual and the quest to uncover the essential properties and universal features of the typical human being" (Nord and Fox 1996: 148). The major areas of knowledge resulting from psychology have been personality, motivation, attitudes, and learning. These elements also have been core components of the Human Relations School of management (as found in works of leading scholars in this area such as Rensis Likert, Chris Argyris, Douglas McGregor, and others).

Management of human resources has been largely influenced by psychological studies, particularly on issues of motivation, perception, learning, job satisfaction, attitudes, and individual needs. However, after reviewing major developments about psychological factors and processes in organizational studies, W. R. Nord and S. Fox (1996: 149) conclude that "emphasis has shifted from viewing individuals independently of context to consideration of the interplay between individuals and their contexts." The recent increase in attention to context and the "clear decline in the centrality of individual role" (1996: 149) have rekindled awareness of the contextual relationships and, thus, underlined the significance of the organizational focus. Accordingly, the comparative behavioral information is indispensable for dealing with contextual and organizational subjects, particularly those dealing with people and their concerns such as civil service reform, employee motivation and morale, attitudes at work, or corruption.

Comparative behavioral analysis focusing on people occupying high positions in organizations (i.e., senior managers) provides useful information in major ways. For example, in a study of sixty-three senior public managers from the Arab world, this author concludes that the Arab manager is not a risk-taker and their actions are constrained by fear of failure. A contributing factor to the fear of making mistakes among the Arab executives is that they work in a control-oriented system. Thus when the authority system is highly centralized and the culture of participatory management or politics is weak, risk-taking and creativity among managers suffer. Thus, administrative actions and behaviors that determine performance often are shaped by external influences: political, economic, and social. Because of such linkages, comparative administration studies will continue to contend with the challenges of human behavior, imprecise techniques of observation and measurement, and uncontrollable environmental forces.

Conclusion

Selection and utilization of appropriate comparative method for research is wide open for choice from many possibilities. While emphasizing flexibility, relevance, and prospects of cumulativeness, I would add the following considerations:

1. Selecting the most fruitful approach for conducting comparative public administration research is inescapably an *eclectic* process. Students of the field have to be able and willing to choose from several options, but with full knowledge of the objectives as well as the potential and the limitations of each option. No one method will suit all occasions. Case studies, middle-range models, focus on structure and function, or a behavioral orientation—each provides valid techniques and perspectives. What is the appropriate approach depends on the nature of the type of questions and the objective of the study. It is important, however, that researchers and analysts realize that functional relationships are vital, and political or administrative systems are continually interactive.

2. When a social theory loses its *adaptability*, it is often transformed from a tool of dynamic analysis and inquiry into a set of static ideological beliefs. But administrative theories are continually revised, modified, and reformulated in light of new data or evidence. Change is an outstanding feature of public organization theory and practice, even when there is no full agreement on what theory is or ought to be. Theory relates concepts and associates them in specific patterns after such concepts have received an acceptable measure of evidence and support. Like all theories, public administration theories are constantly disproved, modified, or rewritten. Yet, despite the variability, sound theories retain a measure of effectiveness as tools for organizing data, explaining actions, anticipating events or speculating about relationships (Jreisat 1997: 31).

3. Social theory is subject to rules of science, and consensus of professionals and experts. Broadly speaking, there are several ways for developing and accepting significant conceptual constructs. The overall preference for one theoretical model over another is a matter of consensus among experts, strength of the logic employed, and level of support by empirical evidence. Implicit in such views is a disavowal of claims of scientific exactitude and precision, rarely attainable in the social sciences. If theoretical formulations are exact then they will be always publicly verifiable. Consequently, prediction should be no problem (as in the natural sciences, where control of the environment

is possible and the property of materials can be precisely determined). But in models of social sciences no such precision is claimed nor is one attainable. Thus, the situation Michael Reed (1996: 32) described as "paradigm proliferation."

4. Administrative theory and process evolve and develop, but rarely through radical or revolutionary change. Despite claims of original, new theories and crusades to reinvent management, the continuous search for more appropriate approaches for helping *public* managers has unearthed very few relevant notions of what may be called radical thinking. One cannot consider restated themes calling for flexibility, the exhortations for a "proactive management," or the "the pursuit of excellence" as solutions to challenges of public organizational management. Nor can public managers find much help in postmodern concepts still being defined and debated among intellectuals with predilection for abstract thinking. The output of postmodernism so far has included discourse on structuralism, post structuralism, deconstruction, post capitalism, critical theory, and so forth. But in terms of organizational management, no drastically new perspectives have emerged. "If postmodernism is to provide a solid base for useful social analysis and if it is to contribute to the formulation of a new theory of organizations," concludes Bergquist, "then it must move beyond the status of fad and find roots in the soil of history and precedent" (1996: 578).

Between the rigidities of the traditional approaches and the uncertainties of speculative relativism, the need is for legitimating approaches that provide a synthesis of these trends. Such approaches, as Reed pointed out, "question both a return to fundamentals and unrestrained celebration of discontinuity and diversity: neither intellectual surfing or free riding on the rising tide of relativism, nor retreating into the cave of orthodoxy, are attractive futures for the study of organization" (Reed 1996: 32–33). Whatever the final features of future managerial perspectives, they need to address the practical and theoretical concerns, maintaining continuity in the midst of diversity and minimizing the frustrations of students of public management facing unnecessarily embellished conditions of chaos and confusion.

Breaking out of the culture-bound view and aiming for broader application, comparative public administration researchers are better able to establish generalizations based on data and research results, effectively connected to policy outcomes (Klingner 2009: 21). This can be achieved without sacrificing specificity and distinctiveness of the situation under examination. The desired generalizations evolve from aggregate facts that have been confidently established. In this regard, one has to be careful in dealing with problems of transfer to the "real world" and resist selectivity of data and oversimplification of usually complex administrative relationships. Skills in statistical analysis and electronic data processing improved the tools of methodology (and the capacity to manipulate large data) but have not always resulted in improved analysis and conclusions.

A group of researchers at the School of Public Affairs, University of Colorado, Denver, examined articles published in refereed journals over 10 years, between 2000 and 2009, on the subject of International comparative Public Administration (ICPA). They identified 151 relevant articles focusing on ICPA. Among the findings (1) the articles most frequently were organized around topics such as accountability, performance measurement, decentralization, and budgeting, (2) the vast majority of the articles made use of existing or secondary data, (2) Methods and data in the 151 articles examined differ markedly, (3) Comparative public administration articles were dominated by studies of European, Asian, and North. No doubt, field research in comparative administration is demanding, expensive, and time consuming. It requires knowledge of diverse societies, cultures, and administrative systems. Thus, large-scale activation of comparative research hinges on the ability to utilize frameworks that are not straightjackets, but inductively elicit empirical evidence able to show successful or unsuccessful experiences, and incorporate variables that represent internal as well as external characteristics of units being studied. In addition, sustained substantive comparative field research is a team effort to use Barzelay's metaphor (1997: 1): "Knowledge building is much more of a team sport than contributors to the current literature seem to appreciate." In a perfect world, sustained comparative research requires a long-term view and follows up with a measure of independent or separate verification and confirmation of data.

References

Aberback, J. D., and B. A. Rockman. 1988. Problems of cross-national comparison. In *Public Administration in Developed Democracies: A Comparative Study,* ed. D. C. Rowat, 419–440, New York: Marcel Dekker.

Adler, N. J. 1986. *International Dimensions of Organizational Behavior.* Boston: Kent Publishing.

Almond, G., et al. 2000. *Comparative Politics Today.* 7th ed. New York: Longman

Almond, G., and J. Coleman, eds. 1960. *Politics in Developing Areas.* Princeton, NJ: Princeton University Press.

Almond, G., and S. Verba, eds. 1989. *The Civic Culture Revisited* Newbury Park, CA: Sage.

Almond, G., and S. Verba. 1965. *The Civic Culture.* Boston: Little, Brown.

Babbie, E. 1998. *The Practice of Social Research.* 8th ed. New York: Wadsworth Publishing.

Barzelay, M. 2001. *The New Public Management: Improving Research and Policy Dialogue.* Berkeley, CA: University of California Press.

Barzelay, M. 1997. Researching the politics of New Public Management: Changing the question, not the subject. Paper presented at Workshop of the International Public Management Network, Berlin, and Germany. (June 25–27).

Behn, R. D. 1995. The big questions of public administration. *Public Administration Review.* 55 (4): 313–324.

Bekke, H., J. Perry, and T. Toonen. eds. 1996. *Civil Service Systems in Comparative Perspective.* Bloomington, IN: Indiana University Press.

Bell, D. 2010. *Ethics and World Politics.* Oxford: Oxford University Press.

Bergquist, W. 1996. Postmodern thought in a nutshell: Where art and science come together. In Shafritz and Ott, *Classics of Organization Theory.* 4th ed. 578–591, Belmont, CA: Wadsworth.

Black, C. E. 1966. *The Dynamics of Modernization.* New York: Harper & Row.

Buller, P. F., and R. S. Schuler. 2000. *Managing Organizations.* 6th ed. Cincinnati, OH: South-Wester College Publishing.

Caiden, N. 2001. Preface to the third edition. In *The New Politics of the Budgetary Process.* 4th ed. Wildavsky, A., and N. Caiden, xix–xxi. New York: Longman.

Chapman, R. A., ed. 2000. *Ethics in Public Service for the Millennium.* Burlington, VT: Ashgate.

Deutsch, K. W. 1987. Prologue: Achievements and challenges in 2000 years of comparative research. In *Comparative Policy Research: Learning from Experience,* ed. M. Dierkes, H. N. Weiler, and A. B. Antal, 5–25. New York: St. Martin's Press.

Fitzpatrick, J. et al., 2010. A comparative public administration: Review of the literature and agenda for future research. Paper presented at the annual meeting of the American Political Science Association, (September 2–5, 2010): 1–24.

Fitzpatrick, J., and R. Hero. 1988. Political culture and political characteristics of the American States, *The Western Political Quarterly* 41 (1): 145–153.

Foster, G. M. 1962. *Traditional Cultures.* New York: Harper and Row.

French, W., and C. Bell. 1995. *Organization Development.* 5th ed. Englewood Cliffs, NJ: Prentice- Hall.

Goodsell, C. T. 1994. *The Case for Bureaucracy.* 3rd ed. Chatham, NJ: Chatham House.

Gross, J., and S. Rayner. 1985. *Measuring Culture: A Paradigm for the Analysis of Social Organization.* New York: Columbia University Press.

Harris, P. R., and R. T. Moran. 1987. *Managing Cultural Differences.* Houston, TX: Gulf Publishing.

Hofstede, G. 1984. Cultural dimensions in management and planning. *Asia Journal of Management.* (January) : 81–99.

Hofstede, G. 1980. *Culture's Consequences: International Differences in Work-Related Values.* Beverly Hills, CA: Sage.

Henry, N. 2001. *Public Administration and Public Affairs.* 8th ed. Upper Saddle River, NJ: Prentice Hall.

Johnson, C. A. 1976. Political culture in American States: Elazar's formulation examined. *American Journal of Political Science.* 20 (August).

Jreisat, J. E. 2001. The organizational perspective in comparative and development administration. In *Handbook of Comparative and Development Administration,* 2nd ed., ed. A. Farazmand, 23–31, New York: Marcel Dekker.

———. 1997. *Politics without Process: Administering Development in the Arab World.* Boulder, CO: Lynne Rienner Publishers.

———. 1997a. *Public Organization Management.* Westport, CT: Quorum Books.

———. 1988. Administrative reform in developing countries: A comparative perspective. *Public Administration and Development.* Vol. 8: 85–97.

Kincaid, John. 1980. Political cultures of the American compound republic. *Publius.* 10 (2): 1–15.

Klingner, D. E. 2009. Using US public administration to support global development. *Journal of Regional Studies and Development* 18 (2): 1–29.

Kopczynski, M., and M. Lombardo 1999. Comparative performance measurement. *Public Administration Review* 59 (2): 124–132.

Laite, J. 1988. The sociology of development. In *Perspectives on Development,* P. Leeson and M. Minogue, eds. Manchester, UK: Manchester University Press.

Linton, R. 1945. *The Cultural Background of Personality.* New York: Appleton-Century-Crofts.

March, J. G., and H. A. Simon. 1958. *Organizations.* New York: John Wiley.

Merriam, S. B. 1988. *Case Study Research in Education: A Qualitative Approach.* San Francisco, CA: Jossey-Bass.

Nath, R. ed. 1988. *Comparative Management.* New York: Ballinger.

Nord, W. R., and S. Fox 1996. The individual in organizational studies: The great disappearing act? In *Handbook of Organization Studies,* eds. S. R. Clegg, C. Hardy, and W. R. Nord, 148–174. Thousand Oaks, CA: Sage.

Peters, T. J., and H. Waterman. 1982. *In Search of Excellence.* New York: Harper and Row.

Pinder, C., and L. Moore, eds. 1980. *Middle Range Theory and Study of Organizations.* Boston: Martinus Nijhoff Publishing.

Reed, M. 1996. Organizational theorizing: A historically contested terrain. In *Handbook of Organization Studies,* eds. S. R. Clegg, C. Hardy, and W. R. Nord, 31–56. Thousand Oaks, CA: Sage.

Riccucci, N. M. 2001. The "old" public management versus the "new" public management: Where does public administration fit in? *Public Administration Review* 61 (2): 172–175.

Riggs, F. W. 1991. Public administration: A comparativist framework. *Public Administration Review,* 51, 6 (November/December 1991): 477.

Riggs, F. W. 1991. Bureaucratic links between administration and politics. In *Handbook of Comparative and Development Administration,* 485–509. Edited by A. Farazmand. NY: Marcel Dekker.

Riggs, F. W. 1964. *Administration in Developing Societies.* Boston, MA: Houghton Mifflin.

Riggs, F. W. 1961. *The Ecology of Public Administration.* New York: Asia Publishing.

Riggs, F. W., and E. W. Weidner. 1963. *Models and Priorities in the Comparative Study of Public Administration.* Washington, D.C.: American Society for Public Administration.

Riggs, F. W. 1963. *Models and Priorities in the Comparative Study of Public Administration.* Washington, D.C: The American Society for Public Administration.

Schein, Edgar H. 1985. *Organizational Culture and Leadership.* San Francisco, CA: Jossey-Bass.

Selznick, P. 1948. Foundations of the theory of organization. In *Classics of Organization Theory.* 1996. 4th ed. Shafritz, J. M. and J. S. Ott, 127–137, Wadsworth Publishing.

Sorensen, G.1990. *Democracy, Dictatorship and Development* New York: St. Martin's Press.

Thompson, J. D., et al., eds. 1959. *Comparative Studies in Administration.* Pittsburgh, PA: University of Pittsburgh Press.

Waldo, D. 1964. *Comparative Public Administration: Prologue, Problems, and Promise.* Washington, D.C.: American Society for Public Administration.

Waldo, D. 1978. *Cases in Public Policy and Management.* Education for Public Service Clearinghouse Project. Boston, MA: Intercollegiate Case Clearing House.

Warren, K. E. 1997. *Administrative Law in the Political System.* 3rd ed. Upper Saddle River, NJ: Prentice hall.

Wiarda, H. J. 1991. Concepts and models in comparative politics. In *Comparative Political Dynamics.*eds. D.A. Rustow and K. P. Erickson, New York: Harper Collins.

Wildavsky, A. 1985. *Budgeting: A Comparative Theory of Budgetary Processes*. Piscataway, NJ: Transaction Publishers.

Wilson, W. 1887. The study of administration. In *Classics of Public Administration,* eds. Shafritz, J. M. and A. C. Hyde. 1997. 4th ed. 14–26, New York: Harcourt Brace College Publications.

Yates, D., Jr. 1991. Management in public and private organizations. In *Public Management,* eds. Ott, J. S., A. C. Hyde, and J. M. Shafritz. Chicago: Lyceum and Nelson-Hall.

Endnotes

1. One of earliest delineation of these variables was by Talcott Parsons. He identified five "pattern variables" as dichotomies of which one side must be chosen: affectivity-affective neutrality, self-orientation-collectivity orientation, universalism-particularism, ascription-achievement, and diffuseness-specificity. Parsons, T. and E. A. Shils, eds. *Toward a General Theory of Action* (Harvard University Press, 1959). Some of these variables also are central to the following studies: Almond, G., and J. Coleman, eds. *Politics in Developing Areas.* (Princeton University Press, 1960); Riggs, F. W. *Administration in Developing Societies* (Houghton Mifflin, 1964); and Hofstede, G. *Culture's Consequences: International Differences in Work-Related Values* (Sage, 1980).

2. ICMA Center for Performance Measurement Web page.

3. A noteworthy exception is the *Inter-University Consortium in Institution-Building,* which designed a framework and funded several studies for testing this framework, mostly doctoral dissertations, in several developing countries. Universities of Pittsburgh, Michigan, Syracuse, and Indiana participated in this consortium. But it ultimately faded away for lack of leadership and follow-through.

Chapter 5

Comparative Public Policy

The test of our progress is not whether we add more to the abundance of those who have much; it is whether we provide enough for those who have too little.

**Inscription on President
F. D. Roosevelt's memorial**

Public Policy and Process

Policy has many meanings, depending on the context and the stated objective. Usually, public policies "encompass all those authoritative public decisions that governments make," also referred to as the *outputs* of the political system (Almond et al. 2000: 131). Policy analysis is a systematic examination of alternative actions aimed at selecting one to deal with perceived needs. To facilitate the selection among several alternative policies, an analysis may apply sophisticated quantitative and qualitative methods of research and evaluation. Broadly, public policy reflects a regime's values, the commitments of relevant institutions, and even the views of the whole society. But more directly, a public policy is an output of the political system that may produce different *outcomes* or *impact*. "The fact that governments exist to make policy does not necessarily mean that the policies a particular society gets are the ones that its citizens asked for or would have wanted" (Almond et al. 2000: 131).

Although policy is usually held to the end result of analysis and selection, it is also a *process* leading to the end result. Inputs, processes, and outputs of policies are in constant evolution and change throughout the recognized phases of conceptualization, authorization, implementation, and evaluation. Whether health care, education, environment protection, transportation, or foreign affairs, policy is seldom a stagnant or invariable construct. As relevant needs and conditions change or different public officials take office, policies are also confirmed, altered, revised, or amended, accordingly.

Despite the apparent agreement in the literature on the main phases of the policy process, one finds divergent views on the use and the meaning of the term *policy*. Mark Turner and David Hulme (1997: 59) identified several applications of the term such as a field of study, an expression of general purpose, a specific proposal, a decision of government, a formal authorization, an output or outcome, a theory or model, and a process.

Perceiving policy as "authoritative public decisions" is useful but insufficient. Further specification is essential. In contemporary governance, policy and administration are connected in a most intricate relationship. Conceptually, public administration has been more connected with policy implementation than with policy making. In reality, however, such distinction is increasingly blurred. As Lane (2000: 2) notes: it is impossible to make a sharp separation between policies and administration in the public sector. Public administration is fully engaged in the various phases of the public policy process. Public administration embraces the policy objectives, participates in their formulation, and employs its resources for achieving these policy objectives. The challenge to theory and practice is how to integrate the various functioning elements of setting policy goals, deciding means of implementation, and designating rules for monitoring and regulating these functions.

Comparative policy analysis improves knowledge and understanding of the crucial relationship between policy and administration. Comparison is indispensible for identifying patterns, recognizing critical variables, delineating the degree of variation of these variables in different systems, and ascertaining relevance to application. Comparison of policies provides insights that are unattainable otherwise. It is often noted that comparative policy overlaps considerably with comparative public administration, justifying better integration and better clarification of the relationships between them. The policy-administration linkages are crucial for effective comparative policy analysis; decisions that do not consider or account for the administrative factor are often destined to futility. The centrality of organization and management to the policy processes is undeniable, notwithstanding claims by some comparative policy researchers that "the comparative approach is not central to the tradition of public administration research" (Antal, Dierkes, and Weiler 1987: 18) due to the ethnocentric and parochial tendencies of public administration. Still, public administration is the applied side of public policy and it is unrealistic to cut off or to ignore the conceptual and application links between the functions of policy making and policy management.

Administrative questions are inseparable from policy considerations when defining a policy issue, bringing it into the public agenda, analyzing it, developing alternative strategies for dealing with it, implementing it, and evaluating results (Reynolds 2001: 49). Although various issues and problems may be encountered at every phase of the policy process, the real challenge is often confronted during the implementation phase. Lacking the capacity and the resources to implement, many policies remain aspirations and desires rather than accomplishments. Policy failures at the policy implementation phase are numerous, particularly in developing countries where the state's capacity for action, in general, is limited. As the policy is made, implemented, or its effects assessed—all types of political considerations are in play, enhancing or hindering the progression of any phase of the process.

Cross-country comparative policy analysis broadens the knowledge base about the world and provides guidance in designing better policies. "The fact that different countries often adopt alternative strategies for dealing with similar problems represents a kind of natural experiment" (Heidenheimer, Heclo, and Adams 1990: 1). Thus, careful comparative research can examine and assess those results that may be due to unique circumstances and those that are more applicable to other countries. In the end, through comparison we learn from the positive results and we can avoid the negative experiences. Another justification for cross-country policy comparisons is the growing globalization and interconnectedness of countries. Problems, policies, and events in one country steadily impact other countries. Thus, "we need to know how other countries deal with problems, not only to learn how we might be able to deal with them ourselves, but also in order to estimate what kind of impact their problem-solving strategies might have on our own situation" (Antal, Dierkes, and Weiler 1987: 15). "When countries study one another to draw lessons about which policies work best to reach particular goals, they are engaged in policy analysis" (Adolino and Blake 2001: 2).

Comparing the workings of governments and public institutions of various countries improves understanding of a range of political contexts and the impact on the management of governmental responsibilities in diverse political settings. Focusing on regular duties and functions of governance, comparative analysis provides valuable indications of the effectiveness of public institutions performance, and the overall competence of governance itself. Again, the implementation phase is largely dependent on management capacity and adequate financial resources, usually made available through political decisions that determine structures and functions of administration. Policy research, therefore, remains firmly connected, conceptually and analytically, to politics and to public administration. While comparative public policy analysis promises to improve understanding of the content and the processes of policy making, it also provides valuable operational information on alternative policy options as proposed by various political parties, particularly those in opposition. Comparison helps to identify the range of choices, successes, problems, constraints, and solutions available to policy makers in one or in several states.

The policy process, like the budget cycle, can be an informative way to analyze a policy and identify actors and factors that matter at each phase. Substantively, one finds a considerable consistency in the process of validating policy choices.

A typical policy process may be described through a five-stage model that is widely described in the literature (Adolino and Blake 2001: 9–29). The major phases of the policy process are agenda setting, articulation and formulation, decision making, implementation, and evaluation.

Agenda Setting

The agenda setting could be more complicated than appears on the surface. Needs and demands of citizens are endless. But government can neither respond adequately to all of them nor have the resources to satisfy all of them. The question, then, is which item of the constantly long list of needs and demands gets the attention of policy makers and is included in the agenda for consideration? Likewise, what tools and techniques are usually employed for getting a specific policy issue on the agenda of the authoritative institutions? Thus, setting the agenda determines which issue or problem is dealt with by decision makers, and what alternative specifications decide the options or solutions to be considered while a decision is being made.

Pressures to influence setting the policy agenda come from various sources and with diverse motives: from within the organization, representatives of special interests, advocates of common interest, politicians seeking election, or civic-minded activists defending certain values—all attempt to influence policy making according to their own preferences and motives. The reasons and the methods for those seeking to influence policy vary as well. Certainly, understanding the agenda setting process is key to knowing how to impact public policy. "Before government can make a policy choice, a particular problem in the society must have been deemed amenable to public attention and worthy of attention of policy makers" (Peters 2007: 47). The methods for getting such attention range from dialogue, negotiation, and persuasion to organized demonstrations, even violent protests. An issue has to acquire a sense of urgency to advance to the governmental policy agenda. Such urgency may come also as a result of natural disasters, riots, epidemics, or similar major events (Barzelay 2001: 57).

Policy Formulation

Policy formulation is the course of action to "solve, reduce, or dismiss the problem" (Adolino and Blake 2001: 14) that entails developing and evaluating proposed solutions. Technical feasibility is not political feasibility in making a policy decision. Usually, a vigorous debate and competitiveness take place at this phase not only on what alternatives to be presented but also about the nature of the problem and how it is described. Typically, actors who participate in this process and attempt to shape the outcome are the bureaucracy, legislators and legislative committees, and senior executive leaders. But, the covert and overt power of special interests, organized groups, lobbyists, and mass media can also be formidable and decisive in steering the discourse prior to the actual decision.

Decision Making

Decision making is when "the political process inside and outside of government has weeded out many potential policy options, the moment arrives to make a decision to create a new policy, revise an existing policy, or, alternatively, take no new action" (Adolino and Blake 2001: 17). Despite some distinctions, policy making is inherently a decision making as well. Certain policy decisions are unstructured, non-recurrent, and have far-reaching consequences. In such cases, "there is no cut-and-dried method of handling the problem because it hasn't arisen before, or because its precise nature and structure are elusive and complex, or because it is so important that it deserves a custom-tailored treatment" (Simon 1960: 6). Thus, in the absence of specific procedures for dealing with unstructured decision situations, a great deal of judgment, intuition, and creativity are required in responding to demands for new programs or new policies. Making authoritative policy choices rarely is a routine matter. Even in attempts to apply a rational process in policy choices, decision makers often find themselves bound by incomplete information, pressures of time, limited available resources, inept staff, and difficulties of overcoming resistance to change from within and from without organizations.

A choice among policy alternatives is only one decision among several that may be required during a policy process. A decision on the chosen alternative may not explain how such a particular policy advanced to the top of the agenda, what alternatives have been considered, or how a choice was made among these alternatives. Also, a choice of an alternative policy is not necessarily an explanation of the impact of the policy. Generally, institutional analysis has been valuable for describing how decisions are made and what problems have been encountered in the process. Prescriptive models emphasize the selection of the optimal choice and how a decision "should" be made, which could also be suggested in a mathematical formula (Bazerman 1986: 8).

Policy Implementation

Policy implementation is putting the policy into effect. It is achieving policy goals and objectives. The instruments vary, ranging from reliance on public agencies to total or partial dependence on the business market and subcontracting. Regardless, whether the public bureaucracy is solely entrusted with the implementation responsibility or the activity is privatized through the marketplace, public management capacity for action is a requirement. Even when the function is contracted out or privatized, it is essential that the administrative institutions have the authority and the capacity to implement the policy or to monitor the implementers when handed over to the private sector. Administration is a complex profession with intricate concepts and techniques that involve a great deal of education, training, and skills. Thus, the policy implementation process may require a particular administrative knowledge and competence as well as creative management approaches to achieve the authorized policy objectives.

The administrative institutions, and the people working in them, are key factors for quantitative and qualitative improvement of policy outcome. Public management is increasingly applying performance audit, utilizing better reporting techniques, and enforcing provisions of higher ethical and professional standards of public management. Application of processes of team building, quality circles, total quality management, and similar tools have improved human efforts to efficiently and effectively implement public policies. While significant progress has been made in many associated managerial functions to improve accountability and linkages between resources used and outcomes delivered in public service, there is little evidence that such extensive reforms are taking root or even starting in some countries. Many developing countries are still lacking the necessary institutional frameworks for effective management of the public policy process: independent judiciary, free press, viable political structures, and civil society.

Policy Evaluation

Policy evaluation is an assessment of the outcome of the policy, and an evaluation of its performance to determine conformity to existing laws and fidelity to designated objectives. Frequently, policy outcomes are contested judicially on grounds of equity and consistency with the law and constitutional provisions. In addition, any assessment of policy output or outcome would not be complete without taking into consideration the level of satisfaction of people affected or targeted by the policy. Thus, evaluation of public policy may involve elaborate measurement techniques to determine quantity and quality of the implementation output and outcome. Among commonly utilized methods of policy evaluation is financial and performance audit by professional independent auditors, and an examination by an impartial committee of experts acting as a jury-like panel.

Since the 1990s, public administration theory and practice have been more focused on results of administrative action and service. Public organizations have expended significant energies and resources in trying to improve processes of setting goals, developing indicators, collecting and evaluating data, and initiating change. The United States passed the Government Performance and Results Act of 1993 that calls "for a vigorous implementation of performance measurement across federal agencies by 1999" (Kravchuk and Schack 1996: 348). Many states and local governments have begun similar processes, including developing strategic plans and detailed systems of performance measurement as components of performance budgeting. Techniques of measurement have improved and have been applied at various levels of government in various countries. Comparing and benchmarking of results among organizations and among countries have widely been utilized. In comparing country models and practices in managing performance, Bouckaert and Halligan conclude that the "performance focus not only has an impact on the key public management functions and components...but also changes the nature of policy and management in the public sector itself" (2008: 20).

Beyond the Formal Process

An effective strategy for comparative policy research defines relevant core questions and specifies the purpose in advance. Accurate delineation of policy objectives and the factors legitimating these objectives require reliable information and impartial analysis. Comparative policy analysis usually seeks explanations, finding out institutional strengths and weaknesses, and producing practical recommendations for improvement of the process of the decision making. It is not surprising that in-depth examination of policy making often reveals a reality that is markedly different from the general perception that assumes policy making follows precise rules and legally prescribed processes. Many influences attempt to sway the discourse and to manipulate the evidence for self-serving interests. Elements in the political parties, mass media, and special interest groups continually produce information and exert a variety of pressures techniques to shape policy in their particular image rather than in the common insert.

An illustration of flawed reasoning and misleading diagnosis is what preceded a major policy decision to invade Iraq in 2003. Major influences on the process of deciding are described in the following sections.

Mass Media

Mass media have a critical role to play in a democratic governance. They describe, analyze, explain, verify, and reveal relevant information on major policy issues so the public is better informed and educated about policies that affect their lives. But when mass media coverage becomes a form of advocacy, promoting certain ideology, or representing certain political interests, they lose more than their professional integrity. Prior to the invasion of Iraq, millions of Americans viewed numerous panels on television discussing the question of invasion. Many of the panels consisted of so-called experts on terrorism, members of the U.S. Congress, representatives from think tanks, and advocates of special interest groups—all seemed to have been deliberately chosen. The discussions were often touted as open discussions by "experts" or policy makers. The participants, typically were guided by a reporter from the television station, who repeatedly offered certain interpretations and conceptions of events, thus, structuring the information and framing the questions in a particular way (Jasperson and El-Kikhia 2003: 114). It was not easy for a dissenting voice to articulate an alternative position in such a discussion. Many participants offered opinions based on assumptions made without any particular knowledge about the country soon to be invaded. Since the invasion, many in the news business admitted that their prewar coverage was "far too deferential and uncritical" and failed to provide "independent" validation of false official statements about Iraq.[1]

Declarations by Political Leaders

On August 26, 2002, addressing the convention of Veterans of Foreign Wars, Vice President Dick Cheney declared:

> Simply stated, there is no doubt that Saddam Hussein now has weapons of mass destruction. There is no doubt he is amassing them to use against our friends, against our allies, and against us.[2]

On October 7, 2002, in Cincinnati, Ohio, President George W. Bush declared that "we cannot wait for the final proof, the smoking gun that could come in the form of a mushroom cloud."[3] According to tabulations by *The Center for Public Integrity* in Washington, D. C., President George W. Bush and seven of his top officials, including Vice President Dick Chaney, "made at least 935 false statements in two years following September 11, 2001, about the national security threat posed by Saddam Hussein's Iraq" (Lewis and Reading-Smith 2010: 1). Consistently, the statements emphasized these points: (1) Iraq has nuclear weapons or weapons of mass destruction; (2) Iraq sought uranium oxide from Niger; (3) Iraq was connected with those who committed the crime of 9-11; and (4) the Iraqi leaders were connected with Al-Qaeda and terrorist groups (Pfiffner 2005: 201–214; Lewis and Reading-Smith 2008: 1).

It is commonly known now that no weapons of mass destruction were found, the uranium story was a forgery, and no connection could be established by the CIA and the FBI between the Iraqi regime and terrorist groups or with the 9-11 perpetrators. Nearly five years after the U.S. invasion of Iraq, and an exhaustive examination of the record, The *Center for Public Integrity* concluded that "an orchestrated campaign [had] effectively galvanized public opinion and, in the process, led the nation to war under decidedly false pretense … It is now beyond dispute that Iraq did not possess any weapons of mass destruction or have meaningful ties to Al Qaeda. This was the conclusion of numerous bipartisan government investigations, including those by the Senate Select Committee on Intelligence, the 9-11 Commission, and others" (Lewis and Reading-Smith 2008: 1).

From an ethical perspective, "questions of governance do not concern themselves with whether the invasion of Iraq was ethical, but instead examine the decision-making processes that led to the invasion of Iraq and make determination as to whether the decision-makers and involved public servants acted with integrity" (Huberts, Maesschalch, and Jurkiewicz 2008: 255). From the perspective of global ethics, Peter Singer explains the invasion this way:

> In the end, it was Bush [President George W.] who made the United Nations irrelevant in regard to Iraq, by demonstrating that it could only stand on the sidelines while its most powerful member, with one or two allies, attacked a virtually defenseless member state that was not itself,

at the time, engaged in any aggressive activity beyond its borders. The United Nations Charter says in Article 2, Section 3, that "all members shall settle their international disputes by peaceful means." Section 4 of the same article reads: "All members shall refrain in their international relations from the threat or use of force against the territorial integrity or political independence of any state." Bush's threats and subsequent military attack on Iraq were in clear violation of the UN Charter, but the United Nations was powerless to do anything about it. (Singer 2004: x)

In addition to the ethics aspect of the decision, the cost of the invasion in human lives and material loss for the U.S and for Iraq is immense. The consequent pain and suffering of the Iraqi people rank among the most tragic in modern history. A dysfunctional quota-based system of governance in Iraq emerged in December 2010 producing a weak government with unpredictable future. Moreover, after nine months of acrimonious negotiations in 2010, the elected parliament of Iraq met only once to vote on who would hold the country's top leadership spots.

Influence of Special Interests

Policy makers were surrounded by officials in strategic positions, particularly in the U.S Defense Department and the Office of the Vice President who belonged to or were supportive of a very active political group with their own agenda, playing up invading Iraq. This group, known as neoconservatives (neocons), had the attention of key individuals in the executive branch of government. Their reasoning of the decision to invade was questioned by professionals (high-ranking military personnel, CIA staff, and State Department diplomats) who had reservations before and during the invasion (Pfiffner 2005). From their key positions in government, utilizing their influence with certain journalists and news organization, the neocons were successful beyond their imagination in orchestration the essential forces for the decision to invade Iraq.

Lessons learned from policy and decision making gone awry can be as or more valuable than those ascertained from successful ones. Questionable evidence, faulty assumptions, hidden agendas, and incomplete transparency are some of the serious breakdowns. The implications of the invasion to policy making in the United States will be felt for generations to come; indeed, some already refer to it as the beginning of the end for the American empire. When decision makers cross over from perceiving reality to creating their own reality, they fail more than their professional ethics; they let down their duty and obligations to the country. Hugh Heclo (2010) suggested the notion of *issue networks* that I find appropriate for explaining policy decisions such as to invade Iraq. An *issue network* consists of small identifiable circles of participants who reinforce each other's emotional commitment and sense of their interest rather than the outcome of a neutral and objective analysis (Heclo 2010: 414). In certain policy issues where emotions rule more than reason, and when mass media outlets with a point of view join *issue networks* supported by special interests groups, the power of advocacy tends to override sense of responsibility. In the *networks*, special interest groups operate behind the scene, escaping accountability. Policy makers do not extend their efforts to eliminate contradictions, validate concepts, and integrate fragmented evidence to produce reliable knowledge of the object of the policy. When advocacy, passion, and self-interests rule rather than reason and evidence, and when contradictions and unreliable information persist, policy decisions are reduced to mere shots in the dark or risky adventures of unknown consequences.

Another illustration of conflicting perceptions is when the U. S. health care policy was debated earlier in 2010. On one side, the opposition charged, among many criticisms, that socialists and communists are the movers of the new policy program. On the other side, dissatisfaction was expressed that the policy was not bold enough to offer general health care coverage to all citizens as in most Western democracies. Throughout the debate, powerful special interests were a major force in shaping the debate, disseminating misinformation, and spreading doubts about the proposed policy and the motives of its sponsors. Mass media, particularly the electronic segment, aligned themselves with one side or another in the debate. The final outcome of the health care policy was a watered down bill that does not resemble what was needed or asked for, and remains ambiguous and subject to an assortment of positive and negative conjectures. In a democracy, opposing views on policy issues can be functional; vitriolic and rancorous exchanges are not. They tend to impair the process rather than illuminate the issues.

In sum, policy making is a complex process that requires full transparency and honest consideration of all known and relevant facts and evidence. Sane policy is neither an outcome of ideological warfare nor a plausible expectation to follow from a battle of self-serving narrow interests. With so many visible and invisible forces in play, the reality of public policy making is often different from what gets described neatly in textbooks. Comparative research has the potential of improving the results of empirical analysis of policy decisions with better utilization of data and by relying on tested organizing frameworks.

A framework that promises a systematic execution of research is outlined by Heidenheimer, Helco, and Adams. The effectiveness of their approach is mainly because of its reliance on a comparative framework and its conception of public policy as "the study of how, why, and to what effect different governments pursue particular courses of action or inaction" (1990: 2–4). The following is an elaboration and extension of these basic elements of the framework:

1. The "how" of this definition calls for focus on what goes on inside government structures, how these structures operate, and how they arrive at policy decisions. The issues here are profoundly consequential, beyond the operational and instrumental values. This is the domain that largely defines what type of governance and to what extent citizens are allowed to practice

the democratic values of expression and participation. Transparent communication in an open society is a critical element in the process of "how" policy objectives are defined. A policy maker is used to massive information flowing to the office where it is processed, stored, interpreted, and analyzed. "Administrators are normally pressed from many sides with informational and data sources flowing into their offices from their superiors, subordinates, other agencies, citizens groups, and the general public" (Stillman 2005: 254).

2. The "why" a government pursues certain course of action is difficult to satisfy. The inquiry may take the researcher into unfamiliar terrain of historical, cultural, and motivational factors that may have been instrumental in shaping the adopted policy. Often, we discover that policy decisions, actually, involve behind the scene maneuvers by powerful special interests, or other unstated motives of powerful political leaders. It is not unusual that citizens' expectations are dashed when elected officials take on policies that are generally judged as neither serving public interest, however defined, nor honoring promises made during election.

3. The "to what effect" question focuses on impact, outcome, or "the payoff" of the adopted policy (Heidenheimer, Helco, and Adams 1990: 5). Here where tools of measurement and evaluation are invested to determine utility as well as fairness and equity of the adopted policy.

Although the "how," "why," and "to what effect" questions may provide useful clues for overall policy analysis, the process of making choices among options and alternatives remains insufficiently informed. The practical steps, even the mechanics of making choices, require greater specificity to be useful to the practitioner. To satisfy such need, primary information (based on actual experiences) is indispensable. Libraries are stuffed with volumes that cover topics on industrial policy, economic policy, urban policy, criminal justice policy, transportation policy, education policy, environmental policy, and others. But the countries compared in the literature are often limited to the United States and Europe. The information and findings disclosed by such literature cannot be regarded as representative of all countries or reflecting the wide range of global practices.

Finally, previous comparative policy research appears to attain comprehensiveness and synthesis through comparative case analysis aiming at greater understanding of change in public management policy (Manning and Parison 2004; Pollitt and Bouckaert 2004). As Barzelay points out: "Public management policy refers to government-wide institutional rules in the areas of expenditure planning and financial management, civil service and labor relations, procurement, organization and methods, and audit and evaluation" (2001: 51). The comparative case study method has been a common research strategy for developing generalizations, identifying patterns, and explaining similarities and differences in national policies of many countries in dealing with a particular function.

Frameworks of Decision Making

The centerpiece in the chain of actions leading to policy making is the actual decision-making activities. The literature on decision making in government and in business comprise works of psychologists, political scientists, statisticians, economists, anthropologists, sociologists, mathematicians as well as public and business administrationists. This broad spectrum of research interests necessitates establishing some boundaries of inquiry. Because the primary concern of this discussion is actual policy decisions and how they are made, several influential decision models are appropriate for consideration. These models range from the rational and bounded rationality constructs to the incremental and a variation of consensus building frameworks. Nevertheless, all these decision models, no matter how enriching to the discussion of policy processes, remain insufficient by themselves. Decision models tend to be mechanical or narrowly focused on the tree rather than the forest. Policy analysis is concerned with understanding and explaining the larger picture and the contextual factors affecting the decision in addition to its procedures, focus on the forest as well as the tree.

A functional model or framework of decision making identifies factors that interact through time to shape final policy choices. A pre-decisional phase of public policy making determines access to decisional agenda, considers important influences, evaluates available information, and compares possible policy alternatives. Frequently, these functions are served in an organizational context. Thus, organization learning is vital because "the processes of direct and vicarious learning provide a flow of ideas for actions that promise to improve routine" (Barzelay 2001: 63).

In many cases of policy change, management was the central issue. Comparing change of management policy in three countries—Britain, Australia, and New Zealand—Barzelay builds a cluster to be used as a benchmark that exemplifies the New Public Management. Without reproducing lots of detail on the research plan and the cases utilized, he reports that the inclusion of public management issues on the governmental policy agenda in Britain, Australia, and New Zealand is attributable to parallel changes in the political stream. The changes were the election of the Conservatives in Britain in 1979, election of Labor Party in Australia in 1982, and election and reelection of Labor Party of New Zealand in 1983 and in 1987. The three countries seemed to have reached similar definitions of the problem but via different paths. In Britain, Thatcher, before becoming a prime minister, was a vocal critic of the civil service, often referring to it as inefficient. In Australia, the center-left Labor was primarily concerned with fiscal austerity and mitigating the impact of budget cuts. In New Zealand, public sector management issues reached the policy agenda as a result of change in government, which also defined the problem in terms of organizational inefficiency requiring radical reform policies. In the three countries, new political leaders sought reforms through changes involving institutional rules, financial management, civil service and labor relations, and organization (Barzelay 2001: 69, 71).

These cases of management policy change, illustrate the mutual influence, even convergence, of policy and administration, constituting a theoretically informed comparative, case-oriented analysis. Similarly, the political leadership of three conservatives democracies: Margaret Thatcher in UK, Brian Mulroney in Canada, and Ronald Reagan in the United States, as Peters and Savoie point out, "sought to perform radical surgery on the civil service." The dilemma is that the political leaders in these three countries misdiagnosed the problems of their governments and applied the wrong remedies (Peters and Savoie 1994: 418).

Public administration decision-making models are particularly relevant to policy making as they offer a powerful explanatory force. Decision frameworks focus on practical considerations such as who makes the decision, what alternatives are evoked, at what cost, and for what outcome. Some of the widely known decision making models are described in the following sections.

Rational Model

The rational model assumes the decision maker is committed to a rational approach that follows logical steps leading to perfect decisions. Rationality requires clear definition of values and goals to be maximized by the decision. Also, a rational decision is premised on a complete knowledge of the alternatives and their anticipated consequences. In this type of decision, analysis is comprehensive and takes into account every important relevant factor. The rational model has been commonly claimed by economists who believe they have clear and consistent system of preferences, knowledge of choices, and tools of computation that permit selection of optimal choices (Lindblom 1959; Novick 1965; Simon 1961; Bazerman 1986). The rationalist model has been restated numerous times by numerous authors. Its essential elements may be outlined as follows:

- Define the goal, the objective, or the problem—clearly and accurately.
- Identify the criteria to be used in evaluating alternative solutions—cost, time, and other specifications.
- Identify all alternative actions or choices to reach the defined goal or solve the problem.
- Gather information about each alternative.
- Evaluate each alternative based on the criteria established.
- Recommend the alternative with the best value (Walters, Aydelotte, and Miller 2000: 352; Jreisat 1997, 136; Bazerman 1986).

To be sure, often the process of choice calls for determination of the rationality and ethics of the choice as well as acquiring relevant knowledge about it. Still, perceiving reality and applying reason and rationality may not be sufficient to overcome various limitations and shortcomings. Some of the assumptions made by decision makers could be proven wrong and the anticipated results of such decisions may never materialize. Under such conditions, theory loses its guiding force to those working on the forefront of the service, and administrators of the policy are left with a rule of thumb or trial-and-error techniques in dealing with problems facing them.

Incremental Model

The incremental model is often presented as a contrast by critics of the rational models (Lindblom 1959; Wildavsky 1984); it regards public decisions as grounded in the tradition of political realities. Instead of optimizing and maximizing results, reality often dictates what Lindblom called "successive limited comparisons" or the *Incremental Model* as the alternative. This model does not assume a clear, final definition of goals (objectives) of decisions in government. The model begins with the existing situation, where means and ends are often intermixed. Analysis is limited and focused on alternatives that can be agreed upon or accepted. This decision-making process is pragmatic and primarily is concerned with reaching an agreement among parties involved. The decisional tools of the incremental approach are less of the objective calculations and systematic evaluations utilized by the rational actor. They are more of the bargaining and compromising techniques that provide for proportional representation of interests, minimize conflict, and lead to an agreement within usually a democratic context.

Just as the rational model is often associated with economists, the incremental model is generally associated with politics and the political process. Until recently, the incremental model has been stressed in studies of public decisions of allocation of resources. Aaron Wildavsky's *The Politics of the Budgetary Process* is one of the most widely known references that promote the incremental approach in budgetary decisions. "The largest determining factor of the size and content of this year's budget," says Wildavsky (1984, 13), "is last year's budget." From this perspective, decisions on the size and shape of the budget are matters of serious contention among presidents, congress, political parties, administrators, and interest groups who vie with one another to have budget decisions reflecting their preferences. Charles E. Lindblom (1959, 1980) has been another leading proponent of the incremental approach in public policy decision making. He and others view the making of public policy as a response to short-term political conditions, by small increments, according to events and developments, and not according to rational, information-based, analysis.

The incrementalist decision maker is primarily concerned with reaching an agreement on a final outcome. The method used is bargaining that utilizes various tools, including policy concessions, side-payments, persuasion, and skillful use of limited information. The process is inherently political and often degenerates into power plays among contending forces who seek to influence the final decision by building alliances and attempting to manipulate the rules of the game more than searching for fair or equitable solutions. The process is realistic and widely used, but often is uncertain and even suspect. The outcomes of incremental decisions, with selective reliance on facts and evidence, largely depend on the participants' ability to reach an agreement over who gets what. The process may involve ethical and fair-minded decision makers who advocate a strategy usually referred to as a win-win strategy for reaching a satisfactory outcome and a resolution that is acceptable to all, even if not optimal.

Bounded Rationality Model

The bounded rationality model is one of the mutations and variations between the two polar systems of policy making: the maximizing rationalistic and the politically incrementalist. The *Bounded Rationality Model* (Simon 1960) is based on the recognition of the inherent limitations of the rational model when applied to government. In a real situation of decision making, the values are not always as clearly defined as the rational model assumes. Knowledge of the consequences is always fragmentary, incomplete, or unavailable. Lack of information on the problem, the alternatives, the criteria, and the impact of choosing certain alternative, seriously limit the judgments of decision makers. Time and cost constraints, in particular, limit the search for full information.

Another limitation is imposed by the imperfections of human perceptions in the selection of information as well as in its utilization. The human cognitive ability is limited naturally and can evoke or retain and utilize only limited information on the problem and the alternatives for its solution. The enormous progress in the development of computational tools and the so-called information revolution have aided and advanced humans' cognitive capabilities. However, they have not freed them from their biases, self-interest, and biological limitations to achieve total rationality of decisional actions.

Consensus-Building Models

The consensus-building models involve more than one decision strategy and may use various decision rules. One such decision strategy widely used in democratic systems of government is *voting*. The voting method is not limited to selection of policy makers at the various levels of government. It is also the main method for decision making used within government, on a daily basis. National legislative bodies as well as county commissions, city councils, unions, advisory citizens' councils, and employees of public organizations usually vote on policy choices. The process assumes the existence of a measure of information, discussion of the problem requiring a decision, and knowledge and acceptance of the decision rules in advance.

Voting also means equal participation in public decisions by affected parties and aggregation of their preferences. Municipalities resort to referenda for settling various debates over public decisions on taxes, zoning, form of government, and other significant policies. Administrative organizations rely on voting by their employees to measure support to certain public policy decisions such as health insurance coverage, salary contracts, or certain rules affecting modes of operation. The outcome of a decision made as a result of the voting method may be binding, as in referenda on local taxes; or may be advisory, when the purpose is to find out preference or level of support for a policy choice. Voting is almost always a decisive method to establish aggregate preferences, and hence a consensus for some choice of action.

Comparative policy analysis of worldwide practices of decision making suggests that the applications of the above frameworks are not universal, to say the least. Most of the processes of decision making, described above, assume a context that approximates Max Weber's "legal-rational" authority structure, and provides a reasonable degree of transparency. The comparative literature has not articulated, sufficiently, the linkages with the system of governance (institutions, processes, and outcomes). Governance involves more than just the political or administrative orders of a society. Governance reaches and influences many aspects of society such as types of institutional structures, legitimacy of the system of authority, authenticity of decision processes, fidelity to society's fundamental values, and respect of human rights. Certainly, policy decisions are not independent from the complex combination of variables usually known as democracy or increasingly referred to as "the civil society." Within such a system, issues of accountability of public officials and the rule of law stand out as crucial elements in determining the overall quality of the regime's performance.

Where political leaders maintain excessive monopoly of power, and governmental actions or inaction have profound effects on the daily lives of citizens, comparative analysis has to be extended outside the traditional domains of government. While the effects of these traditional structures (executive leadership, legislatures, courts, and bureaucracies) is most decisive, complete comparative analysis should include many nongovernmental institutions that labor in the service of public interest. The behavioral patterns of these entities in rendering their assumed functions are not discrete acts performed in a vacuum. They influence and are influenced by existing political and economic power configurations, available resources, and leadership ethics and competence.

In developing countries, processes of policy decisions are less systematic and methodical than in developed countries. In a study of the Arab states, this author found lack of recorded information about public policy decisions to be very restrictive of effective and reliable analysis and evaluation. Also, the absence of citizens' representation and professional institutional input often resulted in public decisions made mainly on the basis of personal preference of the top leader. Consequently, it is difficult to determine with certainty what considerations or what reasoning entered into a specific policy action, let alone holding public officials accountable for their actions. Red tape may be the bane of the bureaucracy but all that paperwork does not necessarily reflect the reality of decision making by public officials (Jreisat 1997: 135). The personal nature of policy making is a characteristic of many developing countries. Senior administrators, too, tied to powerful political leaders, often operate beyond the institutional norms, protected from facing consequences of their inadequate or faulty actions. Many political leaders themselves are little inclined to work through institutions, further contributing to the latter's atrophy, and ultimately even undermining the vitality of governance at large.

Lack of documentation and the personal features of governing in developing countries seriously undermine transparency. Without transparency true account-ability is unattainable. In addition, without transparency the mission of scholarship and research on public affairs become difficult. Credible knowledge hinges on the development of an empirical base, which is always a demanding and painstaking process. To a large degree, this is true for all developing countries as it has been a lasting problem for comparative studies. Consequently, scholars tend to either intel-lectually congregate in the safety of revealed and publicized issues of international conflict or foreign policy decisions, or develop global, over-generalized, and impres-sionistic models about societies they know very little about.

As if the subject is not complex enough, the literature on developing coun-tries often displays a temptation to emphasize dramatic events or to let plentiful consulting money create instant expertise and sketchy analysis. Authentic com-parative scholarship usually results from focused attention to specific societies or regions over long times, substantive knowledge of history, familiarity with lan-guage, understanding of culture, and a genuine interest in the country's problems and aspirations. This is not to say that profound comparative policy research has always to be comprehensive or all-inclusive endeavors. Research that leads to snap-shots, producing focused pictures of specific aspects of policy structure, process, impact—can also provide significant building blocks in a larger and more com-prehensive knowledge of societies. To eliminate contradiction and attain validity and consistency of concepts, they have to be integrated into a cumulative total of knowledge on the larger objective of investigation. Specific information that recog-nizes patterns, similarities, and difficulties of public organizations has been in short supply resulting in knowledge gaps in the literature on comparative administration and comparative policy. Thus, confirmation of many middle-range theories, and developing concepts and generalizations of lasting utility, has made little headway in recent years.

Public Policy and Administrative Discretion

Any system of governance has to resolve the issue of how much administrative dis-cretion to authorize in matters of policy making. In democratic political systems, establishing a consensus on a coherent approach to administrative discretion is a complicated matter. Not only because of abundant pejorative descriptions of public bureaucracy, but also because of changing ideologies and perceptions of political parties that frequently rotate in the command posts of the state. For some of the extreme negative views, the ideal or desirable condition of governance is a state of administration that exercises little or no discretion at all.

A significant part of the opposition to the administrative process is based on a rationale tied to a particular conception and interpretation of the democratic system. One perspective seeks protection of democratic values from an assumed influx of "bureaucratic despotism" in the modern state. A constant source of opposition to bureaucracy is by a neoconservative, anti-administrative state partisanship, based on the absence of a solid line that connects citizens and government appointees. Bureaucrats do not represent citizens, elected officials do. This premise is extended through a neoconservative argument that also defends the role of interest groups, seeks protection of unhindered free market mechanisms, and invariably favors the interests of the private financial capital. This ideology has inverse effects on the state's institutions and policies. It is often manifested in a multipronged attack on the public sector, followed or accompanied by grand privatizing strategies of most government functions. The justification is based on the "assumed" inefficiency of government institutions and incompetence of public bureaucrats. For such advocacy, downsizing, contracting with the private sector, and narrowing public administration functions and responsibilities are justified, even when the private sector delivered inferior products or services at a higher cost, or caused an economic disaster such as in 2008–9.

The fundamental issue here is associated with the type of governance system and the definition of the role of the state in modern society. This issue has several dimensions. A major one is the relationship between the public and the non-public domains—the private, the non-profit, and other organized groups. Until recently, in most countries of the world, the trend has been to restructure government and the economy according to an image espoused largely by the World Bank and conservative economists and politicians. This restructuring favors the private sector as the tool of a free market system that promotes competitiveness and higher efficiencies in production and in services. To a large extent, this trend renders the argument of politics-administration dichotomy somewhat superfluous in the eyes of those who favor neither to have a powerful role in the modern economy. For critics of the public sector, the redefined role of public administration is to be a facilitator and a promoter of the interest of the free market system, which in its own way, shall meet the social and economic needs of citizens.

Another aspect of the role of the state in society focuses on the mutual exchanges, shared interests, and other relationships between public administration and its political context. This aspect is directly connected to the issue of discretion. What is the appropriate level of decentralization to lower levels of authority in public organizations or to local authorities? Extreme decentralization to achieve flexibility and initiative at lower levels of governance "may exact cost in terms of uniformity and control of response" (Stillman 2005: 256). The opposite proposition is also problematic for excessive centralization is achieved at the expense of organizational and managerial accountability and responsiveness.

An influential conception of the political-administrative relationship that received support in the 1970s is based on questioning "the value of passing so many laws creating new social programs without paying adequate attention to whether these laws were effectively implemented or carried out at all" (Stillman 2005: 401). The broad expansion of government activities is criticized because it resulted in the erosion of administrative responsibility and accountability. Such expansion is also linked to the crisis of public authority. Consequently, it became more difficult to set precise legislative guidelines for execution of public policy. This argument has been articulated by Theodore Lowi in his book *The End of Liberalism* (1969), according to Richard Stillman II (2005: 401). Although this position by Lowi overlaps, with certain aspects of the neoconservatives' perspective—both view with alarm the expansive power of the administrative state—but the two positions end up separate and different in their prescriptive component. For Lowi (1969), Congress and the president need to make precise laws, and the courts need to formulate strict judicial standards to guide administrative actions, thereby reducing administrative discretion. This is not the same as privatizing the responsibilities of the public sector, but rather specifying and restricting administrative discretion because policy implementation should be an extension of the power of policy making (Stillman 2005: 401).

Today, one finds plenty of proposed ideas on what is needed to transform the habits, culture, and performance of contemporary public organizations. Some even promise to "reinvent" the government and to redefine it. The ideas for change vary in their range of coverage as well as in their sense of reality. Recommendations for change of governance offer different recipes: (1) Limit or substitute public bureaucracy by promoting mission-driven entrepreneurial leadership, enhancing competition and deregulation, reducing civil service, privatizing and contracting out as much as possible of public functions, and relying on the magic of the market to attain the desired end. (2) Restrict, define, and reduce administrative power and discretion by invigorating oversight and revitalizing the policy making process. (3) Reinvent government, focusing on the customer, fostering "total quality management," decentralizing to local authorities, and privatizing wherever feasible.

Regardless, in adapting the political-administrative exchanges and linkages, the managerial leaders have not only to change their organizations, but also they need to learn how to manage their interdependence with elected politicians and apply political skills in the process of managing performance and change (Milner and Joyce 2005: 1). The various ideas for change are not mutually exclusive, but they are often contradictory (Carroll 1995; Moe 1994). For generations, reformers have been attempting to separate certain activities from the political heat. Public administration at all levels of governance has been making measureable progress in improving definition of mission and objectives, empowering employees, empowering independent regulatory agencies, stressing the values of public service, emphasizing ethics of public service, improving civil service and budget processes, fostering human rights in public service, and actively improving professional education and training for preparing future generations of competent and ethical managers. "There have always been innovators in the public services, but the pressure to reform and modernize the public service are predominantly political" (Milner and Joyce 2005: 1).

The role of public administration is established in enabling statutes and other instruments that provide administration with the necessary authority for rule making, regulation, and administrative adjudication. No private sector organization is qualified or capable of substitution for public management authority or taking over its legitimate duties and responsibilities in the modern state. Actually, the reality of the modern state indicates that administrative discretion is essential for defining, interpreting, and enforcing public policy decisions. The obvious fact is that eliminating administrative—"bureaucratic"—discretion in the modern state is impractical as it will bring about a paralysis of public institutions and governance itself. Even in formulating public policy, administrative discretion is necessary to allow pubic managers the freedom of proposing new policies to be enacted in statutory legislation. The rationale is self-evident. Administrators have experiences in their jurisdictions, knowledge and skills acquired through education and training, and commitment to their functions and organizations, which give much credence to their views and suggestions.

Finally, the representation issue is not a sufficient reason to deny the indispensability of administrative discretion. The legislative doctrine of delegated power of rule making provides authenticity to administrative actions. As to representativeness, beyond questions of trust and technical expertise, civil servants are recognized as a diverse group that replicates society at large. Long time ago, noting the diversity among public administrators and a comparatively high homogeneity among legislators, Norton Long (1962) recognized that the federal civil service of the United States was more representative of the American people, in all significant respects save election, than Congress. "The concept of representative bureaucracy, then, denies the separation of politics and administration ... It accepts a vital policy-making role for administrators, and it emphasizes the importance of administrators who are both competent and represent societal values" (Dresang 1999, 66).

Processes of administrative discretion and empowerment, however, do not mean in any way a weakening of "legislative oversight" and supervision. Indeed, to maintain a responsible management of public affairs, an increasing attention is given to processes of self-control and socialization in the proper ethics and values of public service. Impact of rapidly changing technology and the effects of various tempestuous elements of the environment of public service remain to be carefully researched and their consequences assessed as related to the discretion and the overall performance of public administration.

All this means that the policy-administration dichotomy continues to pose several questions of ideological as well as practical nature. In addition to legislatively delegated authority to administration, career civil servants derive further legitimacy for their actions from their expertise and professionalism, maintained through two main channels (1) compliance with the rules and values of a "merit" system and competitive recruitment, and (b) application of deliberate policy and activities of skill-building and personnel development their members. Advancing professionalism in public management is the most feasible approach to ensuring administrative responsiveness to duties of public service. Also, public managers need to exercise discretion and authority because they continue to be a significant factor in the authoritative allocation of resources in the society.

Clearly, public administration can improve on the common practice of seeking sustained citizen input in administrative decisions and encourage wider citizen participation in policy formulation and implementation. In truly democratic systems, people are linked to public institutions through means other than election. Citizens are served, regulated, protected, educated, consulted, and invited to share their views on policies affecting their lives. Public institutions are the first line of defense for public security, not only military security, but also security of food, water, jobs, health care, safe environment, justice, and general welfare. Security is enhanced by a governance system that employs trusted, coherent, and functional staff. Understandably, developing links with citizens and manifesting public service values and policies vary from one governance system to another.

In most political systems, public administration has been challenged on the representation issue. Achieving broad public participation in public decision making can be costly and uncertain and cause delays (Walters, Aydelotte, and Miller 2000: 349). Even well established democratic systems are facing serious challenges in maintaining credibility in the eyes of their public:

- The struggle to maintain legitimacy of representative governments under very low election turnouts, particularly at the local level, is difficult to overcome.
- Genuine opposition parties are either absent or weak, thus, there is dearth of valid policy alternatives.
- In the United States, as in many other countries, the flow of news on corruption and unethical conduct by political leaders at all levels of government seems never-ending, setting off a constant erosion of public trust. In fact, many public officials have already been indicted and some have been spending time in jail.

Thus, weak citizens' representation in governance, decline of effective political opposition parties, and corruption have deepened mistrust of government, particularly political leaders often regarded as serving special interests rather than public interests. Because practices of countries differ, a methodical application of the comparative approach can serve to clarify and to inform about many aspects of the political/administrative functions. Comparative analysis can define the links of the political and administrative institutions to citizens and determine the degree of balance and fairness in the delivery of public goods and services. Through comparative research we may be able to ascertain to what extent the state is active and involved in the governing the society, and how much autonomy is granted to "market forces" to self-regulate without "undue" government interference. Most important, by considering practices and experiences of various countries, comparative analysis informs us about public policies and actions that worked and those that did not.

Certainly, the nature of public administration mandates in contemporary states tends to generate cross-currents and contentions over its role in governance. Operating within such environment creates many predicaments for public managers and institutions, beyond the usual tensions of acquiring adequate resources for implementing policies. In meeting their professional responsibilities, public administrators depend on these factors:

1. Public administration relies on expert analysis in public policy determination more than on citizens' participation. Citizens, as taxpayers, demand and expect delivery of a variety of public services as well as setting and enforcing standards that protect their safety and welfare, efficiently and effectively. Emphasis on competent knowledge and expediency tends often to overshadow democratic norms and create tensions within governance.

2. The environment of public administration remains uncertain and civil servants continually have to vie for political support. As a result, strain and disagreements are common between advocates of state activism in society and those who consider the state merely as a protector of the "free market" and a server of capital. Such contradictions hamper processes of public policies, impede administrative actions, and cause various negative pressures that press the political domain for budget cuts, low salaries for public employees, dismantling rules and regulations, and demanding outright privatization of most public services.

3. The bottom line argument remains that administrative capacity for action requires meaningful administrative discretion. In a democracy, both of capacity and discretion are regarded by many as inimical to political control, a subject often mired by myths and distortions. Advocates of unfettered free markets habitually use bureaucracy and government regulations as scapegoats for explaining their own failures or setbacks of the economy. As a key institution in the implementation of public policy, bureaucracy has to regularly prove its worth, coherence, ethics, and legitimacy as an indispensable institution in a contemporary democratic state.

Comparative Politics and Comparative Administration

Comparative politics embraces the whole political system in a wide range of countries. Theoretically, public administration is only a part of the multifaceted comparative politics that includes subfields such as political parties, public law, political behavior, executive leadership, and the legislative process. Often comparative politics is more devoted to the macro political than to components or subfields of politics. The study of administration, on the other hand, has been commonly focusing on bureaucracy, its behavior, its personnel practices, its finance, and its decision making.

Distinguishing comparative public administration from comparative politics is possible and is analytically desirable. Yet whatever the complexity of the task may be, the delineation of relationships will always involve a measure of overlapping. In both comparative fields, the policies and objectives of the state and the ways and means for achieving them are common concerns. In practice, it is not surprising that the officials involved in setting political objectives are often also administering them. Irrespective of the level and location of decisional powers, the role of public administration remains crucial. Thus, the new field of comparative policy research, building on preceding policy analysis, reflects the influence of public administration and other areas of social science, particularly economics (Antal, Dierkes, and Weiler 1987: 17). The characteristics that distinguish this new focus "include its problem-orientation and it's multidisciplinary" (Antal, Dierkes, and Weiler 1987: 17). This common recognition is not unmindful of the reality in which a highly centralized, authoritarian political regime tends to reduce public administration to a mere regime-serving instrument rather than a society-serving institution.

With the collapse of the socialist camp, debates on the most suitable form of governance in modern societies have been centered on the democratic models employed in the West. Very few authentic copies of the Western models, however, are found in developing countries. While democratization has been a consistent objective of reform, its practice has been far from real or tangible applications. Raising the banners of noble ideas the like of individual freedom, citizen representation, and application of the democratic values and principles has been anything but successful in the majority of countries. Recognizing this fact, Hubert Vedrine, the French Minister of Foreign Affairs once pointed out that "the Western countries think a little too much that democracy is a religion and the only thing you have to do is converting."[4]

Despite many endeavors and repeated claims since World War II, political science scholarship remains uncertain about the real determinants of democracy. Some even are not sure "whether open democratic societies are affluent because they are open and democratic or whether it is the other way around" (Macridis and Brown 1990: 8). Certainly, a participatory political process with regular election is not *ipso facto* democracy or a sufficient measure of it. Moreover, in the context of developing countries, a democracy accompanied by unchecked free market economy may cause somber concern in the opposite direction. This has been widely acknowledged and may be simply broached in Vaclav Havel's words (quoted in Comaroff 1999: vii) as a "new totalitarianism of consumption, commerce, and money." The main point is that the democratic model is a complex system that requires certain preconditions to achieve successful application in developing countries. In the meantime, until certain preconditions for a genuine democratization trend are possible, analysis should not preclude variations of the model, for example, liberalization of public policies that may result in more effective applications and better service of societal interests.

Comparative politics has been singled out for not adequately and effectively addressing the issues facing the newly independent states. As outlined by scholars of comparative politics (Macridis and Brown 1990: 1–2), its failures include the following:

- Comparative politics dealt primarily with a single culture-configuration, namely, that of the Western world.
- It focused on representative democracies and until recently treated undemocratic systems as aberrations from the democratic "norms."
- It prevented students from dealing systematically not only with nondemocratic Western systems but also with colonial systems and other distinct societies.
- Research was founded on the study of isolated aspects of the governmental process and lacked real comparative application.

Moreover, comparative politics has been criticized for understating the role of public administration in modern governance. It is of a great interest to students of contemporary public administration to realize that widely used text books such as *Comparative Politics Today* (Almond et al. 2000, 7th ed.) and *Introduction to Comparative Government* (Curtis 1997) gives only a rudimentary attention to public administration, even if it is the "cutting edge of government" that Woodrow Wilson spoke about in the 1880s. In fact, one cannot find the words *public administration* in the tables of contents of these references. The term *bureaucracy* is allotted two and a half pages in the 800-page volume by Almond and his associates. The volume by Curtis and his associates has no mention of public administration or bureaucracy in its table of contents; the concepts are simply reduced, assumed, or submerged under other titles. This in itself is indicative. The following is a breakdown of the main parts of both tables of contents.

Comparative Politics Today, 7th ed., Almond et al.:

1. Issues in Comparative Politics
2. Comparing Political Systems
3. Political Culture and Political Socialization
4. Interest Articulation
5. Interest Aggregation and Political Parties
6. Government and Policy Making
7. Public Policy

Country Studies: 12 countries
Introduction to Comparative Government, 4th ed., Curtis et al.:

Why Study Comparative Politics and Government?
Classification of systems

Comparative political theory has fared no better in terms of addressing compelling contemporary issues of governance, let alone focusing on problems of developing countries. There are few contributions from political theory, beyond the familiar and over-prescribed democratic models, which seek to adapt to a particular political structures to make it more relevant to the conditions of other systems. Touting *Border Crossing*, edited by F. T. Dallymayr, the publisher and the author write:

> Comparative political theory is at best an embryonic and marginalized endeavor. As practiced in most Western universities, the study of political theory generally involves a rehearsal of the canon of Western political thought from Plato to Marx. Only rarely are practitioners of political thought willing and professionally encouraged to transgress the canon—and thereby the cultural boundaries of North America and Europe—in the direction of genuine comparative investigation.

Comparative public administration and comparative policy could have gained greater relevance and comprehensiveness in addressing issues of developing systems. Certainly, relevance and saliency of policy formulation and policy implementation would be improved significantly with better accounting of the connections with the political context. Comparative public policy is not a substitute for comparative public administration. Public policy analysis is more focused on process or function; hence, the administrative and organizational structures and roles become less distinct. As Henderson (1982: 170) points out, "The policy paradigm ... tends to blur the distinction between the administrative elements of the polity, often de-emphasizing much of the technical material that has traditionally been considered Public Administration." In reality, the policy focus does not replace the administrative one, but has to incorporate it to develop a more effective combination of the two concerns. Usually, the betterment of the concepts or practices of either comparative public administration or comparative public policy improves the functioning of both. Both have enormous stakes in the continual search for rationalizing public decision-making processes, honing the methodology of comparative research, and validating concepts and practices of governance. One may go further and claim, with good reasons that the ultimate gains from the comparative approach may succeed or falter, depending on the ability to harmonize and integrate the policy and administrative concepts and practices.

Operating within a system of law, public administration is placed in a paradigm of management that connects it with the political system in a partnership as they, together, set policy and develop strategies. Weakening either partner in this union is detrimental to the capacity to govern. This is why public managers are responsible for building competence among their employees, assuming the right choices are made in recruitment. Competence-building requires training with a defined purpose, values, and content. Also, an overall policy of personnel development has to emphasize learning on the job. Evidence indicates that relevant training as a reliable tool of improving performance is indisputable. Finally, the challenge of motivation in the public sector often is brushed aside by leadership: how to motivate public employees when there are fewer incentives available such as pay raises or promotions.

Traditional administrative approaches, emphasizing control and command processes, generate rigidities and dysfunctions that prevent them from adopting many of the new managerial concepts and practices. Unless there is an emerging organizational management with appropriate professional competence, the evolution will be slow. To implement "new" managerial processes with greater attention to results, certain managerial issues have to be elevated on the priority listing of reform ingredients to induce a more receptive climate to innovation and change.

A comprehensive reform policy that involves people, organization, process, and relations with the environment is unavoidable. In nearly all countries, public management has been directed to achieve budget cutbacks and to manage public policies with fewer resources while accounting for what it does in measurable terms. At the same time, public organizations are less familiar with techniques and processes of downsizing. Thus, a crucial mental and behavioral adjustment is essential to avoid the necessity for public managers to accept apparent defeat or to develop a sense of failure and despair. An important element in such adjustment is that resource allocation has to serve and be connected to organizational performance. Effective use of scarce resources necessitates linking awards to performance. Competent management cannot escape for too long offering salary raises, travel money, and symbolic recognitions to the most productive and most valuable people to the organization's mission. Certainly, when fewer people are able to do the same or more work, they should share in the benefits.

Another aspect of the new reality is largely unmet; that is, the demand for effective leaders who can lead in a fast changing organizational context. The need for a new breed of organizational leaders is never more compelling. Such leaders have to revitalize organizations, define the content and direction of desirable change, mobilize commitment to new visions, and secure needed resources. These leaders also face employees' worries of internal organizational politics in implementing policies.

Thus, they suspect and often do resist the suggested change. A discouraging sense among employees is that only individuals lacking political power will suffer the consequences of the financial cutbacks or downsizing. Assuring staff that management is committed to fairness, equity, and serving the collective interest may alleviate some of the anxiety over unfair practices. No doubt, a strategy based on practicing a proactive managerial stance that fosters employee participation is the best mechanism to soften the blow and to minimize the damage to the continuing programs and activities of the organization.

This inventory of measures for building administrative professional competence will result in better implementation of public policies. But, as has been repeated throughout this discussion, the political context is paramount. As Alex Inkeles (1987, 50) pointed out, the special characteristics of policy research is its intention, or great potential, to guide the action of a community, a polity, or its leaders to "correct" action, which most effectively and efficiently achieves the acknowledged goals of these political actors. In this endeavor, comparative administration and comparative policy are indispensable paths for reaching such goals.

References

Adolino, J. R., and C. H. Blake. 2001. *Comparing Public Policies.* Washington, D.C.: CQ Press.

Almond, G. A., et al. 2000. *Comparative Politics Today: A World View.* 7th Ed. New York: Longman.

Antal, A. B., M. Dierkes, and H. N. Weiler. 1987. Cross-national policy research: Traditions, achievements, and challenges. In *Comparative Policy Research,* eds. M. Dierkes, H. N. Weiler, and A. B. Antal, 13–25. New York: St. Martin's Press.

Barzelay, M. 2001. *The New Public Management.* Los Angeles: University of California Press.

Bazerman, M. A. 1986. *Judgment in Managerial Decision-Making.* New York: John Wiley.

Bouckaert, G., and J. Halligan. 2008. *Managing Performance: International Comparisons.* London: Routledge, Taylor & Francis.

Carroll, J. D. 1995. The rhetoric of reform and political reality in the National Performance Review. *Public Administration Review.* 55 (3): 302–312.

Comaroff, J. ed. 1999. *Civil Society and Political Imagination in Africa.* Chicago: University of Chicago Press.

Curtis, M. ed. 1997. *Introduction to Comparative Government.* 4th ed. New York: Longman.

Dallmayer, F. R. 1999. *Border Crossing.* Boston: Lexington Cooks (book cover).

Dresang, D. L. 1999. *Public Personnel Management and Public Policy.* 3rd ed. New York: Longman.

Education for Public Service Clearinghouse Project. 1978. *Cases in Public Policy and Management.* Boston, MA: Intercollegiate Case Clearing House.

Heclo, Hugh. 2010. Issue networks and the executive establishment. In *Public Administration: Concepts and Cases.* 9th ed., R. J. Stillman, II, ed., 413–421. Boston, MA: Wadsworth.

Heidenheimer, A. J., H. Heclo, and C. T. Adams. 1990. *Comparative Public Policy: The Politics of Social Choice in America, Europe and Japan.* 3rd ed. New York: St. Martin's Press.

Henderson, K. M. 1982. Comparative public administration: The United States view in international perspective. *Public Administration and Development.* 2: 162–183.

Huberts, L., J. Maesschalch, C. Jurkiewicz, eds. 2008. *Ethics and Integrity of Governance: Perspectives across Frontiers.* UK: Edward Elgar.

Inkeles, A. 1987. Cross-national research confronts the needs of the policy maker, In *Comparative Policy Research: Learning from Experience,* eds. M. Dierkes, H. N. Weiler, and A. B. Antal, pp. 50–55. New York: St. Martin's Press.

Jasperson, A. E., and M. O. El-Kikhia. 2003. CNN and al Jazeera's media coverage of America's war in Afghanistan. In *Framing Terrorism,* eds. Norris, P., M. Kern, and M. Just, 113–132, New York: Routledge.

Jreisat, J. E. 1997. *Public Organization Management.* Westport, CT: Quorum Books.

Kravchuk, R. S., and R. W. Schack. 1996. Designing effective performance measurement systems under the Government Performance and Results Act of 1993. *Public Administration Review.* Vol. 56 (4): 348–358.

Lane, Jan-Erik 2000. *New Public Management.* London: Routledge.

Lewis, C., and M. Reading-Smith. 2008. Iraq: The war card, false pretenses. The Center for Public Integrity, http://projects.publicintegrity.org/WarCard/default.aspx?sec=project-home&context=methodology, accessed October 11, 2010.

Lindblom, C. E. 1980. *The Policy-Making Process.* 2nd ed. Englewood Cliffs, NJ: Prentice Hall.

———. 1959. The science of "muddling through." *Public Administration Review.* 19 (Spring): 79–88.

Long, N. E. 1962. *The Polity.* Chicago, IL: Rand McNally.

Lowi, T. J. 1969. *The End of Liberalism.* New York: W. W. Norton.

Macridis, R. C., and B. E. Brown, ed. 1990. Comparative analysis: Method and concept. In *Comparative Politics: Notes and Readings.* 7th ed. Belmont, CA: Wadsworth.

Manning, N., and Parison, N. 2004. *International Public Administration Reform: Implications for the Russian Federation.* Washington, D.C: The World Bank.

Milner, E., and P. Joyce. 2005. *Lessons in Leadership.* London: Routledge.

Moe, R. C. 1994. The "reinventing government" exercise: Misinterpreting the problem, misjudging the consequences, *Public Administration Review* 54 (2): 11–122.

Novick, D., ed. 1965. *Program Budgeting.* Cambridge, MA: Harvard University Press.

Peters, G. 2007. *American Public Policy: Promise and Performance.* Washington, D.C.: CQ Press.

Pfiffner, J. P. 2005. The decision to go to war with Iraq. In *Public Administration: Concepts and Cases,* ed., R. J. Stillman II, 203–217, New York: Houghton Mifflin Co.

Pollitt, C. and Bouckaert, G. 2004. *Public Management Reform: A Comparative Analysis.* 2nd ed., Oxford, UK: Oxford University Press.

Reynolds, H. W., Jr. 2001. Public administrators and policy agendas. *International Journal of Public Administration* 24 (1): 1–8.

Simon, H. A. 1960. *The New Science of Management Decision.* New York: Harper & Row.

Singer, D. 2004. *One World: The Ethics of Globalization.* 2nd ed., Yale University Press.

Stillman, R. J. II. 2005. *Public Administration: Concepts and Cases.* 8th ed. Boston: Houghton Mifflin.

Turner, M., and D. Hulme. 1997. *Governance, Administration, and Development: Making the State Work.* West Hartford, CT: Kumarian Press.

Walters L., J. Aydelotte, and J. Miller. 2000. Putting more public in policy analysis, *Public Administration Review,* 60 (4): 349–359.

Wildavsky, A. 1984. *The Politics of the Budgetary Process.* 4th ed. Boston, MA: Little, Brown.

Endnotes

1. The Center for Public Integrity, The War Card, 2008 (http://projects.publicintegrity. org/WarCard/default.aspx?sec=project-home&context=methodology), accessed 10-11-2010.
2. Ibid.
3. George W. Bush speech printed in the *Washington Post*, October 8, 2002.
4. Hubert Vedrine, commenting on the democracy conference in Warsaw, Poland, which concluded with a pledge to promote democratic governments throughout the world. The pledge was signed by 106 countries after a two-day (June 26–27, 2000) conference, France did not sign this declaration (*St. Petersburg Times*, June 28, 2000, p. 10A).

Chapter 6

Administration of Developing Countries

The greatest difficulty lies not in persuading people to accept new ideas, but in persuading them to abandon old ones.

John Maynard Keynes

Every people on earth go through two revolutions: a political revolution that helps them recover their right to self-government ... and a social revolution—a class conflict that ultimately ends in the realization of social justice for all inhabitant of the country.

G. Abdul Nasser,
Philosophy of the Revolution[1]

Understanding Development

More than 75 percent of the human race lives in developing countries. About 35 percent live in two developing countries: China and India. Based on estimates by the U.S. Census Bureau, O'Leary and Slyke report that by 2020 the world population is expected to increase to more than 7.5 billion people; more than 90 percent of that growth is estimated to take place in developing countries (2010: 6). By the end of World War II, fewer than fifty countries had claimed independence. The rest of the countries were ruled by colonial states that endeavored to prolong an outmoded imperialist order. The colonized often had to wage a brutal struggle to gain their freedom and independence. The British and the French regimes were central pillars of the colonial system of the twentieth century, but not the only ones. The UN "millennium summit" in New York (September 2000) was attended by 150 heads of independent states.

The demise of colonialism instigated the greatest structural adjustments of governments in history. One after another, as nations declared themselves free of imperial hegemony, they also proclaimed various plans for comprehensive societal change, even when their leaders were uncertain of the type of political, economic, and organizational structures they were forging for their societies. Independence required substantive adjustments in all aspects of life. In a spiral mode, rising expectations fed escalating citizens' demands for improved standards of living. These demands could not be met without considerable investments in national development. The state was the vehicle of choice for initiating and coordinating all elements of the comprehensive development plans. These plans mostly were conceived as blueprints that guide activities and maintain focus as the state implemented developmental policies.

The broad developmental initiatives of the 1950s and 1960s that dominated intellectual debates and influenced applied public policies were often imprecisely referred to as *nation building* or merely *modernization* policies. The concepts of *modernization* and *nation building* have been equated with application of rational control over the physical and social environments of people (Pye 1962; Black 1967; Myrdal 1968). To achieve such control, the effective employment of advanced technology and science was considered essential. These perspectives are premised on (1) acceptance of the nation-state as the prime unit of the polity, (2) commitment to secularism and justice in public affairs (Pye 1962), and (3) recognition that implementation of societal change is most effective when administered by institutions that have the capacity to learn from and adapt to advancements in human knowledge (Chomsky 1994).

By the 1970s, the literature on nation building and modernization was not conveying a consensus of views, but, rather, was presenting growing ethnocentric interpretations. Similarly, strategies for a comprehensive change (relying on global models or grand theories of modernization) were being criticized for lack of definite content, for being "culture and time bound" (Heady 2001), and for "not taking into account the historical, objective background to underdevelopment in the Third World" (Sayigh 1991: 44). But the real limitation of such macro-aggregate models as *nation-building* or Riggs' *Agraria* and *Industria* is their lack of applied operational content and their failure to grasp the concrete reality of the new nations (Jreisat 2005).

Building institutional capacities as instruments of the universal quest for a transformation to modernity has been a centerpiece of the more recent prescriptive models on development. Although with little integration, concepts of institution building, development, capacity, and sustainability have been widely used in the literature, providing more specificity than before. Certain core ideas have also gained common acceptance. For example, developing countries were in need of organizational structures that are more effective and more compatible with requirements of national development. Whereas compatibility includes having greater commitment to developmental values, effectiveness embodies sufficient technical know-how to carry out legitimate mandates. Also, acceptance and support from the political and cultural environment reinforce the effectiveness of developmental policies. In sum, developing countries found themselves in a dire need for different types of institutions from the inherited traditional ones; and their experience indicated that sustained institutional development required certain conditions (Goldsmith 1992: 586).

The apparent convergence in Western literature toward a view of modernity (commensurate with application of science and technology to control the physical and social environment) also presupposed the unfolding of these views within a liberal democratic state. Much of the literature in the West left little doubt about the underlying political form against which all others are measured. The archetype is democracy with its secular, libertarian, competitive, and multiparty structures. In reality, comparative political science scholarship also suggested and actively supported alternative forms of political systems, as long as they were in consonance with the official policies of the Western states. It is important to note that neither prescriptions for reform nor conditions of financial aid by industrial countries have been consistent in advocating democratic political values or demanding effective and accountable governments in developing countries. Tensions in the larger setting of the international system during the Cold War era were more influential in shaping such prescriptions than the actual needs and demands of recipient nations. Thus, Western governments extended aid and support to authoritarian regimes with unquestionable loyalty to Western countries and policies such as the Shah of Iran's regime.

The assumption that development is the application of science and technology within a democratic system presupposes two essential conditions: (1) the presence of instrumental, rationalized administrative institutions, and (2) acceptance of the process of change as fairly universal. This latter point means the process is not necessarily captive to, or even dependent on, notions of cultural and historical particularism. Accordingly, the solution for less developed countries in reaching the stage of modernity is to discover, learn, and faithfully apply the most likely ways and means that worked for certain nations. The World Bank seemed to be in agreement with such premise when, in 1956, with considerable financial assistance from the Ford and Rockefeller foundations, created the Economic Development Institute (EDI)[2] to offer six-month training courses in theory and practice of development for top officials from borrowing countries (Rich 1994: 75).

The critics claimed that Western theories of modernization have served as ideological legitimation for domination of Third World countries (Luke 1990: 212). The argument has been made that as the political and economic power of the United States expanded in the postwar period, so did preeminence of liberal, developmental thought in the form of modernization theory. But, the U.S. social science has also been considered as the product of a collective Cold War mentality, mainly in the service of U.S. policy makers. Academics supplied the doctrine and rationale and found their allies in the ranks of the U.S. Agency for International Development that extended plenty of consulting opportunities (Klaren 1986, 8; Vitalis 1994: 46).

From another perspective, the ideology of development has been considered anti-political. It has been suggested that what is needed in many developing countries is not the dispersion of power, but the centralization of power. Samuel Huntington (1968) suggested that what distinguishes developed from developing countries is the concentration of power and the ability to rule. Both the United States (and the former USSR) developed because there was enough power at the center. Political development, therefore, has nothing to do with democratic development but can be measured by the degree of institutionalization (Huntington 1968; Packenham 1973; Binder 1971). The political systems most conducive to development, according to Huntington, are those represented by the Brazilian military after 1964 and the Pakistani regime under Ayub Khan, a military strongman.

Yet another view considered modernization as "a non-economic process origi-nates when a culture embodies an attitude of inquiry and questioning about how persons make choices—moral (normative), social (or structural), and personal (or behavioral)" as Apter (1965: 10) concluded. He considered choice as central for the modern individual, and self-conscious choice implies rationality. "To be mod-ern means to see life as alternatives, preferences, and choices" (Apter 1965: 10).

Finally, as Mahbub ul Haq (founder of the Human Development Report of the UNDP) pointed out, "Human Development is a development paradigm that is about much more than the rise or fall of national incomes. It is about creating an environment in which people can develop their full potential and lead productive, creative lives in accord with their needs and interests" (Haq 2009: 1). Consequently, recent development initiatives have increasingly become issue-focused, expressing greater concern with immediate issues such as security, poverty, water, environ-ment, infrastructures, employment, and healthcare. While development continues to involve economic growth, other policies of direct impact are regularly elevated to higher national priority.

Development and Legacy of the Past

Remarkably, whatever alternative scenarios of development were played out in the emerging nations, shortly after independence, their citizens' voices and preferences were not an important factor in the choices of policies made for them. Devising and adopting a strategy for development, whether such strategy is of domestic or foreign lineage, has to primarily contend with the impact of previously instated institu-tions and processes as well as the demands of external donors and lenders of funds. Certainly, any developmental strategy during the Cold War era had to be mindful of the machinations of the super powers, which largely shaped prevalent concepts and practices of regimes in the evolving new world of that time.

The legacy of the past, particularly external domination and colonial rule, continued to affect attitudes and outlooks of the developing countries and underline their apprehensions about recurrence of such imbalance in their international relations. Moreover, the colonial experience has always been an element in a psychological legacy of suspicion and distrust of the powerful industrial nations, accused of creating various political, economic, and cultural dislocations within the newly independent nations. Post colonial theories evolved to underline an anti-imperialist formulations based on experiences in the Middle East, Latin America, and Africa that challenged the cultural and theoretical justifications for European domination (Kohn 2010: 216). "Some argued that European civilization was materialist, individualist, and violent, and therefore did not have the moral authority to govern other peoples" (Kohn 2010: 216). The international postcolonial conduct of the powerful states renewed fear and distrust of the various systemic distinctions manifested in dichotomous structuring and grouping among nations such as rich versus poor, Western versus non-Western, and developed versus less developed. External domination is key explanatory concept in the following three distinct postcolonial theories of structuring the international system.

Classic Imperialistic Hegemony

This is where the power of the imperial state (having a superior military force) dominates inferior political entities and reduces them to satellite status. Historical evidence supports this thesis. In modern history alone we find Spain, Portugal, France, England, Russia, and Japan acting as imperial powers at different times in relation to different geographic areas. Today, the United States is referred to as the only or the last superpower, which acts as an imperial force in its relations with countries of the Third World. The U.S. invasion of Iraq in 2003, on false premises, gave credibility to such perception worldwide. Even before the invasion of Iraq "much of the rhetoric of the 'New World Order' promulgated by the American government since the end of the Cold War—with its redolent self-congratulation, its unconcealed triumphalism, its grave proclamations of responsibility ... all too easily produces an illusion of benevolence when deployed in an imperial setting" (Said 1993: xvii).

With global leadership comes global responsibility. After the World War II era, the United States was thrust into the role of global leadership, a task proved to be too complex and challenging. President George W. Bush's decision to invade Iraq in 2003 on foggy justification, without knowing how this will end, and at what human and material cost to both of the United States and Iraq, soon to be followed by the economic disaster of 2008–9—these and other developments generated deep self-doubts inside the United States and distrust of its global leadership abroad. Although the U.S. role of global responsibility has far more initiatives and accomplishments, the invasion of

Iraq remains among the most consequential, deeply embedded in the consciousness of people in the Arab world.

Dependency Theory

This paradigm explains underdevelopment in terms of imbalance in global economic relationships. Simply, economic domination results in dependency, which fosters underdevelopment. The relationship is one of domination and exploitation by the industrial (few center countries) of the many "peripheral," developing countries, regarded as helpless in their acquiescence and dependence (Sayigh 1991: 52). Thus, for the "dependency paradigm," domination is rooted in the structure of the world economy. The restrictive policies and measures applied by industrial countries result in economic disadvantages to developing countries and perpetuate their dependencies. Dependency theory achieved fame in academia and reached to broader audiences in the 1960s. Economists of the Latin American Institute of Economic and Social Planning in Chile proposed these views of development.[3] Numerous publications by Latin American social scientists and others have inspired a lively debate among development economists worldwide.

Debates within the dependency school share certain common grounds, particularly the view that the force of international capitalism is setting up a global division of labor as well as shaping the future of the developing countries. Dependency theorists claim that under the auspices of multinational corporations, capitalism has created a world economic system binding together the globe but, at the same time, perpetuating the dominance of the industrial states. Irrespective, the dependency paradigm has not been able to satisfy some important considerations. Foremost is the inability of the advocates to advance beyond preoccupation with consequences of imperialism (Smith 1985: 114). Also, success stories coming out of certain Asian countries provide convincing evidence of the possibilities of independent development. The progress of several Asian countries such as Taiwan, South Korea, Singapore, Indonesia, and Malaysia has been remarkable, despite past or present subservience to big industrial countries. A spectacular example is South Korea which, by one appraisal, "has achieved more economically in a shorter period of time than any other country in modern history."[4] These cases from Asia challenge the core assumptions of the dependency theory. Finally, as Sayigh (1991: 43) asks: "is dependence still a relevant and useful explanation of underdevelopment in our changing world, when almost all Third World countries have acquired at least the outward and formal trimmings of political independence and sovereignty, and the power of independent economic decision-making?"

Cultural Domination

Political and economic relationships, however determining they may be, do not fully account for the cultural factors and their impacts on society. Cultural relations are not always symmetrical, particularly in the presence of a dominating culture. In *Culture and Imperialism*, Edward Said (1993) explores European writings on Africa, India, parts of the Far East, Australia, and the Caribbean and finds depictions that are part of the general European effort to rule distant lands and people. He also noted that the *Orientalist* description of the Islamic world often reflected similar attitudes and assumptions.

Postcolonial theories in the humanities, social studies, and literature explored various dimensions of the colonial experience. As Margaret Kohn pointed out, it is in works of literature that colonialism is celebrated, justified, repressed, and contested. "The seminal text in the interdisciplinary field of post-colonial studies is Edward Said's *Orientalism*, which was originally published in 1978" (2010: 203). Influenced by poststructuralist theory, Said argued that the Orient was the constitutive outside of the West. The "constitutive outside" describes the way in which a society takes a series of negative characteristics and projects them onto an excluded group, thereby reinforcing a sense of cultural identity. By representing the Orient as irrational, sensual, and violent, colonizers created a set of images to establish their superior rationality. Orientalism, according to Said, produced expert knowledge through studies of linguistics, anthropology, literature, and religion that ultimately served to define, dominate, and restructure the Middle East. Thus, the supposedly disinterested academic study of the Middle East served to support European colonialism and to provide it with the ideological rationale rather than the construction of an objective and neutral scholarship (Kohn 2010: 203; Said 1978).

Certainly the influence of cultural values on a society cannot be denied. Precisely in this area, the comparative perspective can render one of its greatest contributions to knowledge by developing a contextualized approach to development. Culture refers to the totality of all learned social behavior of a given group; it provides standards for perceiving, believing, evaluating, and acting (Thomas 1993: 12). Culture includes knowledge, belief, law, art, religion, morals, customs, habits, symbols, and rules of discourse in a social system. As such, it is shared values and beliefs that mostly evolve and accumulate through time. As Thomas (1993: 4) points out, culture is studied not only to be described but also to be changed. Many cultural elements evolve and are maintained via institutions and structures such as the school, the family, place of work, and place of worship. Culture not only shapes how we view ourselves and how we view others, but it also translates into, and determines, a wide range of attitudes and behaviors. This conception is the most complex to demonstrate or assess, namely, the impact of culture on individual attitudes and behaviors and, indirectly, on institutions and society at large. Still, culture is changeable; and, among the most effective sources of cultural change are education, international exchange, and intercultural communication.

In sum, the domination thesis (military, economic, or cultural) assumes uneven power relations, creating asymmetrical global reality, which largely dictates approaches to development in less powerful countries. Believers invoke plenty of historical evidence in support of such conclusion. European thinkers, for example, pioneered modernization analysis, and European imperialism popularized it, by dictating many of the educational and cultural norms of the former colonies. Actually the dichotomous classification between modern and traditional is itself traceable to European sociologists in the nineteenth century. A prominent early illustration is the German sociologist Max Weber's polar conception of the state's authority system according to legitimacy claims. In his *traditional system,* legitimacy is claimed and accepted on the belief in the sanctity of traditions and the authenticity of the actions by those who exercise authority under them.

In contrast, legitimacy of Weber's *legal-rational system* rests on belief in the rule of law and the right of those elevated to positions of authority under such rules to issue orders and commands. The combined influence of such polar thinking about modernization is reflected in much of American social science writings in the 1950s and 1960s. Sometimes referred to as *developmentalists,* many of these scholars favored integrated, comprehensive global models that offer intellectual synthesis and comparative perspectives on development. Examples of these contributions are: T. Parsons, *The Social System* (1951); D. Lerner, *The Passing of Traditional Society* (1958); W. W. Rostow, *The Stages of Economic Growth* (1960); G. Almond and J. S. Coleman, *The Politics of Developing Areas* (1960); L. W. Pye, *Communications and Political Development* (1963); S. Huntington, *Political Order in Changing Societies* (1968); and others. All viewed modernization in terms of a comprehensive, systemic process in which societies changed fundamentally from the traditional form to an approximation of a modern system.

For many of the early blueprints of development, central planning was the medium of rational application; and, the state accorded itself final responsibility in overseeing the implementation of "successful" planning (Lewis 1966: 1). In the 1980s, *development* replaced *modernization* and *nation-building* in the literature without a universally understood meaning of the term *development* (Heady 2001). In most contexts, development did not require discarding the old or severing relations with the traditional. *Development* evolved to denote a process of renewal through refinement and reform that encompass material, behavioral, and symbolic assets of the society. To endure, however, national development has to be self-reliant, not dependent on foreign sources for support and sustenance.

The corollary question to *what* development should achieve is *how* to achieve it. It is useful, albeit insufficient, to envision development as a constant improvement in the human condition. Milton Esman (1991: 5–6) specifies five important dimensions of development: (1) economic growth, (2) equity, (3) capacity (cultivation of skills, institutions, and incentives), (4) authenticity (distinctive qualities of each society as expressed in its institutions and practices), and (5) empowerment (expanded opportunities for individuals and collectivities to participate in economic and political transactions). Other prescriptions of development criteria or objectives often bear significant similarities. They emphasize elements of rationality, planning, increasing productivity, social and economic equalization, improved institutions and attitudes, national independence, and grass roots participation (Myrdal 1968).

Perhaps, lack of controversy over objectives is a function of what may be described as the "motherhood and apple pie" syndrome. Objectives are too inexplicitly stated to accommodate any chosen position. Disagreement, however, is most relentless in dealing with means and methods of achieving such objectives. Evidence consistently indicates that *what matters is how development is managed and how its benefits and outcomes are distributed among people* (UNDP 1995). Today, the *what* and the *how* of development are regularly accompanied by a question about *who* benefits by it.

Whatever perspective is most salient, developing countries continue to face gaps of knowledge and information in many crucial fields. As Colin Kirkpatrick and Pete Mann concluded: "Unequal access to knowledge across and within countries is seen as an important source of economic inequality and poverty" (1999: 1). The potential power of information technology systems to make governments more efficient and more able to respond and meet their obligations has not been used fully in most countries. Although developing countries may be limited in their abilities to create new knowledge, they have to learn how to utilize existing knowledge in the market place or through education (Thomas 1999: 5). Investing in education and learning, therefore, has never been more indispensable.

In summary, despite diverse, sometimes incongruous, views on how to transform developing countries into modernity, one finds a reasonable fusion of core concepts and policies. Recognizing or agreeing with these core concepts, however, is not the same as ensuring their successful or consistent application. Based on experiences of many developing countries, these conclusions are widely acknowledged:

1. Genuine national development is not based on a priori economic assumptions, but on empirical understanding of local political, administrative, and economic realities.
2. National development is a collective effort that involves the full capacities of private and public institutions, in a partnership.
3. Sustainable development is not totally dependent on capital infusion from external sources, nor limited to export-orientation of the economy. Development is more dependent on self-reliance and on employing processes that address community needs and demands and employ relevant technologies in creative ways to cause an overall improvement of productivity.
4. The development process is qualitatively enhanced when public decisions are transparent and accountability of public officials and institutions is affirmed.
5. Application of scientific and technological methods to achieve growth and increase production is unavoidable.
6. The process of development faces the continuing challenge of transforming institutions and cultures to embody efficiency, orderliness, rationality, and knowledge-based decision processes.

Finally, today's human development concept encompasses producing enabling environment for people to live productive, healthy, and creative lives, and to develop their full potential. Also, development entails sustainability and affirmation that people are the real wealth of a nation.

The Implementation Challenge

Public managers in developing countries are particularly challenged by the complex requirements and needs of managing national development. Conceptually, development management (administration) is regarded as an outgrowth or a subfield of international and comparative administration. Derick Brinkerhoff and Jennifer Coston (1999) view development management as a broadly eclectic applied discipline whose analytic and practical contents reflect four related facets: (1) Development management is a means to improving the efficiency and effectiveness of foreign assistance programs, and to furthering international agencies' policy agendas. (2) It is a toolkit for promoting the application of a range of management and analytical tools adapted from a variety of social science disciplines, including strategic management, organization development, political science, and others. (3) It emphasizes values of self-determination, empowerment, and equitable distribution of development policies. (4) It has an explicitly interventionist orientation, where the application of tools in pursuit of objectives is undertaken in ways that self-consciously address political and values issues (Brinkerhoff and Coston 1999: 349).

Methodologically, development research encounters often a disarray of priorities and methods. Of particular difficulty is that objectives or criteria of development are heavily qualitative, and seem to defy direct measurement. As a result, appraisals of development have been conducted indirectly by using indicators that are directly measurable such as number of trained doctors, literacy rate, child mortality, average life expectancy, per capita income, even percentage of citizens who own cars, televisions, telephones, and radios. Because "no quantitative indicator is capable of exactly measuring a qualitative criterion" (Colman and Nixon 1986: 8), research is limited to approximations of qualitative levels attained in a society. The elements in Myrdal's development criteria cited above illustrate this issue—namely, how to reliably measure or quantify variables such as "rationality" or "social and economic equalization," for example.

Thus, development is multidimensional and resists attempts to measure it through a single-factor. The common reliance on per capita GDP alone is insufficient to measure economic development for many reasons. As Amartya Sen[5] noted in a "Profile" in the *New York Times* (January 9, 1994), per capita GDP "can easily overstate or understate poverty and mislead policymakers."[6]

As a measure, GDP does not adjust for social costs of productivity either (crime, urban sprawl, or safety hazards). Another important limitation of GDP is that it does not even attempt to account for ecological costs of development such as damage to the environment. Nonetheless, per capita GDP continues to be widely used in classifying countries into categories of high, medium, or low income as in The World Bank annual reports. Thus, the most influential indicator of economic growth is narrow, even deficient, but remains the most prevalent for measuring standards of living in a society.

To construct a more balanced and comprehensive coverage, an index that combines several indicators promises greater reliability. An indexed set of indicators that measure economic, social, political, and cultural dimensions of development proved to be a useful instrument, even if in a practical sense using too many indicators would be difficult and costly to manage. The key is to group significant indicators in an index as the *Human Development Index* (HDI), produced annually by the United Nations Development Program (UNDP), since 1990. This Index combines data on indicators in education (adult literacy rate), health (life expectancy at birth), and per capita GDP to define and measure progress in human development.

Compelled by pressures for relevance and persuaded by the methodological promise of more focused middle-range theories, recent literature loosely differentiated three types of development: *economic, political,* and *administrative*. Each employs its own concepts, methodologies, and disciplinary underpinning.

Economic Development

Whereas economic development has generally been equated with growth of per capita output and income, the expectation is that economic development is better served when there is rising productivity, growing employment opportunities, and a diversified economy. Barry Herman pointed out that by the early 1960s, "[T]he physics metaphor was ascendant in economics and development became economic engineering" (1989: 5). Also at this time, national planning was the fashion in Third World countries. This meant direct state investment in selected areas of the economy, or centrally influencing the economy through taxes, subsidies, and regulations. In 1965, the United Nations set up a Committee for Development Planning, composed of prominent international economists, and charged it with elaborating planning techniques to share with developing countries (Herman 1989: 5). Early policies of the World Bank, too, fostered the central planning approach.

Central planning was the most popular instrument of development, particularly that it was expected by donor countries and by institutions such as the United Nations, the World Bank, and lending private establishments. "In the 1950s and 1960s development theorists prescribed long-range, comprehensive, national planning, and centrally controlled, 'top-down' systems of decision making to formulate and implement development policies" (Rondinelli 1982: 44). The purpose of central planning was to improve standards of living in general by selecting, articulating, and specifying a list of projects for implementation within a comprehensive central plan that encompassed all sectors of the economy: agriculture, industry, trade, education, and infrastructure. Some of the methods and procedures were adapted from the practices in private corporations in Western countries (Rondinelli 1982: 46).

Currently, one hears very little about central planning except in the context of attempting to comprehend its failures, as in East Europe and the former Soviet Union. The record of central planning in developing countries also is uneven. Serious trials of comprehensive development planning, often inspired by programs of international financial aid, proved to be illusory. A variety of ailments have been cited as contributing to failure of comprehensive development planning, including poor data, lack of trained staff, inadequate political support, corruption, and poor coordination (Heady 2001; Jreisat 2001; Caiden and Caiden 1977; Palmer et al. 1989). In many countries, these deficiencies resulted in rampant inflation, enormous public debts, and increased bureaucratic rigidity.

During the 1960s and early 1970s, an influential economic perspective of the central planning genre defined development in terms of *linear stages of growth* (W. W. Rostow and others), successive stages through which all countries must pass. Accordingly, countries need only discover the proper mix of savings and investment to enable them to "take off" toward their cherished developmental goals. This mechanical sort of "economic engineering" was to be realized through national planning and capital investment. Criticisms that point out the futility of the stages or the linear approach mounted in the 1970s. Economic growth has always been a core component of national development prescriptions as if all other aspects would not take place or would not matter in the absence of economic improvement. Despite the narrowness of such conception, it is compelling and needs further exploration. Some of the most influential alternative economic perspectives are described in the following paragraphs.

The developmental element in the economic theory advanced by John Maynard Keynes' *The General Theory of Employment, Interest and Money* (1936) has been relevant and effective. Historian Arthur Schlesinger Jr. referred to Keynes as "the economist of the century" (1994: 1). Schlesinger described Keynes' contribution to economics as

> the work that revolutionized modern conceptions both of economic theory and of public policy. It was here that Keynes invented Keynesianism, disproving the classical laissez-faire theory of self-adjusting, self-regulating, self-sufficient market, demonstrating that a free economy was just as likely, perhaps more likely, to reach stable equilibrium at low as at high levels of employment and proposing the fiscal remedies by which the state could set the economy in motion without abolishing the market structure. (1994: 1)

Keynesian economics dominated the contemporary scene in many countries of the West. Keynes' ideas, for example, provided the intellectual backbone of many of the policies that became parts of the New Deal programs of the Roosevelt administration. But, the influence on developing countries has been mostly indirect. In part, Keynes was not much interested in the development of emerging countries. But his ideas of relying on the state as the principal force in achieving economic growth (along with full employment and price and wages stability) served as a rationale for state economic activism. Consistent with Keynesian economics, governments of developing countries established the policy framework for development, enforced investment priorities, regulated, operated major enterprises, and provided a wide range of essential public services from education to transportation (Esman 1991: 7).

During the 1980s, a neoconservative alternative, a countermovement in economic thinking, gained some ground. It features basic "structural adjustment" to free the market, privatize public corporations, and dismantle public ownership of production means and property. It rejected central planning and regulation of economic activities (Todaro 1989: 82). In essence, this economic perspective seeks to minimize the role of the state in the economy by downsizing government. Also, it advocates deregulation and the privatizing of public enterprises and all possible state functions. Ultimate faith is placed in market incentives, which are trusted to produce greater efficiencies and better utilization of resources to achieve growth of the economy (Esman 1991: 9). The growing economic powers of the World Bank and International Monetary Fund (IMF) are major forces behind such macroeconomic policies, sanctioned by large industrial systems, mainly the United States and Britain.

Despite familiar shortcomings and inefficiencies of public sector economic involvement, advocates of the free market as the solution have not satisfied concerns over the subject of welfare economics, and seem to ignore a host of issues stemming from previous market failures. History indicates that economic competition has never been perfect or fair, and that government action often came to pass exactly because of "market failures" that required government to improve efficiency (Mendez 1992: 13) or attain social justice. A good illustration is the economic crisis of 2008 and the role of governments in the United States and in the rest of the world to stimulate growth, create jobs, and regulate financial and economic behaviors. Moreover, the private sector in many developing systems has been ill prepared to assume its responsibilities as envisioned in the restructuring and privatization schemes.

Typically, the choice of a strategy for development implementation is based on a selection of economic assumptions and perspectives, associated with confirmed economic thinking under comparable conditions. A credible strategy specifies the degree of reliance on internal or external resources, lays out the details of commitment to legitimate values of equity, and takes into account existing and potential administrative capacities. But concepts and theories of economic growth still differ on what causes growth and on what methods should be used in measuring its results. It appears that because of these protracted differences, the field of development economics is going through a crisis of confidence and self-doubt (Colman and Nixon 1986: vi), precipitated in part by the increasingly harsh criticisms by radical political economists. Whether we have been observing the demise or the flowering of development economics, serious developmental problems remain unsolved. And this reality alone constitutes a formidable barrier to strategies of development implementation in developing countries.

Development Administration

The national development of an emerging nation inevitably incarnates particular needs and demands that require specific administrative abilities. This type of administration or management, adapted for the particular needs of developing countries, has been referred to as *development administration* or development management (see Chapter 2). Broadly, development administration is an integral part of societal development and is profoundly influenced by the overall political, economic, and cultural attributes of the society. It is the process of formulating and implementing strategies involving policies, plans, programs, and projects aiming at achieving societal improvement and inducing economic growth and social change.

Development administration is a response to particular national needs and is different from administration development, which could be any administration in any setting seeking change or improvement of its capacity. Development administration involves policies, organizations, and processes particularly adapted to the initiation and implementation of development objectives. Although development administration has a specificity that essentially ties it to development in developing countries (though not exclusively), administration development is a universal objective of governance.

At an early phase in its evolution, the comparative public administration movement recognized the particular administrative conditions and needs of developing countries. During the 1960s and 1970s, comparative research and scholarship produced a considerable amount of literature that, for the first time, methodically addressed the administrative systems of developing states. During this period, various field studies were published, employing diverse techniques of description and analysis. Many of these were case studies that enriched the development administration literature and underlined critical issues and challenges facing certain countries. The following list of publications is only an illustration, not an exhaustive account of these early contributions:

- Ralph Braibanti. 1966, *Research on the Bureaucracy of Pakistan*. Describes the history and the various environmental problems influencing the administrative system of Pakistan, concluding with a program for administrative reform in that country.
- Robert T. Daland. 1967, *Brazilian Planning: Development Politics and Administration*. A study of central planning that inquires whether planning is

necessary or desirable in developing countries. Using Brazil as a case study, he concludes that linkage between planning and development is neither direct nor uniformly positive.

▪ Edward W. Weidner, ed. 1970, *Development Administration in Asia*. Includes thirteen articles on various aspects of Asian Development Administration.

▪ Milton Esman. 1972, *Administration and Development in Malaysia: Institutions and Reform in a Plural Society*. Describes the development of administrative capabilities of senior managers through institution-building and administrative reforms.

▪ John D. Montgomery. 1974, *Technology and Civil Life: Making and Implementing Developmental Decisions*. Criticizes Western theories for their preoccupation with macro-development and for not linking technology to redistribution of political power and to serving those most in need.

▪ Philip E. Morgan, ed. 1974, *The Administration of Change in Africa*. Offers a collection of articles on development administration in the African context.

▪ George F. Grant. 1979, *Development Administration: Concepts, Goals, Methods*. Provides a comprehensive text on the subject.

Fred W. Riggs

I single out Fred Riggs from a long list of important early contributors for his leadership role in comparative and development administration. He was a prolific author whose work is so extensive and creative that it has become an area of study by itself. For several years during the 1960s and 1970s, Riggs was the undisputed leader of the comparative and development administration in the United States. He chaired the Comparative Administration Group (CAG), which evolved into the current Section on International and Comparative Administration (SICA) of the American Society for Public Administration (ASPA). His early work focused on development administration and produced certain models and theories that generated worldwide reactions from scholars in the field. Three works merit discussion here.

In *Administration in Developing Countries*, 1964, Riggs presented the concept of "prismatic society" to explain the unique conditions and the dynamics of politics and administration in developing countries. Applying a structural-functional approach and relying on his fieldwork in the Philippines and in Thailand, he constructed a model that has become synonymous with his name. From the outset, Riggs underlines a basic premise of his work: "We lack, indeed, any consensus on what is characteristic of the administrative situation in transitional societies, on possible stages or sequences in the process of administrative transformation, on relationships between administrative change and corresponding processes of political, economic, and cultural development. There is even disagreement on the relation between administration and culture—whether administrative behavior is uniquely determined by particular cultures or correspond to general levels of sociopolitical integration" (1964: 3).

As an alternative model for conceptualizing developing countries, Riggs offered his "prismatic model," based on the metaphor of a prism. When white light (that is, light made up of all visible wavelengths) passes (fused) through a prism, it is diffracted, broken into a variety of colors—a rainbow. Similarly, Riggs contended, societies in the process of development move from a fused mode, in which little or no differentiation exists, to a diffracted condition in which a high degree of functional specialization. In administrative terms, this means a change from a situation in which a few structures performing a variety of functions, as in very underdeveloped conditions, to one in which many specific structures perform specific functions, as in highly developed societies like the industrial countries of the West. When the system begins to assign specific functions to specific structures, then it is evolving into a higher mode of differentiation. This phase is also referred to as transitional to the ultimate position of a complete differentiation.

Most developing societies, however, belong to this intermediate position called transitional, between the fused and the diffracted. Thus, during this transition, societies continually search to attain a higher level of differentiation and to acquire higher levels of specialization among their organizations and workforces. Other related variables, according to Riggs (1964: 31), are universalism and achievement that rank high with the diffracted (differentiated) systems. In contrast, a fused model would be high on particularism and ascription. The prismatic model covers those states in intermediate phase on the continuum.

Thailand: The Modernization of a Bureaucratic Polity (1966) is a case study of political and administrative change in Thailand. In a comprehensive review of the society and its main characteristics, Riggs concluded that the country's weak political structures were unable to provide the necessary control over bureaucracy, which is incapable of modernization on its own.

In *The Ecology of Public Administration* (1961), Riggs relied on his field experiences in Southeast Asia and the United States in formulating his perspective on public administration in developing countries. The newly independent countries, he recognized, have been faced with the problem of reorganizing and adapting their administrative systems to face the challenges of development. The problem is that administrative concepts and techniques evolved in the context of social, economic, and political conditions of Western countries are not fully valid or applicable in the new contexts. Thus, Riggs concluded that differences in social, cultural, historical, or architectural environments affect the way in which administration is conducted. He refers to all these issues of the contexts as "the ecology of administration." Governmental setting "is one of the fundamental determinants of administrative behavior," Riggs pointed out (1961: 4).

In his analysis, Riggs consistently emphasized that the comparative approach is indispensable. By comparing societies, "we begin to discover whether any particular environmental feature is regularly accompanied by some administrative trait" (1961: 3). Through comparisons, he contended, we can sort out from numerous environmental factors those few that have important consequences for the administrative system. Thus, to explain differences between two administrative systems, "we must look for ecological differences."

Overall, the impact of Riggs's work is greater in generating debate, even excitement, in the literature and among students of public administration interested in cross-cultural studies. Riggs has been an involved scholar who provided organizational leadership and direction to the early comparative and development administration movement. But, his work largely remained at the macro level and too concerned with comprehensive and grand models, a task proved to be elusive or less relevant to the immediate needs of societies and practitioners of management. Despite criticisms of his work such as too abstract, less relevant to the practitioner, and lacks convincing empirical evidence, Riggs publications are among the most upheld scholarship in comparative and development administration so far.

Nevertheless, the focus on administration of developing countries was a departure from the ethnocentric traditional public administration and comparative politics of the post World War II era. Although the end of colonialism magnified interest in developing countries in general, comparative and development administration had a singular focus that sought to explore the emerging world with far greater enthusiasm than any time before. Stimulated by generous grants from U.S. foundations and government agencies and motivated by financial and other advantages that were available as a result of the feverish competition of the Cold War, scholarship in comparative public administration flourished. Cross-cultural studies were significantly expanded, often in association with other field research activities covering most newly independent countries. The few references listed above are illustration of the intellectual productivity of this period. A particularly significant aspect of this trend is the integration and the institutionalization of comparative and development administration in the educational systems of the United States and the rest of the world. Courses on comparative and development administration became central parts in many graduate programs in public administration and in training activities. Comparative analysis developed a greater presence in journal articles; it also received increasing coverage in a variety of publication projects, further expanding interest in the subject.

Clearly, comparative and development administration are acknowledged for rejecting insular parochialism of traditional public administration and for raising the banners of cross-cultural research worldwide. How successful these efforts have been is another question altogether. There was a clear commitment in development administration research to establish some determinants of administrative action across national borders. Early development administration was not absorbed or taken over by a single model (the Western model) and then sought to measure the universe against such model. In other terms, comparative and development administration research managed to avoid what Roy Macridis and Bernard Brown attributed to comparative politics, or a phase of it—"determinism, scientism, and correlational studies that have a distinct trait of superficiality" (1990: 8). Indeed, these qualities have typified a substantial strand of political research and continue to the present. Development administration, on the other hand, recognized and internalized the necessity of coming up with practical insights that help application, solve problems, and serve people. As an intellectual enterprise, development administration was always mindful of the need for theory and practice to converge because it will ultimately be judged by its practical and problem-solving thrusts.

Over time, comparative and development administration gained greater intellectual autonomy from political science, became freer to tread where comparative politics did not or would not. Comparative administration expanded its interest in other societies, learning about their formal and informal processes of governance, historical legacies, and behavioral and cultural distinctiveness. Nevertheless, development administration now faces conceptual and practical questions that manifest dissatisfaction with its constraining limitations:

■ Little progress has been made in the implementation of various administrative reform programs that have been pronounced by many developing countries.

■ International organizations (the World Bank, UNDP) are leading the theorizing and restructuring efforts according to a preconceived formula that favors the free market and the private sector and seeks to limit the role of the state.

■ Institutions of higher learning with long tradition of teaching and scholarship in cross-cultural interactions are having difficulty rationalizing a curriculum on cross-cultural issues, building support for it, and justifying it in terms of real careers and job opportunities. Ironically, this is happening when technology and the information revolution are creating new job options, forcing trends toward globalization, and accentuating needs for multinational comparisons.

■ Dissatisfaction with traditional organizational and management concepts and practices induced new management thinking on how to increase economic and technological outcomes and how to measure outputs of programs and projects, hence the New Public Management.

Evidently development administration concepts at the present are at a crossroads. There are few clear directions on the horizon. The Section on International and Comparative Administration (SICA), the oldest section in ASPA, is all but dormant. In the past few years, its handlers seem to have yielded to minor activities, preoccupied with collecting membership fees and making an appearance at the annual ASPA conference. They have neither produced an agenda for research and development nor provided needed leadership in academic programs. Certainly, the current state of research and teaching of comparative and development administration is awfully short of the needs, potential, and demands of global context.

Political-Administrative Nexus of Development

Political development is the process of stimulating the political system and activating its institutions to acquire *increased capacity to satisfy old and new types of goals and demands*. This means the ability to create organizational configurations within the administrative and the political systems to handle whatever demands placed upon them (Heady 2001: 119; Diamant 1966). The advantage of viewing political development in terms of *state capacity of autonomous action* is freeing the discussion from the perpetual compulsion of transforming traditional systems into Western-style democracies. Such efforts at unfettered imitation or cloning have been utterly futile.

The experiences of developing countries during the past several decades indicate that governance problems tend to be more relentless for a variety of reasons, not the least of which is that adept leadership in these countries has been in short supply. While no instant solutions to lack of political development are on the horizon, it is essential that the search continues for alternatives besides those forms applied in the West. Whatever variation is adopted, however, it has to provide more effective governance through improved processes such as devising new linkages with the public, building viable institutions, increasing transparency of decision making, and upgrading methods for holding public officials accountable. The criterion of evaluation then becomes, not how similar to Western practices governing actually is but how effective in achieving national needs and objectives. Such objectives have to include freeing citizens from hunger, disease, ignorance, political oppression, and protecting the environment. Invariably, authentic political development requires the system be genuinely independent from external hegemony and tutelage to derive decisions from local needs and interests.

Closely associated with political development is political participation, a process that appears to be clouded by a continuing transitional definition. Joan M. Nelson distinguishes the older image from the new image of political participation. The older image "reflects the intimate connection between the concept of participation and the concept of democracy" (Nelson 1987: 103). Indeed, within this image participation is conceived almost entirely in democratic contexts and is deemed suspect or unbelievable in other settings. A more recent alternative image decouples the concepts of participation and democracy. Such new efforts seek to encompass broader intellectual concerns over a wider geographic and temporal range. In this image, Nelson (1987: 104) concluded: "participation is simply the efforts of ordinary people in any type of political system to influence the actions of their rulers, and sometimes to change their rulers."

Scholarship in 1960s and 1970s on political development conveys contentiousness over what happened, and over what should have happened, in Third World countries. As Weiner noted, adequacy assessments of the widely recognized U.S. scholarship on political development indicate inability to anticipate or explain many of the changes in the Third World (1987: xxv). Unable to be free of cultural and political biases and driven by predetermined methodological processes, such contributions often lost the campaign for relevance. In contrast to early economic development that advocated the creation and distribution of wealth rather than its aggregation, political development often appeared more concerned with the aggregation of power to achieve political order and stability, democratic or otherwise (Huntington 1987: 5). In fact, authoritarian central controls became quite common, and in many countries, the military happily obliged by providing an authoritarian style of governance, whether the people wanted it or not.

Thus, the fundamental questions remain: Is administrative development detached from political development? And does bureaucracy exert a hobbling effect on political development?

Certainly, the political-administrative relationship proved to be more complex than expected, involving too many variables and resisting any absolute conclusions. It is commonly recognized that administration takes place in various settings and *public* administration operates in a political one. In societies with low differentiation among legitimate functions and responsibilities, there is often free overlapping, meddling, and mutual accommodations between administrative and political structures. Thus, despite recognition of the many distinctive operational components of politics and administration, they remain closely associated. By the same token, they are as tangled in the design as they are accountable for the outcomes of national development plans.

The issue of bureaucracy and democracy has been visited in Chapter 3. As I indicated earlier, bureaucracy is a primary unit of analysis and a basic, universal structure of contemporary governance. But we would be mistaken to assume there is only one monolithic bureaucratic structure that may be exported ready-made for operating in any environment. Some scholars note that the form that has been exported to developing countries is inconsistent with democratic values functioning in the West. Abdo Baaklini pointed out that "development theories in general and development administration in particular did not benefit from the rich intellectual history of the field in America" (2001: 2). His conclusion: the type of development administration that has been exported to developing countries since World War II is not necessarily a reflection of Western democratic values. What was promoted either directly under the various bilateral programs of the U.S. government, or under the aegis of the United Nations, was an "abstraction" of the American experience. In this abstraction, the democratic environment was deemed tentatively irrelevant at best or totally harmful and anti-developmental at worst. Thus, the ideology of development consciously or unconsciously is an anti-political ideology despite the often-repeated caveat that this is only in the short run (Baaklini 2001).

In Chapter 3, I also indicated that Riggs (2001) formulated the "imbalance thesis" in which he took the position that bureaucratic power and efficiency have contributed to a lack of political development in emerging societies. The apparent centralizing tendencies of development ideologies are interpreted differently by different people. No doubt, neither American foreign policy nor American foreign aid programs during the Cold War era were enthusiastic advocates of developing democratic political institutions and processes in many developing countries. In fact, the evidence is to the contrary. Too many examples illustrate that what took place often resulted in instituting and nurturing dictators who governed in absolute and undemocratic systems as in the case of the Shah of Iran or the variety of dictatorships that continue to receive American protection and support. Under these conditions, the administrative systems could not be anything but reflections of their political contexts.

On the other hand, social science scholarship, regardless of the approach recommended, considers bureaucracies the best and the most objective instruments for achieving development (Illchman 1965). Some authors went as far as to advocate the advantage of military bureaucracies as instruments for development (Johnson 1972; Huntington 1968; Janowitz 1964). These theories, however, rarely discussed whose goals and values bureaucracy should realize and whether bureaucracy can be kept accountable. But comparative public administration has always been concerned with the impact of political authority and political culture on administrative performance. In fact, among the major themes of debate in comparative literature of the early 1960s, were the subjects of power, efficacy, and politics of bureaucracy.

The primacy of political control over administration is not questioned here, irrespective of the level of effectiveness in exercising it. It is a common knowledge that in many developing countries, political leaders have kept very tight rein on all powers of the state, particularly those related to public funds and military control. Actually, "the political features of the state also gave the administrative process many of its current attributes: highly centralized, beset by nepotism and political patronage, and burdened by its own weight of swelled ranks of ill-trained public employees" (Jreisat 1997: 227). Under these political forms and processes, professional management with neutral competence is hard to sustain.

Inescapably, then, administrative reform has become contingent on attitudes of the political leadership and the degree of its support for reform. What elements of the bureaucracy may be changed? How much citizen participation in public decision making is allowed, and how are different opinions dealt with? Who is to benefit by reforms? Beyond studying regime types, it is essential to define under what conditions regime's support is possible. The alternative is committing huge budgets and extensive efforts to changes incompatible with existing political authority and hence with little chance of implementation.

A current, optimistic view is counting on the reemergence since the 1980s of democratic institutions in most countries, a reemergence that has shaken the self-righteousness of public administration and its superior rationality, even if it has not completely eliminated it (Baaklini 2001). Realistically, this perspective acknowledges the fact that newly established democracies are still facing many formidable challenges to their ability to place their administrative institutions under appropriate and effective democratic controls. Crucial challenges remain.

- Political corruption stretches out to include politicians and legislatures, who are viewed as being preoccupied with self-serving, narrow interests rather than with the general public interest. The public distrusts the political process.
- Many legislatures have only a poor ability to undertake any effective oversight of bureaucracy or to initiate strategic public policies. The public and the bureaucracy know that legislative bodies in their countries are rarely freely elected, and thus have only nominal moral authority.
- The redefinition of the role of the private sector in society and the blitz of a global economy place bureaucracies in many developing countries in difficult positions. Trying to adjust to their new redefined roles and to implement reformulated public policies, bureaucracies face a great deal of uncertainty and a lack of political support. It is not surprising, however, that citizens of many developing countries seem to place primary blame for their economic and social problems on their politicians and legislatures. They conclude that bureaucratic influence is largely a result of political weakness rather than a cause of it.

Public Administration Traits in Developing Countries

Despite the dismal results of many national development plans, many developing countries face an ongoing need to build institutions and organizations with abilities to overcome traditional barriers to effective implementation of developmental policies. The creation and use of these abilities have always been primary challenges of development administration. The absence and breaking down of these abilities have often been major factors in development administration's failure to meet satisfactory levels of performance. As a result, development administration has not fared well in some critical areas, such as the conception of an inspiring, compatible vision and managing effectively to achieve this vision. In utilizing modern techniques, development administration, for example, seems to lag behind the private sector in leveraging technology to improve internal operations and to enhance the overall effectiveness of development organizations.

Unable to attain a timely correction of its deficiencies or to learn from its failures, development administration largely remains burdened by a combination of inherited structures and behaviors and deeply internalized local cultural patterns. This combination of legacies has had the effect of impeding performance and wasting badly needed institutional energies on other than productive endeavors to accomplish developmental mandates. One finds a high measure of concurrence

Table 6.1   Traits of Administrative Systems of Developing Countries

Fred Riggs	Ferrel Heady	Others
Overlapping and heterogeneity Formalism Diffusion Particularism Ascription	Imitation rather than indigenous Deficiency of skills Nonproduction-oriented bureaucracy Formalism Autonomy	Overstaffed public organizations Underpaid public employees Low productivity Lack of innovative and skilled public managers Excessively centralized decision making Corruption Administration mirrors the political context

in the literature when searching to identify and to define typical problems and characteristics of these administrative systems. The three clusters (summarized in Table 6.1) describe general attributes of public administration in developing countries:

1. Those attributes defined by Fred Riggs (1964: 13–15, 31) as characterizing transitional systems seeking modernization:
   - *Overlap and heterogeneity.* The administrative system in a developing country gives an illusory impression of autonomy, whereas in fact it is deeply enmeshed in and cross-influenced by remnant of older traditional social, economic, religious, and political systems. Thus, to understand public administration in a heterogeneous social system, one must also study "overlapping" interrelationships.
   - *Formalism.* Forms in developing countries do not always represent reality. Laws passed by legislators are not enforced by the administration, necessitating more rules, which remain as formalistic as the previous ones.
   - *Diffusion.* This is an attribute of a low level of differentiation (or no differentiation) of administrative structures and functions: Everybody is doing everything. The opposite of diffusion—as used by Riggs—is diffraction, where structures of the system are specific and perform particular functions. Here, the system becomes differentiated, and the processes are universal and achievement-oriented. Thus, diffusion is low differentiation—a characteristic of underdevelopment.
   - *Particularism and ascription.* Administration in developing countries tends to apply rules variably according to family connections, wealth, and influence rather than uniformly according to universal rule.

2. A cluster of common administrative patterns typical of administration in developing countries, according to Heady (2001: 299–302):

   ■ *Imitation rather than development of indigenous public administration.* This refers to the conscious effort to imitate some version of modern Western bureaucratic administration or to introduce it into developing countries.

   ■ *Bureaucracies deficient in skilled workers necessary for developmental programs despite high levels of unemployment.* Bureaucracies in developing countries face shortages of trained managers with technical and managerial capabilities.

   ■ *Bureaucracies that are not production-oriented.* Much of bureaucratic activities are channeled toward the realization of goals other than program objectives.

   ■ *Formalism.* A widespread discrepancy between form and reality.

   ■ *Bureaucracies with generous amounts of operational autonomy.* This is the result of several factors, including lack of transparency and poor institutional control.

3. A cluster is derived from an examination of administrative systems of several developing countries, with special reference to the Arab states, confirming some of the characteristics suggested by Riggs and Heady, though with some different emphases. A number of studies have assessed implementation and outcomes of proposed reforms of administration in the contemporary Arab societies, and provided appraisals (Ayubi 1989; Jabbra 1989; Palmer, Leila, and Yassin 1988; Jreisat 1997; 1988). These are some the reported attributes of bureaucracies:

   ■ *Overstaffed public organizations whose employees are underpaid and whose productivity is low.* The growth of bureaucracies in most Arab states has been excessive without commensurate improvements of public services. The magnitude and the type of growth in public employment indicate that the bulk of expansion is at the central offices and not at the local government; the growth is also in the "conventional" rather than "developmental" jobs. Except for major oil-producing countries, in most Arab states, public employment is an opportunity to have a job in countries with chronically high unemployment rates, as in Egypt. The state has always been the largest employer, and its hiring practices aimed at meeting minimum standards rather than seeking the most qualified applicant. In most of these states, wages as well as expectations of productivity are kept perennially low (Jreisat 1999: 29–30).

   ■ *Innovative and skilled public managers in short supply.* Arab bureaucracies lack innovative skills, partly because of low wage structures and poor incentives. Even where financial incentives are no problem, as in oil producing countries, innovation has been low (Palmer, et. al. 1989: 25).

- *Excessive centralized decision making.* Senior managers are reduced to a clerical class thoughtlessly enforcing higher commands.
- *Political and administrative corruption regularly impeding reform.* Corruption commonly involves the misuse of authority for considerations of personal gain, monetary or otherwise. Similarly, corruption involves unethical conduct by public employees and intentional violation of the professional norms of public service. Causes of corruption, however, cannot be definitively decided. Poor pay, inadequate fringe benefits, weak commitment to the state or to the party in power, lack of monitoring and control of public officials, and the culture of the society have all been blamed for rampant corruption in modern governments.
- *Administrative structures, mirroring the political context, that have not adapted to the urgent need for inclusive decision-making processes.* Public employees have not experienced involvement and participation that induce them to improve their performance. Moreover, citizens (at least those directly affected) are not included in deliberations of policies that shape their lives and affect their futures.

These typical patterns of development administration survive as long as the political and cultural contexts have not embraced or internalized fundamental principles of a *civil society*, a term that has been used to denote the rule of law, property right, and human rights. Also, wherever the state is highly centralized and dominant in the economy through direct ownership or excessive regulations, the nongovernmental sector has been generally stymied, its functions limited, and its competitiveness constrained. But, during the past few years, most nations have been attempting to correct traditional shortcomings by adopting more decentralized political and administrative systems, employing more trained workforce, and paying more attention to human rights issues as well as to matters of global concern such as migration, environment, security, and healthcare. Comparative analysis and continuing internationalization trends in public administration have enforced these tendencies (Jreisat 2005). Universal values are stimulating new needs for administrative knowledge and skills, thus the distinctiveness of development administration has been diminishing in the face of increasing internationalization of management and the growing emphases on universal needs and values for public administration.

References

Apter, D. E. 1965. *The Politics of Modernization.* Chicago: University of Chicago Press.
Ayubi, N. 1989. Bureaucracy and development in Egypt today. In *Bureaucracy and Development in the Arab World,* ed. Jabbra, J. G. pp. 62–78. New York: E. J. Brill.
Baaklini, A. I. 2002. Administration in developing countries and the democratic challenge. In *Governance and Developing Countries,* ed. Jreisat, J. E. 57–70. Leiden, The Netherlands: Brill.

Binder, L., et al. 1971. *Crises and Sequences in Political Development*. Princeton, NJ: Princeton University Press.

Black, C. E. 1967. *The Dynamic of Modernization: A Study in Comparative History*. New York: Harper & Row.

Braibanti, R.1966. *Research on the Bureaucracy of Pakistan*. Durham, NC: Duke University Press.

Brinkerhoff, D., and J. Coston 1999. International development management in a globalized world. *Public Administration Review* 59 (4): 346–361.

―――― and N. J. Caiden. 1977. Administrative corruption. *Public Administration Review*. 37 (3): 301–309.

Chomsky, Noam. 1994. *World Orders Old and New*. New York: Columbia University Press.

Colman, D., and F. Nixon. 1986. *Economics of Change in Less Developed Countries*. 2nd ed. Totowa, NJ: Barnes & Noble Books.

Daland, R. T. 1967. *Brazilian Planning: Development Politics and Administration*. Chapel Hill, NC: University of North Carolina Press.

Diamant, A. 1966. Political development: Approaches to theory and strategy. In *Approaches to Development, Politics, Administration, and Change*, ed. Montgomery, J. D. and W. J. Siffin, 15–58, New York: McGraw-Hill.

Esman, Milton 1991. *Management Dimensions of Development: Perspectives and Strategies*. West Hartford, CT: Kumarian Press.

――――. 1972. *Administration and Development in Malaysia: Institutions and Reform in a Plural Society*. Ithaca, NY: Cornell University Press.

Goldsmith, A. 1992. Institutional and planned socioeconomic change: Four approaches. *Public Administration Review*, 52 (6): 582–587.

Grant, G. 1979. *Development Administration: Concepts, Goals, Methods*. Madison: University of Wisconsin Press.

Haq, M. 2009. *The Human Development Concept*. Human Development Report, United Nations Development Program, 1–2. http://hdr.undp.org/en/humandev/ (visited 10-27-2010).

Heady, Ferrel. 2001. *Public Administration: A Comparative Perspective*. 6th ed. New York: Marcel Dekker.

Herman, B. 1989. The outlook of development, In *Debt Disaster? Banks, Governments, and Multinationals Confront the Crisis*. New York: New York University Press.

Huntington, S. 1987. The goals of development. In *Understanding Political Development*. eds. M. Weiner, M., and S. P. Huntington, New York: Harper Collins.

――――. 1968. *Political Order and Change in Societies*. New Haven: Yale University Press.

Illchman, Warren. 1965. Rising expectations and revolution in development administration. *Public Administration Review* 25 (4): 314–328.

Jabbra, J. G. 1989. Bureaucracy and development in the Arab World. *Journal of Asian and African Studies*, xxiv (1–2): 1–12.

Janowitz, M. 1968. *The Military in New Nations*. Chicago: The University of Chicago Press.

Johnson, J., ed. 1972. *The Role of the Military in Underdeveloped Countries*. Princeton, NJ: Princeton University Press.

Jreisat, J. E. 2005. Comparative public administration is back in, prudently. *Public Administration Review* 65 (2): 211–222.

_____. 2001. Bureaucratization of the Arab world: Incompatible influences. In *Handbook of Comparative and Development Public Administration,* 2nd ed., ed. A. Farazmand, 1007–1018. New York: Marcel Dekker.

_____. 1999. Comparative public administration and reform. *International Journal of Public Administration* 22 (6): 855–877.

_____. 1997. *Politics Without Process: Administering Development in the Arab World.* Boulder, CO: Lynne Reinner.

_____. 1988. Administrative reform in developing countries: A comparative perspective. *Public Administration and Development.* 8 (1): 85–97.

Keynes, J. M. 1949. *The General Theory of Employment, Interest and Money.* London: Macmillan.

Kirkpatrick, C., and P. Mann. 1999. Knowledge, training and development: An overview. *Public Administration and Development* 19, 1 (February).

Klaren, P. F. 1986. *Promise of Development.* Boulder, CO: Westview Press.

Kohn, M. 2010. Post-colonial theory. In *Ethics and World Politics,* ed. Bell, D. 200–218, Oxford, UK: Oxford University Press.

Lewis, A. W. 1966. *Development Planning.* New York: Harper & Row.

Luke, T. W. 1990. *Social Theory and Modernity: Critique, Dissent, and Revolution.* Newbury Park, CA: Sage.

Macridis, R. C., and B. E. Brown, eds. 1990. Comparative analysis: Method and concept. In *Comparative Politics: Notes and Readings,* 7th ed. Belmont, CA: Wadsworth.

Mendez, R. P. 1992. *International Public Finance: A New Perspective on Global Relations.* New York: Oxford University Press.

Montgomery, J. D. 1974. *Technology and Civil Life: Making and Implementing Developmental Decisions.* Cambridge, MA: The MIT Press.

Morgan, E. P., ed. 1974. *The Administration of Change in Africa.* NY: Dunellen.

Myrdal, G. 1968. *Asian Drama: An Inquiry into the Poverty of Nations* New York: Pantheon.

Nelson, J. M. 1987. Political participation. In *Understanding Political Development,* eds. Weiner, M. and S. P. Huntington. New York: Harper Collins.

O'Leary, R., and D. M. V. Slyke. 2010. Introduction to the symposium on the future of public administration in 2020. *Public Administration Review.* Supplement to Vol. 70 (December): 5–11.

Packenham, R. 1973. *Liberal America and the Third World.* Princeton, NJ: Princeton University Press.

Palmer, M., A. Leila, and E. Yassin. 1988. *The Egyptian Bureaucracy.* Syracuse, NY: Syracuse University Press and The American University in Cairo Press.

Palmer, Monte, et al. 1989. Bureaucratic innovation and economic development in the Middle East: A study of Egypt, Saudi Arabia, and the Sudan. In *Bureaucracy and Development in the Arab World,* ed. Jabbra, J. G. pp. 12–27. New York: E. J. Brill

Pye, L. W. 1962. *Politics, Personality, and Nation Building: Burma's Search for Identity.* New Haven, CT: Yale University Press.

Rich, B. 1994. *Mortgaging the Earth: The World Bank, Environmental Improvement, and the Crisis of Development.* Boston: Beacon Press.

Riggs, F. W. 1961. *The Ecology of Public Administration.* New York: Asia Publishing.

Riggs, F. W. 1964. *Administration in Developing Countries.* Boston, MA: Houghton Mifflin.

Riggs, F. W. 1966. *Thailand: The Modernization of a Bureaucratic Polity.* Honolulu: East-West Center Press.

Riggs, F. W. 2001. Bureaucratic links between administration and politics. In *Handbook of Comparative and Development Administration.* A. Farazmand, ed. New York: Marcel Dekker.

Rondinelli, D. A. 1982. The dilemma of development administration: Complexity and Uncertainty in control-oriented bureaucracies. *World Politics.* Vol. XXXV (1): 43–72.

Said, E. W. 1978. *Orientalism.* New York: Vintage Books.

Sayigh, Y. A. 1991. *Elusive Development: From Dependence to Self-Reliance in the Arab Region.* London: Routledge.

Schlesinger, A., Jr. 1994. The economist of the century. *New York Times Book Review.* (January 23).

Smith, T. 1985. The dependency approach. In *New Directions in Comparative Politics*, ed. Howard, H. J., Boulder, CO: Westview Press.

Thomas, J. 1993. *Doing Critical Ethnography.* Qualitative Research Methods Series, no 26. Newbury Park, CA: Sage.

Thomas, V. 1999. Globalization: Implications for development learning. *Public Administration and Development* 19 (1): 5–17.

Todaro, M. P. 1989. *Economic Development in the Third World, 4th ed.* NY: Longman.

UNDP. 1995. *Human Development Report.* NY: Oxford University Press.

Vitalis, R. 1994. The Democratization Industry and the Limit of the New Interventionism. *Middle East Report.* 24: pp. 187–188.

Weidner, E., ed. 1970. *Development Administration in Asia.* Durham, N.C.: Duke University Press.

Weiner, M. 1987. Introduction to Understanding Political Development. In *Understanding Political Development*, M. Weiner and S. Huntington, eds. NY: Harper Collins.

Endnotes

1. Quoted in Diamant, A. 1966. Political development: Approaches to theory and strategy. In *Approaches to Development, Politics, Administration, and Change.* Montgomery, J. D., and W. J. Siffin, eds. 15–58, New York: McGraw-Hill. P. 15.
2. Bruce Rich (1994: 76) indicates that in subsequent years EDI expanded its offerings to include more practical instruction on the World Bank techniques for project appraisal and country programming. More than 1,300 officials participated and many of them have risen to the position of prime minister or minister of planning or finance in their respective countries.
3. This was a UN organization which originated from the Economic Commission for Latin America (ECLA).
4. *Business Week.* 31 July 1995, p. 57.
5. Amartya, Sen. Profile. *The New York Times.* January 9, 1994. p. 8F.
6. *Developing countries* is the preferred designation instead of terms such as *less developed, underdeveloped, emerging,* or *poor countries.*

Chapter 7

Administration of Developed Systems

> We are in a new era. Today we have to deal with those problems we inherited from that time: the boom-and-bust economics, the social division, the chronic under-investment in our public service.
>
> **British Prime Minister Tony Blair,**
> **marking the tenth anniversary of**
> **Margaret Thatcher's departure from office**[1]

Checking Central Powers, Building Institutions

Advanced, developed, or industrial democracies are common designations denoting a group of countries that include Canada, Europe, Japan, and the United States. Among other attributes, each of these countries has a governance system that is relatively effective in making and implementing public policies. Generally, these countries also have a high consonance between adopted public policies and society's needs and demands. Citizens actively participate in governance, usually through constitutionally established and maintained privileges. The enforcement of public policy is assigned to institutions that are legally entitled to make decisions and that have the ability to act on them.

For a variety of reasons, developed countries enjoy higher overall standards of living than most others. Their citizens generally have higher levels of income, better health care, higher literacy rate, and equal protection under the law. Benefitting from the use of sophisticated and regularly refined technologies for production and for the delivery of services, these countries manage to consistently increase the outputs of their organizations and to augment their managerial efficiencies.

What administrative concepts and practices are commonly employed in industrial countries and how they evolved are subjects of universal relevance, irrespective of levels of development. To understand how administrative systems of developed countries have been instrumental in reaching fairly high levels of performance, one has to examine, broadly and retrospectively, institutions as well as the prevalent systems of governance. Generally, public administration literature passes over the tasks of creating a sense of tradition and of viewing institutions and societies as constantly evolving. Although this discussion is not intended to be an exhaustive analysis of this aspect of industrial systems, it is an attempt to highlight critical events that left indelible marks on their institutions and processes of governance.

Contemporary literature extends a measured recognition that the European practices of the seventeenth century were the precursors to the emergence of modern bureaucracies. The seventeenth and eighteenth centuries were a foundational phase and are excellent sources of information on administrative structures and the influences that shaped them. Early in the seventeenth century, power drew away from the provinces and localities of Europe and became concentrated in the central government, requiring the active aid and development of administration and finance (Gladden 1972: 141). During this time, Germany led the West in "professionalizing" the public service. Government activities and services expanded, creating a need for appointees with particular knowledge and skills. Prussia had the distinction of being the first modern state to introduce and develop a system of entrance examinations for the public service (Gladden 1972: 158, 163)

At an early phase, the need became quite clear for education and specialized training in the skills necessary for managing government operations. The German state took the initiative to ensure that suitable instruction was available at the universities. As early as 1727, Frederick William established a chair in *Cameralism* at two German universities to give instruction in efficient administration. By 1808 an aristocratic regulative bureaucracy had replaced the royal autocracy of king and council. The career bureaucrats were invariably selected from the intellectual elite of the nation by means of rigorous examinations. This created a sort of aristocracy of experts who claimed to be true representatives of the general interest (Gladden 1972: 165).

Between 1650 and 1850, the West experienced significant political and economic upheaval that resulted in reexamination and restructuring of its administrative systems. Historically, the West experienced revolutions against the *status quo*; but soon the consequences became far-reaching and universal. The English Revolution of 1688, the American Revolution of 1776, and the French Revolution of 1789 preceded the industrial revolution, which produced far-reaching consequences by the early twentieth century. The single and the collective impacts of these historical events have been profound political, economic, and administrative changes, reaching far beyond any one country (Jreisat 1997: 13).

A revolution is the subversion and the abandonment of the *status quo* for the promise of a better alternative. Thus, these British, French, and American political revolutions did more than usher in dazzling political alternatives. They also laid the foundations of the "organizational society" as we know it and advanced modern values such as reason, liberation, and egalitarianism. By official design as well as a consequence of new socioeconomic realities, formal organizations and professional management became indispensable for the new states. Organizations, as newly invigorated social structures, and professional management, which had gained more autonomy in practicing their specialized craft, both became the trusted enforcers of public decisions. These public decisions have already become bound to the public will rather than to the ruler's personal authoritarian commands. Thus, the representation of societal interests rather than individual wants in public decisions finally was inescapable.

The French Revolution was driven by hungry citizens who revolted against the whole sinking political and economic structure of privileges and monopolies granted by the king. This revolution made it the duty of government to provide for welfare of the people. It transformed the nature of politics and administration by the dramatic introduction of notions such as *citizen, rights, liberty, equality,* and *justice* (Jreisat 1997: 14).

The American Revolution, on the other hand, was managed differently by men of different outlooks and experiences. As the common wisdom had it, these men sought to reflect the Anglo-Saxon tradition, particularly the political and economic ideas of John Locke, David Hume, and Adam Smith. However, contemporary historians and researchers are finding evidence that ideas borrowed from native peoples and their influence on European immigrants to America goes much deeper than has been acknowledged. In all of this, the American experience made the autonomy and will of the individual paramount no matter what final political and economic designs were to be forged.

By the middle of the nineteenth century, the feudalistic economic order dissolved and commercialism emerged, followed by the Industrial Revolution. As commercialism expanded, new urban centers took shape. Power struggles intensified for seaways, colonization of other peoples and territories, and domination of world trade. Western imperialistic expansions affected almost every area of the known world, particularly Asia and Africa.

Comparative analysis of this early period indicates that many important philosophical and practical changes were in the making. In England, the birth of constitutionalism inhibited the arbitrary rule of the Crown and instituted the supremacy of the Parliament. In France, the attack on the excessive central authority set the stage for new centralized structures, such as those governing local authorities initiated during the Napoleonic period. In both France and England, the orientation as well as the structures of public institutions was dramatically altered. Managing the affairs of the state in the context of the new political and economic realities required different levels of skill, commitment, and values. Moreover, political and economic events left distinct prints on public administration. The abolition of the absolute monarchy, and the transfer of power to a liberal constitutional state, meant that government's primary role became the protection of rights and liberties such as the right of property, free-market capitalism, and individual human rights. The state became law-based, and its main functions became the making and enforcing of laws. Thus, the study of public administration shifted to the study of administrative law. Lawyers replaced managers as "the elite" in upper and middle ranks of government (Kickert and Stillman 1996: 65).

The predominance of law in the French liberal state of the nineteenth century emphasized guarantees of citizens' rights and limits on state power but it "eclipsed social science-based public administration" (Chevallier 1996: 67). Still, the state continued to expand its functions and interventionist approach to serve functions of economic regulation and redistributive social equity. The increase of the state's interventionist powers inevitably provided the appropriate conditions for the rapid emergence and indispensability of public administration for the effectiveness of state actions. It might seem, therefore, that the growth and independence of public administration were uncontested. In reality, administrative law studies continued to compete with and to rival public administration in France and throughout the European systems. During the 1960s, France experienced "a spectacular growth of studies claiming to draw their inspiration from administrative science," as Chevallier (1996: 69) points out. He concluded that, in reality, French administrative knowledge has been enriched by a variety of approaches, and he singled out three models in existence today (1996: 69):

■ A legal model, whose essential goal is to arrive at a better knowledge of the structures and functioning of public administration while emphasizing the reference to legal texts
■ A managerial model, which is geared toward finding and implementing the most efficient management techniques and intended to go beyond the public-private split
■ A sociological model, which aims to improve the understanding of administrative phenomena with the aid of sociological concepts and methods

The structure of the British model of governance changed infrequently over the twentieth century. A constitutional arrangement reduced the powers of the monarch to defined ceremonial duties. Executive powers are concentrated in the office of the prime minister and in the cabinet; legislative powers reside mainly in the Parliament. By the end of the nineteenth century, the British system had refined the merit system for the recruitment and retention of civil servants. The civil service system evolved and came to be organized around clearly demarcated classes of employees: clerical, executive, and administrative. The contemporary administrative class provides the leadership expected with traditional neutrality towards the competition of political partisans. Another significant feature in the modern British system is the Treasury's role in handling a variety of civil service functions (that is, until the early 1980s when some of these functions were placed under the prime minister).

The British public administration "is still more that of a North American satellite than a core European State" (Pollitt 1996: 81). During the 1980s, an unmistakable movement at the political level sought radical change of the administrative structures and functions. The government emphasized economy and efficiency, required improvements in financial skills of public officials, stressed the importance of evaluation, and created new national audit bodies to perform duties beyond traditional audit. Moreover, as Barzelay pointed out, in negotiating with public service unions, the government was able to produce settlements that were much more consistent with cash limits than thought possible (2001: 24). "The government's stance in these negotiations appears to have been of considerable significance in controlling the growth of public expenditure" (Barzelay 2001: 25). These changes dictated shifts in public organizational cultures, according to Pollitt (1996: 83), to particularly serve three objectives:

- A new, output-oriented, cost conscious, decentralized public service.
- A customer-focused public service
- A reduced role of government in favor of privatization

The British program of the 1980s for reforming the public sector has often been referred to as Prime Minister Margaret Thatcher's program because of her leadership during its implementation, even if its main ideas were not hers. The program has received a great deal of praise, and no less criticism and skepticism. Among Thatcher's widely publicized changes is the creation of machinery at the center of government, staffed by people closely identified with her, to oversee management improvement. This measure was viewed as deepening disharmony between her and the civil service, particularly after the introduction of the Financial Management Initiatives (FMI), which was followed by scrutiny of the efficiency of government departments. Civil servants perceived this as her attempt to replace neutral, disinterested civil servants with outsiders who have her ideology of economic liberalism (Mascarenhas 1993: 322). Also, the change meant she relied less on the Treasury and the Civil Service Department, which she abolished in 1981, turning back some of its functions to the Treasury (Barzelay 2001: 26).

The verdict on Thatcher's program, several years after its inauguration, is mixed and increasingly critical. A combination of factors has contributed to the negative assessments. One is that attitudes and organizational cultures proved to be more resilient than anticipated. Another, that the opposition viewed Prime Minister Thatcher's actions as primarily motivated by ideological impulses as by pragmatic considerations of change. The final effects of these changes is to separate policy making from service delivery. Policy making is to be concentrated in central offices where skills and leadership capacities have been enhanced, and service delivery is to be directed towards appropriate lower levels of organization. All this is subject to new emphasis on accountability through measured results. In the end, opposing forces saw her partisanship not only as pro conservatism but also as anti-public sector and anti-welfare state as well as anti labor. These perceptions seem to have culminated in significant resistance to her program, or in reciprocity of disdain between her and the opposition.

Impact of Science and Rationalism

The industrial revolution sharpened, refined, and rationalized the managerial concepts and practices to serve capitalist objectives, particularly maximization of capital returns on investments. The new organizational focus turned to rational theories that emphasize science, technology, and improved managerial practices. Thus, the organization became more confirmed as a socio-technical instrument, essential for the attainment of big objectives such as those envisioned by entrepreneurs and political leaders with expansionist views of the roles of their countries. In Europe, the evolution of the state and the development of public administration have been closely linked (Kickert and Stillman 1996: 65). In Germany and France, the expansion of state functions was followed by an increase in the number of public employees and a growing complexity of government responsibilities.

Still, no other conceptual framework captured the spirit of the time and acquired as much following as Max Weber's bureaucratic model, which approximated Western systems in depicting their legal-rational systems of authority. Variations of this model permeated Western countries over the years. The bureaucratic model achieved almost universal acknowledgment and acceptance within capitalist economic orders.

Other frameworks followed, extending, negating, criticizing, or modifying the bureaucratic model. Administrative management, human relations in its various subsidiaries, systems analysis, decision-making models, the New Public Administration, and most recently the New Public Management—all were efforts to devise most appropriate organization and management processes to accomplish pressing administrative tasks. Despite continual challenges and criticisms, basic managerial concepts proved exceptionally durable. *Classic, traditional, rational,* or *machine models* are designations used in reference to the same three powerful and widely debated approaches: (1) Scientific Management or Taylorism, a U.S. genre; (2) Administrative Management or the "Principles" School, an American refinement and maturation of ideas presented in 1916 by Henri Fayol, a French engineer, and (3) The Bureaucratic Model by Max Weber, a German sociologist. The evolution of administrative knowledge in the United States between the 1880s and the 1940s demonstrates tremendous continuity and consistency. Woodrow Wilson, Frederick Taylor, Luther Gulick, Max Weber, and others offered constructs that are surprisingly harmonious and, to a large extent, complementary. The organization presented by classical management, however, accommodates only rational behavior by its members. It promises superior technical efficiency and administers rational rules of conduct to control human failures and predispositions. It is hierarchically structured, with authority and responsibility clearly defined. The organization accepts neither confusion nor ambiguity on the question of who is in charge. Unity of command is observed and graphically portrayed in the organization chart. Individual values, goals, and preferences are recognized only when they enhance organizational goals (Jreisat 1997).

Attaining the benefits of specialization for the organization is crucial, as is balancing the centrifugal forces of specialization (through coordination exercised at higher levels of authority). The classical organization is isolated from the turbulence of its environment. It efficiently and effectively serves the authoritative masters at the top, who set goals and objectives for the system. Thus, it is insulated from the troublesome exterior and oriented toward an orderly and manageable interior. The tradition of administration in the West, therefore, is rooted in developing and operating rational systems, bent on the use of scientific-technical know-how. Such systems cultivate specialization, define responsibilities, organize tasks, and coordinate results so that, in the end, they generate the necessary capacities to accomplish goals and objectives entrusted to them.

Another important aspect of these rational organizational systems that served the industrial countries so well is a built in search for continuing improvement. Consider the U.S. government as an illustration. Almost every U.S. president in the twentieth century initiated some review of the public bureaucracy in a search for improvements. Invariably, the stated purpose has been to streamline, reshape, improve, restructure, and even reinvent public bureaucracy. As a result, it is possible to identify methodical attempts to change the system of public administration since the 1880s, when the merit system was introduced to public service. Over time, many structural and functional adaptations were introduced, such as the following:

- *The Budget and Accounting Act of 1921* gave birth to presidential budget and finance, as a result of recommendations by the William Howard Taft's Commission on Economy and Efficiency in 1913.
- The *Executive Office of the President* was created in 1937, giving President Franklin D. Roosevelt the staff he needed to implement his New Deal programs and to manage World War II as well. Establishing the Executive Office was a recommendation of the Brownlow Committee, named after Louis Brownlow, a public administration scholar.
- Many recommendations for administrative reform resulted from reports submitted by the first Hoover Commission in 1947. The changes aimed at

strengthening the managerial functions and included introducing the idea of performance budget and revitalizing the Bureau of the Budget, which became the current *Office of Management and Budgeting.*

- Other reforms were introduced by recent presidents such as restructuring the civil service system during President Jimmy Carter's administration.
- The initiatives of the National Productivity Review (NPR) and the "reinvention of government" movement dominated the reform debate during the 1990s, particularly during President Bill Clinton's tenure, and continue to stir debate.
- President Barak Obama initiated various changes aimed at improving efficiency of public administration, restructuring programs, streamlining operations, and revitalizing the regulatory processes.

With the end of World War II, a major departure from the classic models was underway, advanced by the human relations model. The human relations school of management was a fundamental break from the rational-machine models of management that had provided the frameworks for administration through fifty years of evolution. Influenced by a powerful behavioral perspective that overwhelmed all fields of social science, the human relationists focused on people in the organization and what motivates them to work. Other frameworks such as system analysis, decision-making models, and a variety of schemes and theories all intended to provide answers to vexing administrative issues and problems.[2]

At the end of two centuries of development, then, it is possible to state some conclusions about various influential conceptual frameworks that shaped managerial practices of the industrial countries. One must add that many aspects of these management concepts and practices have some universal elements that are transportable. Thus, attempts at imitation, copying, and adaptation can be found in many countries, developed or developing. This review across time and space illustrates that the comparative method is crucial for providing a deeper understanding of the concepts and the social and political factors that affect their emergence. Comparative analysis, while indicating a continuing shifting of focal points, also illustrates the unmistakable common and constant search for reform and renewal of administrative systems. This by itself is a clear sign of the viability and dynamism manifested by public administration, as a field of learning and application, over the years. Today, the big debates in public management, not only within the industrial countries but globally, is centered on what is new and effective in improving performance of administration as well as governance.

The New Public Management

Although it remains imprecisely defined, the New Public Management (NPM) has been touted as a remarkable change sweeping public management in the industrial systems and around the world (Kettl 2005: 1). "Public administration across the world is supposedly converging around a new paradigm of public management" (Common 1998: 59). The problem is that this new paradigm of NPM is hard to define and has become a collection of concepts and practices that vary according to the user. The NPM has been described as contradictory, haphazard, lacking precise definition (Common 1998: 59), and a "shopping list" that countries choose from (Pollitt 1995: 133). In the United States, the NPM conjures familiar images of "reinvention," applying market economic practices, fostering competitiveness, privatization, and downsizing of government programs. Advocates of the NPM in the United States were well represented in the government movement to reform the federal management through the efforts of the National Productivity Review, during the Clinton-Gore administration.

Across the Atlantic, despite the well-known criticisms, the image of NPM is somewhat different from that in the United States. "NPM has been understood as a trend exemplified by the United Kingdom, New Zealand, and Australia," wrote Barzelay (2001: 9). Even if no agreement can be established on what exactly NPM is, let alone pinpointing where it started, the general conception is different. European scholars believe that the approach of the United Kingdom, Australia, New Zealand, and some European countries was more focused on the institutional and the policy side of change, relying on economic and political science concepts and methods (Lane 2000; Hood 1995; Barzelay 2001; Pollitt 1996).

Nevertheless, enormous managerial changes are in progress in many locations, involving all aspects of public management, at both the conceptual and at the operational levels. The call for administrative reform has become universal, induced by legacies of costly failures of many governments that have been attempting to implement their policies and reach their national objectives. Administrative reform successes in some countries also have encouraged a much wider pursuit of change. "The integration of the American governmental reform movement into a larger international movement" (Roberts, 1997: 466) is only one outcome of such efforts. Other significant drives for management improvement have been initiated in countries such as members of the Organization of Economic Cooperation and Development (OECD), Canada, Australia, New Zealand, and the United Kingdom, among others. Although these cases of administrative reforms constitute a reliable source of information, they have not yet resulted in definitive generalizations, which can only evolve through systematic comparative assessments and evaluations. Within a dimly defined domain of the NPM, comparative analysis is largely underdeveloped, and generalizations, however tentative, remain underspecified (Jreisat 2001: 540).

Nor has the profusion of scholarly contributions and country reports, regularly recounting cases of management reforms, produced an agreement on a reliable and coherent approach for achieving reform (Pollitt and Bouckaert 2004). At the dawn of the twenty-first century, public administration literature is overflowing with examinations and reviews of various attempts to modernize and to adapt the management of public organizations in changing political, social, and economic contexts. Even when the NPM is presented as a major "paradigm shift" (Kettle 1997; Osborne and Plastrik 1997: 15; Roberts 1997; Mascarenhas 1993), ushering in a "new world order" of management, there is no consensus on the content, much less on the practice, of this NPM. As Helmut Klages and Elke Loffler noted, "From an empirical point of view, there is almost no systematic knowledge about applied NPM" (1998: 41).

Global practical experiences and scholarship on management reforms indicate that some governments have been profoundly influenced by the change. Since the 1970s, many case studies have presented examples of the "aggressive" application of management reforms: New Zealand (Kettl 1997; Scott, Ball, and Dale 1997; Pallot 1996), United Kingdom (Barzelay 2001; Barberis 1998; Ferlie, Ashburner, Fitzgerald, and Pettigrew 1996; Mascarenhas 1993), the United States (Thompson and Ingraham 1996; Moe 1994; Gore 1993), Canada (Roberts 1998; Seidle 1995), to mention only a few examples. Many other countries also are at various phases of reform.

Debates during the past few years over competing perspectives on management and reform have stimulated one of the most exciting exchanges in public administration since World War II. For the purpose of this study, it is possible to divide the stakes in this debate, at least analytically, into two major thrusts: an *economic-based* "new paradigm" and *organization and management* tradition Comparison indicates that each has its own premises, diagnosis of the problems, prescriptions for solutions, vision of desired conditions, and strategies for achieving them.

Economics-Based "New Paradigm"

Canada is one example of the countries that have substantially restructured their public services in line with what the OECD has called the "new paradigm" in public management, which has accepted many of the NPM prescriptions. The restructuring of the Canadian federal and provincial governments is similar to reforms undertaken by other Western democracies, particularly the United States (Roberts 1998). The precise purpose is to make government "work better and cost less." This "new paradigm," the foundation for the recent Canadian reform efforts, has been applied by OECD countries in the 1990s. Basically, the reforms have had three key objectives: (1) cut all "nonessential" or "noncore" public spending, (2) rely less on conventional government bureaucracies for delivering public services, and (3) make public institutions rely less on tax revenue to finance their operations and more on nontax revenues such as fees for services (Roberts 1998: 1).

Christopher Hood (1995, 1991) and June Pallot (1998, 1996), for example, consider the dominant features of the NPM as the removal of private-public distinctions and the imposition of explicit standards and rules on management practices. According to Pallot (1996: 2), the following are the main characteristics of the NPM:

- Greater segregation of public sector organizations into separate "product" centers
- A shift toward competition among the separate units offering the services
- The use of management practices (e.g., accrual accounting, organizational design, career structure and remuneration practices) broadly drawn from the private sector
- An emphasis on efficiency and cost reduction
- The rise of new managerial elite
- More explicit and measurable standards of performance
- Attempts to control public sector organizational units through preset output measures

On the surface, many of the proposed elements of the NPM do not appear particularly controversial. The premises behind them, however, and the processes used to carry them out are. In a symposium on the New Public Management, Linda Kaboolian (1998: 190), referencing Jack Nagel and Peter Self, declared that "common to reform movements in all these countries [United States, United Kingdom, Korea, Portugal, France, Brazil, Australia, Sweden, New Zealand, Canada] is the use of the economic market as a model for political and administrative relationships." The institutional reforms of the NPM, Kaboolian concluded, "are heavily influenced by the assumptions of the public choice approach, principal-agent theory, and transaction cost economics" (1998: 190). Other theoretical grounds conveyed in this perspective for restructuring public agencies include new institutional economics, bureau maximization theory, quasi-market theory, and principal-agent theory (Ferlie et al. 1996: 10).

The connection between NPM and certain economic concepts is made clear and direct by those who view "the new public management as an ideological thought system, characterized by the importation of ideas generated in private sector settings within public sector organizations" (Ferlie et al. 1996: 10). One conclusion is amply clear: "[The] NPM builds on the basic economic premise that private-sector management and economic principles are transferable and functional in the public sector" (Klages and Loffler 1998: 42). Others go further, even advocating the removal of such distinctions between public and private sector organizations altogether (Hood 1991, 1995; Pallot 1996).

Generally, to advocate a new paradigm in management is to assume an existing one is deficient or unsatisfactory. In this case, not surprisingly, the target of dissatisfaction is bureaucracy or public administration in general. One view (Lane 2000: 6) holds that the "NPM is managerialism focusing upon contract making and enforcement seems to take government once and for all out of the Weberian framework of bureaucracy." Another study presumed that "[I]n the affluent post-war era of governmental expansion public administration and management essentially receded to the background (Barzelay (2001: 1). A variety of critical views habitually singled out public organizations and associated them with a list of real, exaggerated, or imagined shortcomings. Criticisms often claimed that public organizations were unresponsive to the demands of citizens, hampered by "bureau-pathology," and led by bureaucrats with the power and incentives to expand their administrative empires (Kaboolian 1998: 190; Nagel 1997: 350). The assumption here is "that government is ill organized, poorly managed, very costly and generally ineffective" (Frederickson 1999: 9). To justify peddling such notions, reformers regularly voice their concerns about a "crisis" in government, and exaggerate public management's failings. The irony of this, as Frederickson pointed out, is that contemporary public administration is increasingly committed to "government reform" (1999: 9).

Organization and Management Tradition

A different perspective on administrative reform is firmly rooted in established organization and management traditions and is entirely in conformity with conventional values and ethics of professional public service. Reforms in this approach seek to extend administrative theories and processes and to improve their utility in serving the traditional administrative values of efficiency and effectiveness in delivery of public services. To achieve better results within the public sector, this perspective seeks to improve the state's administrative capacity and to revitalize its mission of public service by introducing measures aimed at many aspects of governing, including mending the formulation and administration of public policies. The public organization remains the main unit of analysis. Thus, reforming it and building its capacity, not dismantling or bypassing it, are the primary concern.

An organization-management based perspective rejects key notions of the "reinvention of government" movement (Osborne and Gaebler 1992) such as "the old public bureaucracies failed to change when the world began to change," or bureaucracies designed before World War II are anachronistic, "not fitting into the rapidly changing, information-rich, knowledge-intensive societies of today" (Koven 2009: 149). A careful reading of the public administration's traditional literature, as Lawrence E. Lynn, Jr. points out, reveals that the "bureaucratic paradigm" routinely attributed to public administration, is "at best, a caricature and, at worst, a demonstrable distortion of traditional thought that exhibited far more respect for law, politics, citizens, and values than the new, customer-oriented managerialism and its variants" (2001: 144).

The assumption that an overarching traditional bureaucratic form is prevalent in public management negates the consistent identification of public management with basic values such as those pointed out over half a century ago by early scholars of public administration. In his *Ideal and Practice of Public administration,* published 1958, Emmette Redford argued that despite the "indictment" that public administration "have no well-defined ideals," the reality is that the quests for efficiency and dedication to the rule of law, competence and responsibility, public interest, and democratic values have always been fundamental commitments of the field of administration. "The study of public administration must deal with the total process of administration. It will be incomplete if built upon concepts which fit only the input-output relationship (Redford 1958: 23).

Another problem with the assumption of a "traditional, non-changing bureaucratic model" is that such thinking denies all the changes over several decades that continually and invariably adapted management practices. Concepts and measures from non-bureaucratic traditions such as human relations, cooperative systems, due process, team building, egalitarian and social equity values, non-discrimination laws, and many others have been inseparable parts of public management concepts and practices since World War II. Improving public management was continually a high priority policy to every U.S. president since the Taft Economy and Efficiency Commission of 1912 to the present. Experimentation with new administrative approaches has been a central part of the evolution of governance at all levels from the introduction of the merit system in the 1880s to the present.

Public organization and management tradition, then, shows a constant search for improvement, which is different from promoting dismantling or bypassing public organizations for some ideologically bent proposals. Management-based reforms often signify improvements of the managerial processes as well as the development of a culture of organizational learning and innovation. Appraisals and evaluations are continually utilized for correcting or adapting non-workable solutions. Public administration today emphasizes accountability, measurement, evaluation of outputs, and ethics among its high-priority norms, realizing that such concepts are not evenly or universally practiced. In recent years, public financial management, particularly budgeting, has been accentuating specific changes that met a robust measure of success. The literature and a survey by the UNDP and the Swedish International Services (1998: 5–6) of most common administrative reforms introduced in many countries include the following:

- A tendency toward specification of government goals and objectives
- Greater delegation of authority and responsibility to line-agencies, coupled with attempts to set spending ceilings
- Use of multiyear frameworks for allocations of resources in the annual budget
- Expanded operating authority and flexibility for executives and agencies in financial management
- Increased use of comparative information in the form of measures and indicators of results, to be combined with financial information on spending of resources
- Increased reliance on follow-ups and evaluations in the form of regular financial and results reports
- Intensified use of performance audit and evaluation of financial transactions

Thus, the inventory of refined organization and management concepts and practices is substantial and diversified. A century's accumulation of growth and development enriched public administration with extensive choices for organizing functions and managing policies of the modern state. The claim that public administration has to disavow its publicness to be hospitable to reform ideas misses the point. Clearly, an appropriate evaluation is essential before one can endorse any of the assortments of market-oriented ideas and bottom-line approaches that are presented as remedies to the perceived managerial ailments of the public sector. Such evaluation has to be in the context of public policy. True, market-based perspectives for administering the state occasionally overlap with traditional public administration concepts, but this is far from some elements of the so-called a "new paradigm" of public management. Part of the ambiguity is that considerable amounts of tautological descriptions and explanations have not evolved into a concurrence on the substance or the boundaries of the NPM. Ewan Ferlie and his associates have described the NPM as an "empty canvas" on which one can paint whatever one likes (Ferlie et al. 1996: 10). Others have conveniently offered a flexible characterization such as the NPM varies depending on your perspective. David Osborne and Peter Plastrik (1997: 8) introduced their new public management as "reinvention" and "redesign" that will reform public sector management by applying an "entrepreneurial model" to "maximize productivity and effectiveness." About this "entrepreneurial model," they say: "We believe that it represents an inevitable historical shift from one paradigm to another. It is a shift as profound as that which took place at the beginning of the century, when we built the bureaucratic public institutions we are busy reinventing today" (1997: 15).

Thus, the NPM has been many things to many people, and reforms endorsing its shifting tenets remain work in progress. "From a theoretical point of view, NPM is still in a pre-theoretical stage" (Klages and Loffler 1998: 41). The NPM often shifts focus with ease among teachings of public choice, organizational economics, transaction cost-economic, or neo-managerialism despite dissimilarities. Scholarship on the NPM "has gone off in many directions—a tendency even within some individual works" (Barzelay 2001: xii). All this adds to a general feeling of uncertainty about the NPM utility.

As I pointed out above, some European reform initiatives adopted versions of NPM that emphasized the market as an instrument for efficient resource allocation and for reducing the role of the state in the economy. The expected outcome of this was social and economic progress based on business-type competition and greater freedom of choice (Mascarenhas 1993: 320). Thus, the NPM prescriptions often look outside the usual domain of public administration and seek sweeping private sector involvement in a variety of schemes such as privatization, contracting out, joint ventures, or simply a wholesale downsizing of government. Very few advocates of the NPM actually continue to think in terms of public management improvements (i.e., Seidle 1995). Instead, what is proposed appears to be either the replacement or the dismantling of public management as it has been known. A central tenet of this thinking, also, is that the individual, whether manager or citizen, is a rational actor whose behavior is motivated by the quest for maximization of self-interest. Satisfying society's economic and other needs to the maximum degree possible is achieved through private businesses operating in competitive markets.

Core concepts of market-based prescriptions and their emphasis on satisfaction of individual self-interest as a key motivator are contested on several grounds:

- The premise that individual self-interest is the major motivating factor, as Herbert Simon (1998: ii) pointed out, "is simply false." He indicated that human beings make most of their decisions, not in terms of their perceived self-interest, but in terms of the perceived interests of the groups, families, organizations, ethnic groups, and nation-states with which they identify. Moreover, self-interest is too general to explain behavior and all individual choices, as it is often shaped by existing contextual influences (Jreisat 1997: 124).
- Economics literature on market failures indicates that no good or service can be allocated efficiently by leaving it to the private sector (Klages and Loffler 1998: 42). Markets are not always competitive. Mergers, manipulations, incomplete information, and dominance of the market by few producers—all reduce competitiveness. Thus, the assumption by advocates of privatization that the private sector is always more efficient and more productive than the public sector is questionable in light of the record of the business sector during the past thirty years. Herbert Simon, a Noble Prize Laureate in economics, effectively debunked a major argument for privatization. The idea that "privatization will always (or even usually) increase productivity and efficiency is ... wrong," he said (1998: ii). He pointed out that such "empirical evidence as we have on the relative efficiency of private and public organizations shows no consistent superiority of one over the other" (Simon, 1998: ii). Thus, the appropriate answer to the question to privatize or not to privatize is an empirical rather than a predetermined one.
- The NPM assumptions seem to deflate the social and political dimensions of governing, or relegate them almost to irrelevance since the market will be resolving allocative decisions. The British efforts at reform of the public sector in the 1980s, for example, shunted to the background efficiency through management improvement. Those efforts had other, far higher priority objectives, such as reducing the power of public-sector unions and promoting popular capitalism (Mascarenhas 1993: 323).

The public sector delivers services and goods that are primarily evaluated according to citizens' satisfaction rather than according to a criterion of economic efficiency. The public seems to be supportive, even demanding, of government involvement to manage programs and policies to protect the environment, to meet health and education needs, to ensure equal opportunity to citizens, and to manage the social security system. Privatization and reforms, motivated by anti-government ideologies, have largely been advanced as tools to reduce the role of the public sector. In Britain, for example, Thatcher's changes have been motivated by ideological or political commitments such as promoting the private sector, with the intention of altering the balance of power between the business and public sectors rather than for reasons of efficiency (Mascarenhas 1993: 325). The same is said about change in the United States during Roland Reagan's administration. Certainly, under such conditions, a major concern is how well is the public interest being protected against private interests, and how to ensure accountability of important functions carried out outside the domain of the public sector.

Still, significant parts of the British- and U.S.-sponsored changes found their way to the core of a familiar package of reforms that have been advocated by the World Bank economists. Depending on the country, the recommendations are often referred to as the International Monetary Fund's (IMF) framework for restructuring. This package includes measures to privatize, to rationalize public expenditures, to improve efficiency and effectiveness of public policies, and to limit or eliminate social spending, such as government subsidies for food and other essentials. Accordingly, many developed and developing countries have implemented policies to privatize public enterprises, to downsize the public sector, to reform civil service, to stimulate entrepreneurial management, or to contract out government services.

Recommendations to improve public sector performance are consistent with the goals and values of public administration. The controversy begins when reduction of the public sector's role in society is made an end by itself. The public administration community generally objects to embracing private sector methods and objectives, irrespective of fundamental public service values. Issues of equal treatment of employees, serving public interest, transparency, and democratic accountability are central to public administration. Managing "business-like" and certain economic assumptions do not have the same commitment to and concerns for these values. Moreover, the depiction of public administration as an unchanging field in the midst of a fast changing world is an exaggeration. In reality, a primary attribute of public administration throughout its history has been its continuing search for improvement of concepts and practices. As Gordon Kingsley noted, the history of public administration is one of reform and change (1997: iii). This is even more the case in developing countries, particularly after the end of the colonial system.

I have reviewed the NPM at such length to point out two basic conclusions: (1) The NPM is a response to limitations of traditional public administration processes, particularly those producing bureaucratic dysfunctions. But this response has largely been premised on spurious assumptions, and it is often intended to serve other than administrative purposes. Not surprising, the elements of the proposed changes, titled "New" Public Management, are often off the mark or contradictory, thus, failed to produce an agreement on content and process. (2) This analysis also emphasizes the necessity of a methodical appraisal of information, supported by further field research that applies the comparative approach to resolve incompatibilities. Only then a meaningful cumulative process is possible. A synthesis of various scattered findings is imperative for producing coherent comparative administrative knowledge that will prompt an advancement of theory and an improvement of utility.

Common Administrative Features

Despite some disagreements over defining the salient features of public administration in developed or industrial systems, they do unmistakably have common characteristics: (1) a balanced system of power distribution, (2) a focus on results, (3) technology at the service of management, (4) a profound concern for ethics and accountability in public service, and (5) a redefined role for public administration and its linkages with the private sector.

Balanced System of Power Distribution

Public administration in advanced, mostly democratic societies operates within fairly synchronized systems of checks and balances that regulate interactions among vital institutions of the society. In a developed country, the bureaucracy usually functions within a civil society that allows it sufficient independence to practice its professional expertise. As the system of laws specifies bureaucratic powers and prerogatives, it also protects citizens' rights, freedoms, and common interests. Administrative linkages with other branches of government (particularly the judicial and the legislative), interactions with the market, and dealings with nongovernment organizations (NGOs) are also conducted within the rule of law.

An independent and effective judiciary is a crucial aspect of a civil society. Judicial review provides relief to individuals who have been harmed by a particular agency's action. In contrast, political oversight shapes or determines entire programs or policies. Judicial review differs from political controls, according to Ernest Gellhorn and Ronald Levin, "in that it attempts to foster reasoned decision making, by requiring the agencies to produce supporting facts and rational explanations," not necessarily financial savings (1990: 73). In essence, judicial review provides an independent check on the validity of administrative decisions; that is, it ensures compliance with the law and constitutional rights, statutory jurisdiction, required procedures, and proper use of administrative discretion.

In comparison, such a balance of powers is generally lacking in many developing countries, where bureaucracy often follows the footsteps of the political order and turns into either an overpowering institution or corrupt and incompetent one. In these countries, not only does bureaucracy act obsequiously to a similarly inept political order, but other crucial elements of a civil society (judiciary, legislative branch, and NGOs) are also weak or entirely absent. This explains how bureaucracy is part of a larger context and why its effectiveness is not limited to its inherent attributes.

Focus on Results

At the beginning of the twenty-first century, performance-oriented management and its lineage performance budgeting are unmistakable trends worldwide. One of the most significant changes in managing contemporary governance systems is the steady expansion of the concept and practice of performance management internationally. A visible and specific application of performance management is what Allen Schick described as "a wave of change in the management of public budgets [that] has swept through developed countries and has begun to engulf many developing countries as well" (1998: v). The measurement and management of performance consist of various components and relationships among these components that constitute the performance system.

Geert Bouckaert and John Halligan compared management of performance in six developed countries: Australia, Canada, The Netherlands, Sweden, United Kingdom, and United States. "In order to make meaning of the diverse uses and combinations of performance, measurement and management, a framework has been developed" that allows analysis of the evolution of performance management over time and the comparison of country orientations to performance (Bouckaert and Halligan 2008: 3). Performance management is a growth of the tradition of rationalism in public management. Its success requires methodical efforts of evaluating alternative approaches to performance management to continually improve the quality and the quantity of results. "Using performance information includes a systematic comparison of results, a coherent vision of learning to improve, and a strategy of change that is externally oriented" (Bouckaert and Halligan 2008: 100).

The process of performance measurement is demanding. Its return benefits depend on the availability of systematic and documented performance data, ability of management to integrate data into action, and evidence of improvement of consequent quality and quantity of public service following implementation of a performance oriented management system. In addition to the achievement orientation of performance management, the process of implementation requires also that management focuses on serving citizens (stakeholders), use critical thinking, develop professional competence, and collaborate with others. Despite the complexity of implementation, the potential advantages are several and significant: performance measurement helps to save resources and to increase citizens' satisfaction and trust as well as to improve decision making and to ensure accountability of public management.

In recent years, developed countries have introduced many important changes in public financial management that affected all aspects of governance. A profound shift in public budgeting from a focus on input (how much should we spend?) to a focus on outputs (what was produced, at what cost, and to what consequence?) is transforming contemporary management. A renewed emphasis on efficiency and cost reduction is often coupled with explicit processes of performance measurement.

For years, demand-driven public agencies defined success by how much money is budgeted, how many people are hired, and how many activities are funded. Now, result-driven governments define success by outputs and outcomes of spending. The change has been viewed as a part of a larger transformation sweeping public management around the world under differing banners, such as result-oriented management, performance management, productivity improvement, and Total Quality Management (TQM). The change is not limited to budgeting and finance and often varies from one administrative system or subsystem to the next. Frequently, performance management aims at increasing accountability, reducing costly errors, minimizing customers' complaints, improving employees' skills, and developing overall management improvements (Berman 1998: 4).

Technology Serving Management

Administration in developed systems of governance is enabled to adapt and to apply new technologies in public organizations. Besides the need for overall effectiveness, public managers very early recognized the need for relevant, reliable information to help improve their decision-making processes. Thu, policy commitments have been made and extensive resources have been dedicated to designing systems that gather, classify, and retrieve data according to manager's needs. Although measuring performance is a work in progress, even after several years of practice, employing advanced information technologies are making a big difference in how individual agencies are run.

Concern for Ethics and Accountability

Developed countries are in the midst of a revived attention to various reform initiatives in public administration that aim to improve standards of ethics and accountability among public officials. Procedures to reduce corruption and improve recruitment of public employees are regularly refined. Policies to enhance ethics through training and development have been accentuated. The establishment of codes of ethics and the improving general education among public servants also indicate the growing importance of the subject. There is no doubt that today's public management attaches great importance to such values as basic honesty and conformity to law, refraining from actions that involve conflict of interest, and service orientation that is committed to procedural fairness (Willbern, 1984).

At the legal and procedural levels, various mechanisms are employed to ensure accountability. One set of activities seeks to achieve more effective measures of investigation and adjudication of violations. A second set offers programs that emphasize education and training in ethics. A third type of measures ensures dependable processes of inspection and performance audit. Finally, a clear commitment to greater transparency and documentation of government actions, augmented by regular reports and independent evaluation of performance, are all intended to realize greater accountability.

Redefined Public Administration Role Toward the Private Sector

The role of public administration is being reexamined, and proposals for employing market mechanisms of competition for achieving higher efficiencies in public organizations have been at the center of debate. Public policy making in advanced states often seems to face the dilemma of choosing between efficiency, on the one hand, and government's obligations to realize accountability, equity, and justice, on the other. The market claims commitment to and competence in the domain of efficiency. The state seeks a balance of the two, never totally sacrificing one at the expense of the other. As Larry Terry pointed out, "The blind application of business management principles and practices can undermine the integrity of public bureaucracies and so threaten our democratic way of life" (1999: 276).

Other alternatives have been considered with some success. The possibility of joint public-private ventures is increasingly appealing, particularly in Europe. In these ventures, links with the private sector are kept consistent with the principles and values of public service. The most notable example is the practice of creating joint public-private partnerships (PPPs) instead of cloning business practices and substituting them for public management. The "partnerships between the private and public sectors to fund and operate infrastructure projects are set to take off in Europe" (Timmins 1999: 3). The use of private money and private companies to finance and operate infrastructure that used to be entirely publicly funded is a "profound cultural change" (Timmins 1999: 3). PPPs may become an alternative to a wholesale privatization, which often seeks to exclude government entirely, except as a remote regulator. In a partnership, government is a party to the activity, and private funding is a factor in expediting the implementation of such ventures. This is an example of how public administration remains involved and how public service values are kept as an important factor of governing.

Developed countries have not ignored the internal processes of public organizations. In fact, they have introduced many administrative changes aimed at building overall managerial capacities. The objective of capacity building in advanced systems has been served through a combination of initiatives such as: (1) implementation strategies that foster public managers' self-direction and ability to delegate responsibilities effectively; (2) greater monitoring of compliance with assigned duties and fulfillment of substantive requirements of laws and procedures; (3) improved managerial responsibility and accountability through the development and adoption of organizational goals, measuring outputs, feedback evaluation, problem identification, adoption of creative solutions, improving transparency, performance audits, and the use of a variety of techniques to ensure fiscal discipline; (4) the discovery of more-effective strategies to develop human resources and to foster the learning capability and analytical skills of public employees.

Although advocating reform is no guarantee of successful implementation, in the private as well as in the public sectors, reform initiatives in developed systems are continuous and many do result in more productivity and better services. Despite lack of agreement on what changes should be made and why, improved managerial practices have been attained. Some countries have made significant progress. But fending off ideological intrusions and resisting tendencies of fads and fashions made rampant by consultants and peddlers of exhausted ideas, require greater definition of the fundamentals, the big questions, the things that matter. In this regard, comparative public administration research can render a pivotal service. Only through the comparative method can certain questions be satisfactorily answered such as which reforms work, which do not, and under what conditions.

There is no doubt that public administration must continue to emphasize change and innovation. But it is incorrect to assume that public administration principles are irrelevant, and consequently, they need to be replaced by principles and concepts from economics, as in some versions of the NPM. Public administration in the industrial countries continues on the path of development and change, preparing public management for the new global reality. The evolving management perspectives are strained in the attempt to preserve the core values of public service while partaking in new technologies and actively updating their practices to suit the new conditions. A synthesizing process may offer a possibility of an alternative that regards the NPM "not a simplistic Big Answer" but rather "a normative reconceptualization of public administration consisting of several inter-related components" (Seidle 1995: 23). In this case, the NPM would have had "heightened the challenge to traditional cannons of public administration," as Peter Barberis indicated (1998: 454). Perhaps the net effect of reform initiatives will finally transform traditional public administration into a livelier and more effective field.

Conclusions

Comparative analysis of public administration in developed countries indicates that these countries share important common attributes. First and foremost, these countries are constantly searching for administrative improvements and for creative strategies and solutions to achieve these improvements. The experiences of developed countries also underline the significance of the context in which public administration functions. Public administration is not merely a bundle of techniques that can be planted anywhere with equal success. The techniques and processes are usually tied to many contextual factors—political, legal, economic, historical, and cultural—that constitute the distinctive features of a civil society. Ignoring this reality, as the attempt to eliminate the differences between the public and the private sectors, would lead to serious misunderstanding of the whole idea of governance. The administrative practices of developed systems illustrate that public administration is able to improve its cost consciousness without becoming obsessed with a "bottom line" management that sacrifices its commitment to values of equity, social justice, and public service ethics.

Whereas public administration has noticeably been increasing its reliance on data and technology for improving outputs and outcomes of public management, the political impact remains a major factor in causing variation of administrative structures and functions in governance. The political authority is the main source of legitimacy for public organizations, their budgets, and their authority to operate in their areas of responsibility. While the political context has a defining influence on administration, it is also a source of incongruities. The political environment is shaped by larger forces of legislators, interest groups, mass media, political parties, and political appointees whose interactions with professional public managers are often strained by different, even conflicting, goals and values. Although taxpayers ultimately fund public organizations, it is a reality that those who appropriate and authorize spending are usually removed from operations.

Thus, professional concerns of management are not always identical or in accord with political preferences or actions, creating tensions that affect not only the daily operations of public organizations but also the long-range focus on public interest. Elected officials, beholden to lobbyists and financiers of special interests, habitually blame the "bureaucrats" for failures of policy. To explain deficiencies of public policies they helped enact, politicians often join mass media and special interest groups in finding and embellishing public management failures, however episodic or unrepresentative. Thus, public service and public managers become convenient scapegoats for bad public policies (Lynn, 1987; Goodsell, 1983). Within such environment, public managers often retrench into safer terrains of inaction or survival techniques.

In developed countries, the Judicial Context is another crucial element of the environment of public administration. The growing number of laws usually translates into greater powers for public organizations, which already command significant power of functional specialization. Certain public agencies and commissions performing regulatory functions have also been delegated powers that allow them to perform semi-legislative and semi-judicial roles. As a result of these large accumulated administrative powers, judicial review has become an important safeguard against arbitrary use of administrative authority. Courts review administrative decisions and interpret existing laws to ensure protection of constitutional rights and liberties granted to individuals and groups. Over the years, the judicial impact has increased through implementation of defined operational standards in public agencies, as required by federal and state administrative procedures acts.

Moreover, the legal constraints on public administration from strengthening protection of individual rights, from applying the doctrine of qualified immunity, and from the stricter observance of the procedural due process mean that public administrators are under greater pressure to justify their decisions and to demonstrate their legal validity. In public personnel administration, judicial decisions have had significant impact on public employment. Various court decisions, during the 1970s and 1980s, affirmed public employees' basic constitutional rights (freedom of speech, freedom of association, political activity, and equal protection). Court decisions rejected the traditional notion of public employment as a "privilege" and extended to public employees the procedural due process protection (Jaegal and Cayer, 1991: 212). To a considerable degree, in some Western countries, these legal protections provoked the ideological onslaught of conservative politics against public agencies and those working in them.

Thus, the legal context of contemporary public administration demarcates the mission, structure, resources, power of decision making, and overall practices of public agencies. Laws specify standards of operation as well as methods of challenging arbitrary and capricious decisions made by these administrative units. With the expansion of government responsibilities in society, the need for protection of individual rights, by augmenting the political oversight and bolstering the judicial review, is significantly greater. Consequently, the complexity of the public administration environment increased. In addition, public managers had to deal with fiscal pressures at all levels of government such as cutbacks, retrenchment, downsizing, efficiency drives, and a growing focus on productivity improvement. The adjustments of public organizations to these constraints have not always been problem-free.

By the end of the twentieth century, comparative public administration devoted considerable attention to these contextual factors that affect the performance and operations of bureaucracy. Extensive literature has been produced on various aspects of public management in various cultures. The concepts and practices in developed countries have increasingly been presented as global standards to be emulated everywhere. Riggs argued that public administration must be comparative to compel us to rethink the context of what we call public administration. He believed that "we need to develop frameworks and theories for the study of public administration that are truly universal in scope—they will be based on a comprehensive ecological understanding of the place of public administration in all governments, historical as well as contemporary" (1991: 473). Such a framework has also to provide explanatory conclusions that account for the continuously changing conditions facing public policy implementation. Infusing the normative guidelines of comparative administration with empirical knowledge of institutions and society would increase the utility of the comparative method in advancing administrative knowledge globally. Breaking down the ethnocentric fences would enhance the role of comparative research, promoting the discovery of better solutions for administrative problems, and achieving greater universal validity of administrative principles.

References

Barberis, P. 1998. The new public management and new accountability. *Public Administration,* 76 (Autumn): 451–470.

Barzelay, M. 2001. *The New Public Management: Improving Research and Policy Dialogue.* Los Angeles: University of California Press.

Berman, E. M. 1998. *Productivity in Public and Nonprofit Organizations.* London: Sage.

Bouckaert, G., and J. Halligan. 2008. *Managing Performance: International Comparisons.* New York, Routledge, Taylor & Francis Group.

Chevallier, J. 1996. Public administration in statist France. *Public Administration Review* 56 (1): 67–74.

Common, R. 1998. The new public management and policy transfer: the role of international organizations. In *Beyond the New Public Management,* eds. Minogue, M., C. Polidano, and D. Hulme, 59–75, Northampton, MA: Edward Elgar.

Ferlie, E., L. Ashburner, L. Fitzgerald, and A. Pettigrew 1996. *The New Public Management in Action.* Oxford, UK: Oxford University Press.

Frederickson, G. H. 1999. Highjacking public administration. *PA Times,* 22(3) March: 9.

Gellhorn, E., and R. M. Levin. 1990. *Administrative Law and Process.* 3rd ed. St. Paul, MN: West Publishing Co.

Gladden, E. N. 1972. *A History of Public Administration.* II. London: Frank Cass.

Goodsell, C. T. 1983. *The Case for Bureaucracy.* Chatham, NJ: Chatham House.

Gore, Al. 1993. *From Red Tape to Results: Creating a Government That Works Better and Costs Less.* (Report of the National Performance Review) Washington, D.C.: U. S. Government Printing Office.

Hood, C. 1995. The "New Public Management" in the 1990s: Variations on a theme. *Accounting Organizations and Society* 20 (2/3): 93–109.

———. 1991. A public management for all seasons? *Public Administration.* 69 (1): 3–19.

Jaegal, D., and N. J. Cayer. 1991. Public personnel administration by lawsuit: The impact of Supreme Court decisions on public employee litigiousness. *Public Administration Review.* 51 (3): 211–221.

Jreisat, J. E. 2001. The New Public Management and reform. In *Handbook of Public Management Practice and Reform,* ed. Liou, K. T. pp. 539–560. New York: Marcel Dekker.

———. 1999. Comparative public administration and reform. *International Journal of Public Administration,* 22 (6) 855–877.

———. 1997. *Public Organization Management: The Development of Theory and Process.* Quorum Books, Westport, CT: Greenwood.

Kaboolian, L. 1998. The New Public Management: Challenging the boundaries of the management vs. administration debate. *Public Administration Review* 58 (3): 189–193.

Kettl, D. F. 2005. *The Global Public Management Revolution.* 2nd ed. Washington, D.C.: Brookings Institution Press.

———. 1999. The future of public administration. *Journal of Public Affairs Education,* 5 (2): 127–134.

———. 1997. The global revolution in public management: Driving themes, missing inks. *Journal of Policy Analysis and Management* 16 (3): 446–462.

Kickert, W., and R. Stillman II. 1996. Introduction: Changing European State; changing public administration. *Public Administration Review* 56 (1): 65–67.

Kingsley, G. 1997. Reflecting on reform and the scope of public administration. *Public Administration Review* 57 (2): iii–iv.

Klages, H., and E. Loffler. 1998. New Public Management in Germany. *International Review of Administrative Sciences,* 64: 41–54.

Koven, S. G. 2009. Bureaucracy, democracy, and the New Public Management. In *Bureaucracy and Administration,* ed., Farazmand, A. 130–154. New York: CRC Press.

Lane, J.-E. 2000. *New Public Management.* London: Routledge.

Lynn, L. E., Jr. 2001. The myth of the bureaucratic paradigm: What traditional public administration really stood for. *Public Administration Review,* 61 (2): 144–155.

_____. 1987. *Managing Public Policy.* Boston: Little, Brown.

Mascarenhas, R. C. 1993. Building an enterprise culture in the public sector: Reform of the public sector in Australia, Britain, and New Zealand. *Public Administration Review* 53 (4): 319–327.

Moe, R. C. 1994. The "reinventing government" exercise: Misinterpreting the problem, misjudging the consequences. *Public Administration Review* 54 (2): 111–122.

Nagel, J. H. 1997. Radically reinventing government. *Journal of Policy Analysis and Management* 16 (3): 349–356.

Osborne, D., and T. Gaebler. 1992. *Reinventing Government: How the Entrepreneurial Spirit Is Transforming the Public Sector from Schoolhouse to State House, City Hall to Pentagon.* Reading, MA: Addison-Wesley.

Osborne, D., and P. Plastrik. 1997. *Banishing Bureaucracy: The Five Strategies for Reinventing Government.* Reading, MA: Addison-Wesley Publishing.

Pallot, J. 1996. "Newer than new" public management: Financial management and Collective Strategizing in New Zealand. Paper prepared for the conference on The New Public Management in International Perspective, Institute of Public Finance and Fiscal Law, St. Gallen, Switzerland, 11–13 July.

Pallot, J. 1998. New Public Management Reform in New Zealand: The Collective Strategy Phase. *International Public Management Journal.* 1 (1): 1–18.

Pollitt, C. 1996. Antistatist reforms and new administrative directions: Public administration in the United Kingdom. *Public Administration Review* 56 (1): 81–87.

Pollitt, C. 1995. Justification by works or by faith: Evaluating the new public management. *Evaluation,* 1 (2): 133–154.

Pollitt, C., and G. Bouckaert 2004. *Public Management Reform: A Comparative Analysis.* 2nd ed., Oxford University Press.

Redford, E. S. 1958. *Ideal and Practice in Public Administration* Birmingham, AL: University of Alabama Press.

Riggs, F. W. 1991. Public Administration: A comparativist framework. *Public Administration Review* 51 (6): 473–477.

Roberts, A. 1998. Closing the window: Public service restructuring and the weakening of freedom of information law. Paper submitted to the 1998 International Public Management Network Conference (June 28–29, 1998), (roberta@qsilver.queensu.ca).

_____. 1997. Performance-based organizations: Assessing the Gore plan. *Public Administration Review* 57 (6): 465–478.

Seidle, L. F. 1995. *Rethinking the Delivery of Public Services.* Montreal, Canada: Institute for Research on Public Policy.

Schick, A. 1998. *A Contemporary Approach to Public Expenditure Management.* Washington, D.C.: Economic Development Institute and the World Bank.

Scott, Graham, Ian Ball, and Tony Dale. 1997. New Zealand's public sector management reform: Implications for the United States. *Journal of Policy Analysis and Management* 16 (3): 357–381.

Simon, H. A. 1998. Guest editorial: Why Public Administration? *Public Administration Review* 58 (1): ii.

Terry, L. D. 1999. From Greek mythology to the real world of the New Public Management and democratic governance. *Public Administration Review,* 59 (3): 272–277.

Thompson, J. R., and P. W. Ingraham. 1996. The reinvention game. *Public Administration Review,* 56 (3): 291–304.

Timmins, N. 1999. Private sector partners share government's traditional role. *Financial Times* (April 29).

UNDP and Swedish International Services. 1998. *Jordan.* Unpublished Technical Report. Stockholm: Sweden: 5–6.

Willbern, Y. 1984. Types and levels of public morality. *Public Administration Review* 44 (2): 102–108.

Endnotes

1. *New York Times* in *St. Petersburg Times,* November 24, 2000. P. 14A.
2. As the administrative concepts and practices have been revised and refocused in the industrial nations, Japanese management merits recognition. We know less about Japan's public management than about its corporate management. In fact, U.S. managers and organizational theorists spent considerable time seeking to discover the "secret" of Japan's organizational and managerial success during the 1970s and 1980s. The search often led to the notion of organizational culture. The Japanese seemed to have been more successful than the rest of the industrial countries in solving problems related to labor relations. In the Japanese company, people, not machines, are the most important asset and are, therefore, to be valued, nurtured, and retained. The Japanese run their companies by consensus and teamwork; important ideas and decisions bubble up from below as frequently as they come down from on high.

   In the genre of organization theories that emphasize culture and rely on the cultural element in explaining organizational management and behavior is William Ouchi's Theory Z (1981), which seeks to reconcile Japanese management with certain U.S. practices into a framework that crosses cultural boundaries. Also, in the United States, Organization Development (OD) shares some of the premises of Theory Z. Interventions by the practitioners of OD are invariably examining organizational culture and subcultures behind management values and norms within the organization.

Chapter 8

Global Ethics and Public Service

> Corruption is an insidious plague that has a wide range of corrosive effects on societies. It undermines democracy and the rule of law, leads to violations of human rights, distorts markets, erodes the quality of life.
>
> **Kofi A. Annan,**
> **former UN Secretary-General**[1]

Introduction

Today's human society is profoundly different than that of our ancestors. Theirs was simpler and did not face many of the challenges confronting modern-day generations. The world is currently enduring some momentous global events and developments: the environment is at risk, natural resources are diminishing, population is exploding, nuclear and other weapons of mass destruction threaten human civilization, and poverty is vastly growing. If this seems as a disturbing picture, it is. But, also, it is a realistic view of indications of likely future developments unless modified by sane collective policies. Proliferation of nuclear weapons is not an abstract notion, nor is the degradation of the environment or the demographic explosion. Shortages of food and water, and concerns about disease and poverty, are verifiable facts that mean dangers to the human society. Citing a UNDP report, Duncan Bell points out that "approximately 1 billion people around the world are living 'at the margin of survival' on less than $1 per day; 2.6 billion people, or 40% of the world's population, live on less than $2 per day" (2010: 1).

Threats of war, occupation, and violence as well as insufficiency of food and water are menacing people and society in many parts of the world. The pressing problem of shortages of water supplies where some countries such as Egypt, Jordan, Syria, and many African nations are already struggling to cope with current demands is alarmingly destabilizing. As Cindy Gill explains:

> To sustain life, we need adequate supplies of fresh *clean* water. Population growth, pollution, climate change, and other pressures are threatening this indispensable global resource. Despite the vastness of water on our planet [70 percent of the planet], *National Geographic* reports that only 2.5 percent is fresh water, and much of that is captured in glaciers or trapped well below the surface—inaccessible. (Gill 2010: 2)

What all this means for the future, and what challenges it creates for governance, is unpredictable. At this point, I would like to emphasize two factors: (1) Global developments have not all been in one direction. In some areas, significant progress has been made to bring about solutions or to control negative trends. Technology, for example, has been a major facilitator of many of these changes culminating in international agreements on core principles such as global ethics, human rights, economics, trade, and transportation. (2) As the main actors of the international system, governance ethics and collaborative stance are foundations of a global collective will. Developing strategies for solutions to world problems depends largely on the quality of governance systems and their sense of international responsibility. Thus, the politics and the administration of governance have to reasonably consent to direct their organizational abilities to participate and to contribute to the new global order. In recent years, international organizations and leaders of many countries came to realize the danger of corruption on the effectiveness of governance. Corruption disrupted national development policies and projects, increased the cost of managing, alienated citizens, and disturbed cooperative relations with other governments.

The effects of corruption are incalculable, reaching beyond national boundaries in its negative consequences on international commerce, trade, finance, and investment. How is corruption defined? International organizations such as the UN, the World Bank, and Transparency International as well as the literature on ethics, in general, accept the definition of corruption as the abuse or misuse of entrusted power for private gain. Georg Cremer pointed out that social scientists understand corruption "as the misuse of an office or a comparable position of trust for private purposes" (2008: 9). This definition is based on prerequisites of (1) a person holding an office that needs not be a public office, (2) there are standards set by law or anchored in social consent that determine how an office or a position of trust should be fulfilled, and (3) the breach of office norms occurs consciously and intentionally to the advantage of the person holding the office (Cremer 2008: 10). Bribery, misappropriation of resources, and nepotism are in the category of corrupt acts.

Public administration as a profession has been increasingly cognizant of the negative impact of corruption on effective management. As Gilman and Lewis (1996: 517) conclude, "Professional public administration must remain intellectually open to global dialogue on shared values, norms, and structures." Within the field of public administration, two important developments may be cited: (1) developing a code of ethics for the American Society for Public Administration (ASPA), and (2) requiring teaching the subject of ethics in graduate public administration programs. In fact, teaching ethics has become a requirement for accreditation of the Master of Public Administration (MPA) programs by National Association of Schools of Public Administration and Affairs (NASPAA). Today's focus on ethics in public administration is a modest response to "a shift in the public's capacity and desire for scrutiny and insistence upon adherence to moral standards defined by appropriate behaviors from those holding public authority and the public trust" (Huberts, Maesschalck, and Jurkiewicz 2008).

Applied Global Ethics

Global ethics refers to the emerging consensus among states on standards of conduct for achieving justice, respect of human rights, and improving overall performance of countries in their intergovernmental dealings. The conceptual analysis of global ethics is not always uniform or consistent. Peter Jones (2010: 112) makes a distinction between *international society* and *global* or *world* society. The latter terms convey a conception of all humanity as a single community; *international* refers to interstate, describing a community of states and other nongovernmental organizations as multinational corporations. David Crocker (2006: 21) is more concerned with *international development ethics* or the *ethics of global development* that involves moral reflection on current and future development in dealing with poverty, degrading inequality, violence, and tyranny that continue to afflict the world. Still, as Peter Singer concluded, "how well we come through the era of globalization will depend on how we respond ethically to the idea that we live in one world" (Singer 2004: 13).

Global ethics is a wide area of study that aims ultimately to establish consensus on universal principles that would improve global justice, emphasize environmental stewardship, encourage global responsibility, and ensure respect of human rights. Motivated by concerns for enforcing ethical standards, the UN and other international associations have been attempting to set ethical standards among nations, develop international agreements, and suggest measures for enforcement. Although significant progress has been made in this regard, enforcement and compliance remain work in progress at best. As the former UN Secretary-General Kofi Annan concluded, corruption is found in all countries—big and small, rich and poor—but it is in the developing countries that its effects are most destructive, and combating it has been less successful. "Corruption hurts the poor disproportionately by diverting funds intended for development, undermining a Government's ability to provide basic services, feeding inequality and injustice and discouraging foreign aid and investment. Corruption is a key element in economic underperformance and a major obstacle to poverty alleviation and development" (Annan 2004: iii). Countries have their particular reasons for compliance or noncompliance with global ethics standards but certainly cannot ignore the effects domestically.

International ethics "involves the assessment of rules, practices, and institutions of global society in light of relevant moral norms" (Amstutz 2008: 9). Debates on international ethics, however, have occasionally been discordant, particularly in the conduct of foreign relations. Opinions of prominent diplomats who had significant impact on the U.S. foreign policy during the last century vary significantly. For Dean Acheson, for example, "What passes for ethical standards for governmental policies in foreign affairs is a collection of moralisms, maxims, and slogans, which neither help nor guide, but only confuse, decision" (quoted in Amstutz 2008: 12). While George Kennan accepted the idea of ethics in the conduct of a person, he makes a distinction when that conduct is through the machinery of a political organization; then it "undergoes a general transmutation," and the same moral concepts are no longer relevant to it (quoted in Amstutz 2008: 12).

Whether a relativistic view of ethics in foreign policy, as by Dean Acheson or a reluctant acceptance as by George Kennan, ethics today have surpassed theoretical and practical limitations and confinements. Gaining a wider acceptance and support, ethics today is a national and an international concern, receiving unprecedented attention at all levels of governance. Ethics codes, laws, and agreements are now obligating political and administrative leaders to comply with specified standards of good conduct, at the local, national, and international levels. Various relativist theories and minimalist approaches to ethics in the public sector have been rejected or modified in favor of clear standards of ethics in public management and in governance. Dennis Thompson (1985: 555) argued persuasively that administrators in public organizations can make moral judgments and can be the subject of moral judgments. This required debunking the arguments of ethics neutrality (managers simply follow orders) or ethics of structure (administrators should not be held morally responsible for the wrongs of their organizations).

"Moral challenges have confronted every society, regardless of locale or state of industrial development" (Huberts, Maesschalck, and Jurkiewicz 2008: 239). Similarly, reform initiatives are common and continuous among nations, seeking improvement of performance of their governance. Invariably such reform initiatives acknowledge the critical need to extend such reformist position to include ethics factors in public service. Accordingly, research and application have been attempting to clarify some of the conceptual vagueness of ethics issues, and to provide clearer definitions and better linkages between ethics concepts and ethics practice in the conduct of public officials. Applied ethics requires focus on the practical and relevant elements of the subject. This is crucial when governance is facing a compelling demand for integrity of performance at all levels. "In effect, international ethics is concerned with the moral architecture of the international system: that is the moral legitimacy of the patterns and structures of global society" (Amstutz 2008: 9). This is why questions rarely discussed in the past have attracted worldwide attention and debate. Some examples include the following:

Is torture justifiable even when ordered by superiors?
Is the murder of noncombatant women and children acceptable for any reason?
Is ethnic cleansing defensible on any ground or for any justification?
Is discrimination on the basis of religion, gender, color, or ethnicity justifiable?

These are examples of the specific moral issues that are within the terrain of applied ethics. One wonders what an outstanding diplomat as Dean Acheson would say today when faced with such questions. Applied global ethics had expanded beyond honesty and integrity in public institutions to create a comprehensive and integrated approach to ethics in society that includes also nongovernmental establishments and institutions of civil society. Through technology, education, citizens' demands, and continuous attempts at reform, individual states have made public employees more informed and better equipped to manage ethics within their organizations. The effects of ethics on policy outcomes can be tangible and measureable. Leaders of public and private organizations are increasingly recognizing the risks to their organizational accomplishments from failures to make sure that ethics considerations infuse their decision making. The end objective is respect of the dignity and the rights of all human beings, regardless of gender, race, ethnicity, religion, age, or residence.

Institutional Context of Global Ethics

To ensure justice in the existing world order, impartial implementation of global policies and fair application of international rules are requirements. Many institutions have been involved in the difficult task of shaping global policies and influencing rules and standards that have effectively resulted in the construction, approval, and promulgation of various international ethics accords. Most important of these institutional channels are:

1. United Nations and affiliated special institutions and commissions such as Food and Agriculture Organization (FAO), International Labor Organization (ILO), World Health Organization (WHO), Atomic Energy Commission, and Human Rights Commission. The UN General Assembly initiates and approves global policies as well as legitimizes recommendations by its specialized structures.

2. Regional associations generating important agreements are another main source for setting international standards. They represent collaboration among large blocks of connected nations such as the European Union (EU), North American Free Trade Agreement (AFTA), League of Arab States, Association of Southeast Asian Nations (ASEAN), African Union (AU), and Organization of American States (OAS). All have concluded international agreements among their members that endorse certain principles of ethics and recommend actions by each country in its respective domain.

3. Special international structures and forums that have reinforced global interdependence and generated significant balancing of views on critical issues, particularly in world economics and finance, climate control, and national security. The World Bank and the International Monetary Fund (IMF) are also known for their influence in the area of economics and finance. Other instruments of growing global impact during the past few years are the World Economic Forum and the Group of 20 (G-20) that made significant strides in harmonizing international relations and produced important agreements on key global economic and political issues.

These international organizations and forums signify (1) a worldwide recognition that many of today's problems and challenges extend beyond the boundaries of one country and, therefore, require collaborative international efforts to manage them; (2) the total efforts have put forth some vital foundational policies and projects that continue to serve well the currently unfolding global order; and (3) the overall thrust of these and other international initiatives have accentuated the global reality and strengthened the collective aspirations for improved global rule making and rule application. Thus, ethics and combating corruption is one area where harmonious views have been able to accomplish specific universal objectives. Despite some reservations and criticisms, an international consensus has been evolving in dealing with certain global principles of ethics such as the collective relief to countries hit with natural disasters, defense of human rights, support of fair trade, and other cooperative ventures to solve various chronic world problems. Finally, a specific anti-corruption global convention was finalized and approved by the UN General Assembly in 2003, that may be regarded as a new reality of international cooperation in rejecting corruption in its various forms, particularly bribes, fraud, conflict of interest, misuse of information, and unjustifiable or disproportionate violence against others.

The concept of corruption is continually expanding to include more than a citizen paying a bribe to receive a regular service from a public organization. Various UN field studies on corruption have reported that the consequences of corruption have been more pervasive and severe than these small bribes suggest. Corruption caused reduced investment or even divestment, with many long-term effects, including social polarization, lack of respect for human rights, undemocratic practices, and even diversion of funds intended for development and essential services.

Thus, in December 2003, the UN General Assembly approved the *UN Convention against Corruption,* establishing acceptable standards of ethical conduct for the contemporary states of the world in the form of codified rules. The adoption of the *Convention* was an opportunity for a global response to the problem. The high level of support was demonstrated when 106 countries had already signed the *Convention* document within four months of its adoption by the General Assembly, and over 159 nations signed it within two years. The UN General Assembly's Resolution of 2003, approving the *United Nations Convention against Corruption*, included an attachment, as an Annex of nine articles, which may be regarded as a global code of ethics. By signing off, nations had also accepted and endorsed the provisions of this Annex. Because of their importance and specificity, a few of the provisions in the Annex are summarized here:

- "States Parties shall carry out their obligations under this Convention in a manner consistent with the principle of sovereign equality … non-intervention in the domestic affairs of other States" (UN 2003: Article 4).
- "Each State Party shall, in accordance with the fundamental principles of its legal system, develop and implement or maintain effective, coordinated anti-corruption policies that promote the participation of society and reflect the principles of the rule of law, proper management of public affairs and public property, integrity, transparency, and accountability" (UN 2003: Article 5).
- "Each State Party shall, in accordance with the fundamental principles of its legal system, ensure the existence of a body or bodies, as appropriate, that prevent corruption" by such means as implementing the policies of this Convention and increasing and disseminating knowledge about the prevention of corruption. It is noteworthy, that each state is required to inform the UN secretary-general of the name and address of the authority entrusted with developing measures of implementation (UN 2003: Article 6).
- "Each State Party shall, where appropriate and in accordance with the fundamental principles of its legal system, endeavor to adopt, maintain and strengthen systems for the recruitment, hiring, retention, promotion and retirement of civil servants" based on merit. To combat corruption, equitable pay scale and promotion of education and training are recommended. (UN 2003: Article 7).

The UN initiatives have persistently viewed corruption as what it is, a cancer in the body of the modern state and a serious impediment to normal evolution of global interdependence. The UN *Convention* of 2003 is the culmination of many years of cooperative negotiations among nations and professionals in the field of ethics. The UN and its organizational instruments have labored effectively and competently to educate, articulate, codify, and promulgate basic tenets of ethics for the international system to adopt and to enforce.

A Broader Definition of Ethics

Combating corruption is not a single act or decision but a consistent strategy of multidimensional elements. A worthy strategy requires persistent collaboration of many peoples and institutions, and constant monitoring and vigilance, to discover and to prosecute incidents of corruption. This is true for a single institution as well as globally. In reality, despite all measures that have been introduced and approved to rationalize and to professionalize various levels of governance, ethics remains a profound concern. Evidence suggests that corruption continues to spread, threatening developments achieved so far.

A recent poll indicates that one person in four worldwide has paid a bribe during the past twelve months before December 2010, according to a study released to mark the *International Anti-Corruption Day,* established by the UN in 2003 to raise awareness of graft and promote the global fight against it. The study by *Transparency International* focuses on small-scale bribery and was put together from polls conducted among more than 91,000 people in eighty-six counties and territories. The police was the most corrupt, according to the study which reported that 29 percent of those having dealings with police said they had paid a bribe. Worldwide, sub-Saharan Africa was the region reporting the greatest incidence of bribery with more than one person in two saying they had made such payments to officials in the past twelve months. Europe and the United States reported the lowest percentage (4%) of such bribes.[2]

Such statistics can be misleading, however, by overstating and understating the problem. Overstated in magnitude and pervasiveness are bribes by ordinary people to receive ordinary public services. Understated are the huge sums of side payments to policy makers in many developed countries by lobbyists and special interests. Accounting for these payments is like watching a submarine race, the main activities are under the water and mostly invisible. If the principle of conflict of interest, for example, is honestly applied to the members of the U.S. Congress, almost all of them will be prohibited from voting on most legislative proposals before them because of conflict of interest caused by their financial personal gain called "campaign contributions." Whether it is called *bribe* or *political donation,* the end result is to influence decisions on matters small or large. Under the heading "lawmakers seek cash during key votes," the *Washington Post* revealed: "Numerous times this year [2010] members of Congress have held fundraisers and collected big checks while they are taking critical steps to write new laws, despite warnings that such actions could create ethics problems. The campaign donations often came from contributors with major stakes riding on the lawmakers' actions" (Leonning and Farnam 2010, December 26).[3]

Similarly, a Grand Jury Report was made public in Florida (December 2010) with a bleak picture of ethics in state government. After several months of investigations, the report concluded: Corruption is "pervasive at all levels of government... Fraud, waste and abuse of state resources" punishes taxpayers by driving up the cost of services" (Zink and Bender 2010: A-1). The report called for several reforms, including:

- Expand the definition of public employees to include private employees participating in government contract.
- Require lawmakers to abstain from votes if they stand to gain or lose money as a result of the vote's outcome.
- Ban for life any contractor or vender from doing business with the state if the person has been convicted of a public theft or procurement crime.
- Expand the authority of the Ethics Commission to initiate investigation and impose penalty.[4]

Despite the information conveyed by the Transparency International poll on small bribes, some developing countries have been able to improve their ethical standing on global integrity benchmark by TI, achieving higher ranking than some large advanced, industrial countries, generally regarded as less corrupt. The TI *Corruption Perception Index 2010* ranks Qatar (19) ahead of the United Kingdom (20), the United States (22), Belgium (22), and France (25) on the integrity scale. Chile (21) is ranked higher than the United States, Belgium, and France. Cyprus (28) and United Arab Emirates (28) are ranked higher than Spain (30).[5]

In many countries, ethics reform is difficult to attain, particularly when those in leadership positions lack the necessary capability or commitment to make the hard choices. A likely effect of international agreements on standards of ethics in governance is to prod and to pressure these reluctant leaders to institute ethics reforms and to observe appropriate standards of conduct in public service. These agreements and conventions obligate their members to comply with certain principles and guidelines in conducting their duties and responsibilities. Today, ethics (fighting corruption) has become a condition for economic growth, quality of life, equal justice, and sustainable development. In addition to the UN Convention of 2003, other relevant global events include:

- The UN General Assembly adopted a resolution in 2001, which affirmed previous conventions against crime and corruption, and emphasized the need for effective international legal instrument against corruption. This was followed by other resolutions in 2001 and 2002, affirming the same principles and seeking to strengthen international cooperation in preventing and in combating corruption in general or some specific acts of corruption such as laundering of funds. These various initiatives culminated with the landmark General Assembly Resolution in 2003 (October 31) that is most specific and detailed proposals on fighting corruption.

■ The Summit of the Americas in Miami, Florida, in 1994 focused on corruption, and the majority of the thirty-four leaders in attendance vowed and signed what was billed as the world's first international agreement to stop corruption and "embezzlement" of public assets (Jreisat 2009).

■ A 2001 Report by UN agencies (UNDP, Department of Economic and Social Affairs, and Division of Public Administration) compared public service ethics policies and programs in over a dozen African states, provides country reports, analysis, and supporting database. The purpose is to generate more awareness of the needs for ethics, accountability, and transparency in public service. Two particularly important conclusions in this UNDP report: (1) The impact of unethical and criminal practices in the public sector resulted in a loss of confidence in public institutions and an erosion of the rule of law itself. (2) "Among the many calls for urgent action, improving governance and resolving conflict are seen to be the pre-eminent preconditions to sustainable development."[6]

■ In the past few years, many countries, outside Europe and the United States, have developed their own codes of ethics and the tools of enforcement. Within such codes, individual agencies have also constructed their own standards of ethics that often exceed those set in the code of the national government.

These activities in the area of applied ethics suggest that ethics of governance is becoming a universal pursuit and a global policy (Jabbra and Jreisat 2009). Although nation states remain the main formulators of policies, they do so in the context of an increasingly thick web of transnational networks, with different, often overlapping mandates. To be sure, many of the transnational agreements on ethics lack the power to enforce compliance; nevertheless, they draw attention to questions of ethics and accountability, and generate moral pressures on leaders for compliance. International agreements sensitize leaders and deepen awareness of the issues within public service at all levels of governance. The press, formal education, and practical training have been particularly effective tools of communicating the message in public organizations and within societies.

As international agreements and conventions sanction appropriate modes of internal and external conduct and consolidate norms and values that have been legitimated in many modern states, a culture of ethics is being endorsed and encouraged. Despite the limitations, international organizations such as the United Nations, the World Trade Organization (WTO), and the World Bank have been proactive in their attempts to influences and to be purveyors of values and promoters of transnational ethics.

Because academic research of public sector ethics has been "dominated primarily by American researchers focusing primarily on American topics" (Huberts, Maesschalck, and Jurkiewicz 2008: 1), ethics education and knowledge is in serious need for information generated through cross-cultural comparative scholarship. Cross-national comparative research is essential to enrich concepts, validate standards, increase relevance, and synthesize findings. Comparative analysis is also vital for informing the practitioners about smart practices worldwide, and for developing universal, reliable generalizations about professionalism in public administration. Limiting scholarship to primarily Western or single-culture configuration impairs knowledge development and public administration education in general, prevents students from dealing systematically with a variety of cultures and governance systems, and invites myopic abstractions about practices of "the others" in a globalizing world. Applied ethics has to refocus its coverage and continue to expand its intellectual horizon beyond the Western domains.

The study of ethics within a globalizing world faces the challenge of determining the criteria of relevance as well as developing effective methods of enforcement. Applied ethics covers behavior and conduct of people in various contexts. It has to evolve as a foundational value for validating the new emerging global order. A broad definition of applied global ethics is not easy to enforce within over 190 nations, small and large, poor and rich, developed and less developed. Still, global ethics has to evolve beyond the current state of the discipline to build a collective theoretical base supported by empirical evidence. Thus, the challenges described in the following sections are critical.

A Broader Conception

Developing ethics standards for a society cannot be limited to the public sector or to acts of offering and taking bribes and committing sexual indiscretions by a public official. A holistic approach to ethics has to rely on a comprehensive strategy for improving ethics and/or fighting corruption: (1) Such a strategy cannot be limited to public institutions and the people working in them. It has also to encompass institutions and individuals other than those in public sector organizations such as business, religion, and nonprofit organizations. (2) Leadership is a critical element in all organizations, having the greatest influence in galvanizing and directing energies of individuals and institutions to higher standards of moral conduct. Leaders with competence and integrity make things happen in the organization; they create a ripple moral effect among employees by setting examples in their own conduct and overall performance. Global leaders have to lead in the efforts of achieving global objectives such as environment protection, commitment to equality, responsibility to the poor, respect of human rights, resisting prejudice, devotion to peace, and prevention of war and violence against people. Peter Singer argued "that as the nations of the world move closer together to tackle global issues like trade, climate change, justice, and poverty, our national leaders need to take a larger perspective than that of national self-interest. In a word, they need to take an ethical perspective on globalization" (Singer 2004: ix).

Business Factor

Business ethics is crucial and needs to be examined from different perspectives, evoking different theoretical and practical grounds. Business entities, for example, may serve different interests that are not always in harmony among themselves or with other outside social interests. Interests of the stockholders in maximizing profit may collide with environmental considerations and with interests of society in social responsibility. The huge pay for top corporate leaders regardless of performance may not be good for the employees or the stockholders. And mismanagement, misleading financial information, security fraud, inside trading, false accounting, excessive payments to chief executives, and a variety of other corrupt practice are not in the interest of society, employees, or stockholders. This is why a score of corporate executive ended in prison over the past few years.

Another relevant issue is the corruptive influence of money on politics in most countries. The corporate sector in the United States is a major determining factor in politics, and corporate money made the 2010 U.S. election the most expensive ever in the history of the country and in the world. Consequently, the claim of corporate money is corrupting politics made business ethics relevant or even linked to governance ethics. Another relevant question is that the business school curriculum is lacking an ethical component or at least has a feeble component. Despite a perception that ethics and values are increasingly crucial in business education, few business colleges have responded sufficiently to this societal need.

Top corporate leaders, who collect excessive pay irrespective of performance, have also been identified among those who presided over disastrous corporate failures in the United States over the past decade, stimulating a drive for urgent reform. Although some of the most egregious violations of the environment, health, investment, and general welfare of citizens were committed or caused by business enterprises, the global ethics initiatives have primarily been preoccupied and focused on governance. The abuses of multinational corporations in various societies are many and consequential. Weak or corrupt governments, however, have not been able to regulate multinational corporations, or unwilling to enforce certain universal standards. Nevertheless, some countries have taken serious steps in this regard.

The U.S. Foreign Corrupt Practices Act, for example, forbids companies from bribing people overseas to win business. The Foreign Corrupt Practices Act of 1977 was enacted for the purpose of making it unlawful for persons and entities to make payments to foreign government officials to assist in obtaining or retaining business. The anti-bribery provisions of the FCPA prohibit the willful use of any means to corruptly further "any offer, payment, promise to pay, or authorization of the payment of money or anything of value to any person, while knowing that all or a portion of such money or thing of value will be offered, given or promised, directly or indirectly, to a foreign official to influence the foreign official in his or her official capacity, induce the foreign official to do or omit to do an act in violation of his or her lawful duty, or to secure any improper advantage in order to assist in obtaining or retaining business for or with, or directing business to, any person" (U.S. Department of Justice, Criminal Division).[7]

> The FCPA also requires companies whose securities are listed in the United States to meet its accounting provisions. These accounting provisions, which were designed to operate in tandem with the anti-bribery provisions of the FCPA, require corporations covered by the provisions to (a) make and keep books and records that accurately and fairly reflect the transactions of the corporation and (b) devise and maintain an adequate system of internal accounting controls (U.S. Department of Justice, Criminal Division).[8]

Enforcement of the FCBA is also serious. On May 28, 2010, Mark Brzezinski wrote in the *Washington Post* that the "Obama administration gets tough on business corruption overseas." The article specified some of the changes in enforcement. Brzezinski concludes that among the more underreported developments are the initiatives in international "anti-bribery" enforcement. The surge in investigations and prosecutions regarding the Foreign Corrupt Practices Act has produced real buzz that the days of doing business with a wink and a nod are over and that even decisions made years ago may result in serious punishment. The effort is motivated in part by the principle that business should not be conducted one way in modern countries and another way in developing nations. The Justice Department Criminal Division framed the goal as "the creation of a global consensus that corruption is unacceptable, that it harms the least well-off of us the most." The administration also links corruption with national security challenges. Ten years ago there were roughly eight federal investigations at any time regarding foreign bribes. Today, the Justice Department has more than 130 open investigations. The Securities and Exchange Commission, which enforces accounting provisions of the act, has also set up a task force.

Those charged have included senior corporate executives, intermediaries and, where jurisdiction exists, even some foreign officials. This leaves executives more focused than ever on what distant salespeople and consultants are doing to land business, because executives are being held accountable even if they were never alleged to have personally engaged in improper payments. No longer does the Justice Department rely solely on tips from whistle-blowers or business competitors to build cases. Today, officials are turning the tools of organized-crime investigations to anti-bribery. It is widely understood, however, that true deterrence requires other jurisdictions to enact and to enforce similar laws to prosecute violators.

As the United States seeks to match and coordinate efforts, bilaterally and multilaterally, the FBI is deploying "legal attaches" in more than seventy-five embassies worldwide, partly to focus on bribery investigations. But how can FBI agents prepare for this kind of work? Corruption differs from one country to another. How can governments work together to achieve coordinated and effective punishment of those who offer bribes and those who take them, and advance real deterrence? Finally, as the United States claims the moral right to pursue corruption around the world, its own record is not beyond reproach (Brzezinski 2010).[9]

Information and Transparency

To have an impact, global ethics has to develop awareness, accurate information, and ensure transparency in governance. Transparency is essential for improving public recognition of corruption and its dangers as well as for effective monitoring and investigation of unethical conduct. No doubt, public transactions today are more in the sunshine than any time before. Again, the consistent efforts by the UN, the use of the internet, and the availability of information through the use of polls, measurements, and benchmarking by impartial sources, kept the issue of corruption in the public eye. An excellent illustration is Transparency International's Corruption Perceptions Index. It is "an aggregate indicator that ranks countries in terms of the degree to which corruption is perceived to exist among public officials and politicians. It is a corruption index drawing on corruption-related data by a variety of independent and reputable institutions."[10] Despite some criticisms, programs and activities by Transparency International (TI) have been immensely helpful in raising awareness worldwide. The global activities of TI in measuring corruption and disseminating information about it have been highly influential in generating knowledge, creating awareness, and even stirring some competitiveness among nations seeking to improve their ranks on the Index.

The *UN Convention against Corruption* and various other international agreements developed policies and created vehicles for collective action. The signatories on such international agreements have agreed also to obey and to honor their commitments to combat corruption in their domains. The following example suggests that concrete actions, consistent with the new emphasis on global ethics, are being implemented in some developing countries. The case of the small developing country of Jordan illustrates the effects of the global policy on the domestic policy on ethics:[11]

On December 10, 2010, the Prime Minister of Jordan emphasized the government's commitment to combating all forms of corruption through a comprehensive strategy that ensures the collaboration of all concerned commissions and entities. During a ceremony marking International Anti-Corruption Day, organized by the Anti-Corruption Commission, the PM indicated that combating corruption has always been a top government priority. He added that the government has been working on creating a legislative environment to boost the performance of the Anti-Corruption Commission. The PM declared also that the government will work on implementing "effective policies" that detect corruption before it takes place and will respond strictly to all "corruptors and the corrupted."

Jordan ranks fiftieth on the TI Corruption Perception Index in 2010 among 178 countries surveyed, and the sixth among the twenty regional countries covered by the Index. It is worth noting that the PM expressed commitment of his government to maintaining constant coordination and cooperation with local, regional, and *international* parties in the fight against corruption. In addition, the ceremony was organized in cooperation with the United Nations Development Program (UNDP), whose director's speech reiterated that corruption constitutes a major threat to democracy, development, and stability (*Jordan Times,* December 10, 2010).

The illustrations from the United States and from Jordan may not be typical cases, but, clearly, they underline some relevant and vital information. One is that the effort to promote global ethics is bearing some fruits. Another notion is that an enactment of ethics laws and prosecution of violations are increasingly becoming national policies in many countries. Some countries are already updating their laws to include restrictive measures that prevent potential corrupt practices. There is little doubt that the global ethics movement has stimulated anti-corruption measures by many countries. The question is how far such actions are reaching and how effective. These questions can be reliably answered only through extensive data gathering and comparative empirical analysis.

Ethics Education

Knowledge, education, and training are effective instruments for changing behavior. Education is also a source for generating awareness throughout the workforce. Education systems across countries, with few exceptions, have not accorded ethics a high priority in research or in education and training of the workforce. In general, citizens of modern societies are not sufficiently schooled in the liberal tradition of democracy and the cherished moral values such as liberty, compliance with the law, and justice for all. Education in basic civic culture is not common in schools' curricula of most countries. Still, generating a culture of organizational and societal ethics has to be a strategic objective of education systems. This is unavoidable if corruption is to be fought at the grassroots. Setting values through education is a slow but sure method to create the desirable effects and to elevate public understanding and support of anti-corruption policies. Whereas globalization increased interdependence of countries, movement of capital, and the complexities of governance, education and training are viewed as two equally weighted components of a "holistic capacity building process" and preparing individuals for the changed public service (Kroukamp 2007: 2).

Monitoring, Investigation, and Adjudication

Without effective tools and processes of enforcement, violations of ethics would go undetected and managing ethics programs will be inconsequential. Monitoring and investigative tools enable greater oversight of ethics programs and transform and sustain a values-based management culture. Different enforcement mechanisms and structures have been established in various countries for the purpose of dealing with corruption. Many countries have already created independent commissions, courts, or similar structures to specifically prosecute corruption cases. Codes of ethics are increasingly a common tool of information about standards as well as grounds for monitoring and investigating violations of rules of good conduct. Some codes of ethics have a statutory authority for imposing penalties on violators. Clearly, more empirical research is needed to measure efficacy and consequences of these codes of ethics and the processes of implementation as commonly practiced. As Joseph Jabbra (2007) concluded, it is an effective and competitive governance system in place that makes the fundamental difference. The building of an effective public sector is the sure path for cutting cost, reducing bottlenecks, improving service, and affirming the integrity of the governing processes. This latter point affirms the idea that good governance is to be understood and analyzed as a whole system and not as separate or independent individual components. As a concept with multiple dimensions, not the least of which is honesty and integrity, the governance system is to be evaluated with its many mutually reinforcing components.

Conclusion

The development of global ethics and the ratification of the UN Anti-corruption Convention, committing nations of the world to specific standards of ethics and to specific measures of enforcement are among the most profound global achievements. Global ethics has been viewed narrowly by limiting focus to combating petty acts of corruption in their various detectible forms, ranging from graft and bribery to unprofessional and wasteful management of public resources. Regardless, professional management continually seeks to ensure honesty and integrity of public decisions. On the other hand, a broad view of ethics in public service is more inclusive, far reaching, and deals with a wider range of issues. A broad perspective on ethics includes issues such as transparency, professional responsibility, democratic values, civil liberties, respect of human rights, and compliance with the rule of law. Also, a broad coverage of ethics has to include the ethical impact of nongovernmental institutions as well as large corporations on the overall processes of governance.

Although a narrow or focused view is easier to convert into concrete measures to serve a clearly defined objective such as fighting bribes, it remains limited in its effect on society. A broad ethics perspective requires a reconsideration of the content of educational systems and the conduct of inquiries on the real and potential intellectual contributions of philosophy, history, political thought, public administration, and social sciences in general to develop the ideals of a civilized society. Global ethics can evolve and flourish in combating corruption when supported by educational approaches that instill the universality and the fundamental values of society. Education and research foster and promote the principles of good governance in modern society and within the global context. Global ethics, for example, renews the attention to the need to eliminate discrimination and to developing international accords that institutionalize values of integrity and mandate adjudication of war crimes and crimes against humanity, regardless of country of origin. Although monitoring, investigating, and adjudicating violations of ethics is easier when the standards are specific and definable, it is necessary to consider the overall picture and the many linkages. In all this, appropriate education and proper leadership are the most critical factors for continuing the progress made.

References

Amstutz, M. R. 2008. *International Ethics: Concepts, Theories, and Cases in Global Politics.* 3rd ed. New York: Rowman & Littlefield.

Annan, Kofi A. 2004. Foreword. *United Nations Convention against Corruption.* New York: United Nations.

Bell, D., ed. 2010. Ethics and world politics: Introduction. In *Ethics and World Politics*, ed. Bell, D., 1–14. Oxford: Oxford University Press.

Brzezinski, Mark. 2010. Obama administration gets tough on business corruption overseas. *Washington Post*, May 28, A23.

Cocker, D. A. 2002. Development Ethics and Globalization. *Philosophy & Public Policy Quarterly.* 22 (4): 13–20.

Cremer, G. 2008. *Corruption and Development Aid: Confronting the Challenges.* Boulder, CO: Lynne Reinner.

Gilman, S. C., and C. W. Lewis. 1996. Public service ethics: A global dialogue. *Public Administration Review*, 56 (6): 517–524.

Gill, Cindy. 2010. Watershed times. *Pitt Magazine.* Pittsburgh, PA: University of Pittsburgh (Spring): 1.

Huberts, L., J. Maesschalck, and C. Jurkiewicz, eds. 2008. *Ethics and Integrity of Governance: Perspectives across Frontiers.* UK: Edward Elgar.

Jabbra, J. G. 2007. Global competitiveness and public administration: Implications for education and training. Paper presented at the Joint IIAS/IASIA Conference, July 9–14, Abu Dhabi, United Arab Emirates.

Jabbra, J. G., and J. E. Jreisat. 2009. Administration of the Arab State: Synthesizing diverse traditions. In *Winning the Needed Change: Saving our Planet Earth*, I. P. Pagaza and D. Argyriades, eds. 112–126, Amsterdam, Belgium and Washington, D.C: IOS Press.

Jones, P. 2010. The ethics of international society. In *Ethics and World Politics*, ed. Bell, D., 111–127. Oxford: Oxford University Press.

Jordan Times. 2010. Government committed to fight corruption, December, http://www.jordantimes.com.

Jreisat, J. E. 2009. Applied ethics and a global culture. In *Ethics Today*, Newsletter of the ASPA Section on Ethics. Vol. 11, No. 2 (Summer): 17–19.

Kroukamp, H. 2007. Public sector education and training in a developing South Africa: The impact and responses to global competitiveness. Paper presented at the Joint IIAS/IASIA Conference, July 9–14, Abu Dhabi, United Arab Emirates.

Singer, D. 2004. *One World: The Ethics of Globalization.* 2nd ed., Yale University Press.

Thompson, D. 1985. The possibility of administrative ethics. *Public Administration Review.* (September/October): 555–561.

Zink, J., and M. Bender. 2010. Grand jury: Corrupt Florida needs reforms. *St. Petersburg Times.* (December 30: P. 1A).

Endnotes

1. Kofi A. Annan, former UN Secretary-General, Foreword, *United Nations Convention against Corruption,* New York: United Nations, 2004.
2. Transparency International. 2010 Global Corruption Barometer, http://www.transparency.org/policy_research/surveys_indices/cpi/2010/in_detail. Aljazeerah. December 9, 2010. http://english.aljazeerah.net/news/europe/2010/12/20101297627332580.html.
3. Leonning, C. D., and T. W. Farnam. *Washington Post,* December 26, 2010. http://www.washingtonpost.com/wp-dyn/content/article/2010/12/25/AR2010122502236.html?wpisrc=nl_headline.
4. *St Petersburg Times.* FL. 2010. December 30, page 1A. Also, *Sun Sentinel,* Orlando, FL (December 29, 2010, A1).
5. Transparency International. Corruption Perception Index 2010, Long Methodological Brief, http://www.transparency.org/policy_research/surveys_indeces/cpi/2010/in_detail.
6. UNDP. 2001. *Public Service Ethics in Africa, Executive Summary.* Vol. I, p. 1, UN Department of Economic and Social Affairs, Division of Public Administration, New York, UN.
7. U.S. Department of Justice, Criminal Division: http://www.justice.gov/criminal/fraud/fcpa/.
8. Ibid.
9. Mark Brzezinski. 2010. Obama administration gets tough on business corruption overseas. *Washington Post* (May 28): A23. (The writer is an attorney at McGuireWoods.)
10. Transparency International. Corruption Perception Index 2010, Long Methodological Brief http://www.transparency.org/policy_research/surveys_indeces/cpi/2010/in_detail.
11. *Jordan Times.* 2010. Government committed to fight corruption. (December 10): 1. http://www.jordantimes.com/print.html.

Index

213